Deported to Death

CALIFORNIA SERIES IN PUBLIC ANTHROPOLOGY

The California Series in Public Anthropology emphasizes the anthropologist's role as an engaged intellectual. It continues anthropology's commitment to being an ethnographic witness, to describing, in human terms, how life is lived beyond the borders of many readers' experiences. But it also adds a commitment, through ethnography, to reframing the terms of public debate—transforming received, accepted understandings of social issues with new insights, new framings.

Series Editor: Robert Borofsky (Hawaii Pacific University)

Contributing Editors: Philippe Bourgois (University of Pennsylvania), Paul Farmer (Partners In Health), Alex Hinton (Rutgers University), Carolyn Nordstrom (University of Notre Dame), and Nancy Scheper-Hughes (UC Berkeley)

University of California Press Editor: Naomi Schneider

Deported to Death

*How Drug Violence Is Changing
Migration on the US-Mexico Border*

Jeremy Slack

UNIVERSITY OF CALIFORNIA PRESS

University of California Press, one of the most
distinguished university presses in the United States,
enriches lives around the world by advancing scholarship
in the humanities, social sciences, and natural sciences. Its
activities are supported by the UC Press Foundation and
by philanthropic contributions from individuals and
institutions. For more information, visit www.ucpress.edu.

University of California Press
Oakland, California

Library of Congress Cataloging-in-Publication Data

Names: Slack, Jeremy, author.
Title: Deported to death : how drug violence is changing
    migration on the US-Mexico border / Jeremy Slack.
Description: Oakland, California : University of
    California Press, [2019] | Series: California series in
    public anthropology | Includes bibliographical
    references and index. |
Identifiers: LCCN 2018058267 (print) |
    LCCN 2019000207 (ebook) | ISBN 9780520969711 (ebook) |
    ISBN 9780520297326 (cloth : alk. paper) |
    ISBN 9780520297333 (pbk. : alk. paper)
Subjects: LCSH: Immigrants—Violence against—Mexico. |
    Violence—Mexican-American Border Region. |
    Immigration enforcement—Mexican-American
    Border Region. | Deportation—United States—21st
    century.
Classification: LCC HV6250.4.E75 (ebook) |
    LCC HV6250.4.E75 S54 2019 (print) |
    DDC 303.60972/1—dc23
LC record available at https://lccn.loc.gov/2018058267

Manufactured in the United States of America

28 27 26 25 24 23 22 21 20 19
10 9 8 7 6 5 4 3 2 1

For Carla, for everything you have lost and for accompanying me on this journey.

CONTENTS

ILLUSTRATIONS

MAPS

FIGURES

TABLES

ACKNOWLEDGMENTS

First and foremost, I want to acknowledge the invisible labor that goes into my fortunate life circumstances that allow me to have a job, a family, and a productive research agenda. My wife, Carla Soto, has accompanied me on hundreds of my research-related experiences: trips to visit people at the shelters; touching base after a long hiatus; attending marches, protests, and organizing meetings for the immigrant rights community; or simply enduring excruciatingly boring, endless conversations about research, academia, and the politics of migration over a meal or drinks (*Sorry, amor. I'll try not to, but I would be lying if I said I could stop*). You have been a companion on so much of this difficult journey, and your support has made all the difference. I look around at my friends and colleagues, realizing in starkly personal and often embarrassing terms how the work you do makes it possible to me to have everything. You do so much of the work of life, the work of a family, raising our newborn son, and keeping our household from falling down as I abscond to write, give talks, testify, and teach classes. I could not do what I do and still have a functional, happy, healthy life without you.

I also want to thank Daniel E. Martínez for being my collaborator and friend throughout this work and beyond. It feels somewhat disconcerting not to co-author our work this time around, as our different perspectives and approaches to social science create a tension that I feel elevates this research beyond what I am capable of alone. I really could not have written this book without your support, insight, and collaboration. I can't wait to see all the new research and publications that we accomplish in the future, although, as always, there will be little time to stop and appreciate it with so much more to do!

I also owe a special gratitude to Scott Whiteford for supporting me throughout this journey. From the time I was an MA student until my first job, he always encouraged me to push the envelope and dream big. He provided the contacts and framework to make this research possible and taught me a lot about navigating the often unpredictable academic world.

I am also lucky to find myself employed by a university where my interests and approaches do not sit in isolation. I would like to thank all of my colleagues in the Department of Sociology and Anthropology, but particularly Josiah Heyman and Howard Campbell for their support, encouragement, and uncanny ability to push me harder. It is tempting to stay in a safe zone and publish relatively easy work with recycled or somewhat obvious conclusions, but being around such accomplished border scholars has helped me to think deeper and work harder. Dr. Heyman is the model of an applied scholar that I aspire to follow, successfully balancing the production of academic knowledge with contributions to the never-ending activist struggles for change in our border community. Dr. Campbell provides my steady reminder to let go of the baggage of academia and focus on what matters: the people, the streets, and the unique world that is Ciudad Juárez and the border. Fidelity to place and love of a region is what has kept me going in this research and it is what I hope to hold dear for the rest of my career.

I want to thank Diane Austin, who had a formative influence on my knowledge of research methods and on my ability to conduct projects that push me beyond my boundaries. She drove me harder than anyone else, held my feet to the fire to get my notes written and reports finished, and I emerged the better for it. I will be eternally grateful for that education.

This project would not have been possible without the generous support of the Ford Foundation, Mexico and Central America Office. I must thank them not only for their financial support but also their logistical support in connecting our project with others working diligently on issues of migration and drug violence in Mexico. This network has proven invaluable for increasing the impact of our work by getting it into the hands of people who can use it to complement their own efforts. Of particular importance is the work of Kimberley Krasevac and her support but also her critiques, which helped push this research into new areas and answer important, relevant questions that expand beyond the boundaries of academia.

I also need to thank the Drugs Security and Democracy Fellowship funded by the Social Science Research Council and the Open Society Foundation for their support of my ethnographic research. This funding, as well as the network of scholars, has been invaluable to the improvement and development of this project. In addition, a special thanks to the National Institutes of Health BUILDing Scholars program for summer sabbatical funding to write this book and Dr. Luis Zayas for his comments and suggestions on early drafts of the proposal.

The Center for Latin American Studies, the Center for Mexican American Studies, the Department of Sociology, the School of Geography and Development, and the College of Social and Behavioral Studies at the University of Arizona also provided support and funding throughout this research. The supportive atmosphere of the University of Arizona made it possible to conduct this unique work and blend the academic and policy aspects, making its impact far greater than it otherwise would have been.

I also owe a particular debt of gratitude to all of the people who conducted surveys throughout the U.S.-Mexico border region. This project would not have been possible without their commitment and hard work in sensitive and often uncomfortable environments.

Wave I

Kraig Beyerlein

Prescott Vandervoet

Kristin Klingman

Paola Molina

Shiras Manning

Melissa Burham

Kylie Walzak

Kristen Valencia

Lorenzo Gamboa

Wave II

Tijuana: Ramona Pérez (SDSU), Alaina Gallegos (SDSU)

Mexicali: Alfonso Cortez-Lara (COLEF)

Ciudad Juárez: Sonia Bass Zavala (UACJ), Tony Payan (UTEP), Consuelo Pequeño (UACJ), Martha Estela Pérez (UACJ), Raúl Holguín (UACJ)

Nuevo Laredo: Blanca Vázquez (COLEF), Soledad Tolentino (COLEF)

Ciudad de México: Paola Velasco (UNAM)

Interviewers

Patricia Hohl (UA)

Murphy Woodhouse (UA)

Richard Casillas (UA)

Ana Julieta González (UA)

Cynthia Rodríguez (SDSU)

Karla Elisa Méndez Delgado (COLEF, Mexicali)

Diana Correa (COLEF, Mexicali)

Cecilia Martínez (UACJ), Adrian Valenzuela (UACJ)

Alejandra Payán (UACJ)

Luis Isaac Rocha (UACJ)

Jorge Leyva (UACJ)

Yadira Cortés (UACJ)

Mayra González (UACJ)

Yaneth Cossio (UACJ)

Armando Taunton Rodríguez (COLEF, Nuevo Laredo)

Carlos Gerardo Cruz Jacobo (COLEF, Nuevo Laredo)

Jose Ignacio Aguinaga Medina (COLEF, Nuevo Laredo)

Adriana Guillermina Wagner Perales (COLEF, Nuevo Laredo)

Armando Orta Pérez (COLEF, Nuevo Laredo)

Naomi Ramírez (SDSU)

Sean Tengco (SDSU)

Charles Whitney (SDSU)

Jose Huizar (SDSU)

Oscar Hernández (UNAM)

Andrea Bautista (UNAM)

Uriel Melchor (UNAM)

Janett Vallejo (UNAM)

Monserrat Luna (UNAM)

Adriana Acle (COLEF, Tijuana)

Diana Peláez (COLEF, Tijuana)

Gabriel Pérez Duperou (COLEF, Tijuana)

Sandra Albicker (COLEF, Tijuana)

I also owe special thanks to my thesis committee: Elizabeth Oglesby, Jeffrey Banister, Sallie Marston, and Scott Whiteford. Their invaluable comments and support made graduate school a happy and productive experience that differs from so many of my peers. You were the model of a civilized and thoughtful committee. I also need to thank the dedication of Francisco Loureiro Herrera and Gilda Irene de Loureiro from the San Juan Bosco shelter for working on this issue as long as I have been alive.

A special thanks goes to Murphy Woodhouse for his amazing photography that helps to bring this work to life. In addition, he and I worked on chapter 4 together. The difficulty of spending time with Juanito's horrific story should not be understated, and I owe a debt of gratitude to Murphy for the care and insight that is reflected in this chapter. Also, thanks to Raquel Rubio-Goldsmith, Kraig Beyerlein, Prescott Vandervoet, Kathryn Rodríguez, Celeste González de Bustamante, Anna Ochoa O'Leary, Margaret Bellini, Mario Vasquez-Leon, Ricardo Martínez-Schuldt, Lindsay Rojas, Michael Bonilla, Alyssa Borrego, Guillermo Yrizar Barbosa, and Christine Scheer. Also, my heartfelt thanks to the hosts at COLEF–Matamoros, Cirila Quintero and Oscar Misael Hernandez, and the hosts at COLEF–Tijuana, Laura Velasco, Dolores Paris Pomba, Rafael Alarcon, and Alonso Meneses. Special thanks to Edith Tapia for her collaboration on work with asylum seekers in El Paso and to Taylor Levy for reviewing chapter 8.

Of particular importance to this research is the hard work being conducted at the shelters along the U.S.-Mexico border, which feed and provide shelter for thousands of people every day. They are the front lines of mass removal from the United States and must deal with grueling schedules as people are dropped off at all hours of the night, often overflowing into the kitchens and dining rooms. While I have interacted with far too many volunteers and employees to thank by name, I must thank Polo, Fernando, Erik, and Jose, and Constantino Velasquez, Izolda, Lupita, and Manuel uno and Manuel dos. These two teams have spent years giving their all to the day-to-day needs of migrants as they arrive confused and scared at the border. This unappreciated and hard work needs to be more widely recognized.

I would also be remiss if I did not acknowledge the gratitude that I feel toward the thousands of migrants who shared their lives and stories with me over the years. The tenacity of people struggling to improve their lives or return to family in the United States despite the dangers of the desert and penalties they face if they are caught is always awe inspiring. To talk to people day after day who risk their lives for the chance at a happy life demonstrates the cruelty and misguided nature of our current approach to immigration and border enforcement.

CHAPTER ONE

The Violence of Mobility

Nuevo Laredo, Tamaulipas

"He stuck his hand in between the door when I turned my back. I didn't see them coming. Before I knew it they were inside with their guns pointed at us, threatening to do something to my wife, or to me or burn down the institution (a migrant shelter). It was a very serious threat ... One of the Zetas, because he identified himself as a member of the Zetas cartel, spoke to me very calmly, in a certain way. 'We want to take these two people. There is a *patero* (human smuggler) who is not reporting to us. We want to know who crossed them. We will ask them for code words. If they have the codes we will leave them alone and not bother them anymore. If they don't give us the codes, well, it's because someone crossed them and they are not with us.'" The longtime staff member Lázaro froze: "I immediately contacted the priest (in charge of the shelter) and told him, 'Padre, we have a situation here.' 'Lázaro, let them go. We can't do anything else,' the priest replied, so I said, 'You have to leave, *muchachos*, la Casa (del migrante) can't do anything for you.'" The migrants started to scream and plead not to let them be taken. "I let them take them (the deportees) and I never saw them again. What else could I have done?"[1]

These incursions into migrant shelters have become common in northeastern Mexico. "I still hear their screams," Lázaro said as we sat in a restaurant in D.F. shortly after the event. I had just ended my fieldwork along the border and we got the chance to catch up at a workshop held by the ACLU in Mexico City to discuss migrant possessions. This incident happened shortly after I left the shelter, but similar events had happened throughout the Northeast. The two young men who were taken were originally from Michoacán, a central Mexican state and also an area controlled by one of the mortal enemies of the Zetas cartel: La Familia Michoacana. Being deported to Tamaulipas placed them in danger because the Zetas are always suspicious of deportees coming from territories controlled by rival gangs. When the Michoacanos were walking to the shelter, two young lookouts, known as *halcones,* who monitored the people coming and going from the shelter, stopped to interrogate them, a common practice. "They were big guys, as tall as you," Lázaro explained, "and did not pay attention to the halcones, who were little kids." The deportees pushed past the lookouts, shoving one hard against a fence. "The other (lookout) went and called on his radio and the reinforcements arrived. The trucks came with armed men." Simple missteps like this one may have cost these two young men their lives. Being a deportee along the border is a dangerous world, one with complex rules and a shifting terrain that has put immigration squarely in the sights of drug cartels.

Events like this are rarely publicized—the organizations that run shelters do not want the negative publicity and potential closure, nor do the police and organized criminal groups from the area want these activities known. But *what* precisely is going on here? What would drug traffickers, once famous for their gaudy lifestyles and excessive wealth, want with relatively poor deportees and migrants? These hidden horrors are the backdrop for the high-profile massacres in the region, particularly the killing of 72 Central and South American migrants in San Fernando, Tamaulipas, in August of 2010.[2] This massacre has become yet another gruesome footnote in the drug war that has wrecked havoc on Mexico during the first two decades of the twenty-first century.

This book explores a fundamental problem with the U.S. immigration system. Deportation is not considered a punishment but rather an administrative action because people are simply being sent home.[3] And yet, people like these two young deportees from Michoacán are routinely placed in danger, many becoming the victims of torture or death. The mass deportation of people from the United States to Mexico has exacerbated an already hyperviolent situation whereupon organized criminal groups and corrupt authorities prey upon deportees. With the conflict over control of the drug trade raging between drug cartels and the authorities, criminal activities and the pervasiveness of violence into more and more aspects of daily life along the border have led to a concentration on migrants and deportees that is largely new. Long a staple of border cities, the small groups of individuals waiting on street corners, dressed in black and exhausted after days of walking through the desert, were once pitied or simply ignored by residents,[4] but now they are interrogated, extorted, kidnapped, forcibly recruited by organized crime, and even killed.

This violence can be attributed to two major social processes. First, the figure of the migrant, or deportee for that matter, someone defined by his or her movement and always belonging to someplace else, is uniquely exposed to violence. The limited protections afforded to migrants because they are in transit make them easy targets for being abducted, brutalized, or simply made to disappear without anyone searching for them for long periods of time. While, in theory, international conventions protect migrants and refugees, at the local level the ambiguity of belonging, of being in transit, neither from the space where they live nor at their final destination, means there is no one to answer for crimes committed against them. Second, the increasing presence of death, both in terms of the danger of the journey itself but also its social and emotional counterparts, has become an important aspect of the journey. This is highlighted by the blurring of boundaries between deaths caused by the sprawling conflict over the control of drug trafficking and those that are the result of migration. As more and more people pass through these zones of conflict, either while traveling through Mexico from Central America or upon deportation to Mexico's northern border, they are placed in extreme danger and have become the unlikely targets of organized crime.

SAN FERNANDO: VIOLENCE AND
MIGRATION COLLIDE

The massacre of 72 migrants, "the 72" as they came to be known, marked a sea change in the conflict. For the first time it became impossible to contend that this conflict was confined to the ranks of drug traffickers and criminals; clearly many others were also exposed to this violence. Therefore, it became one of the events that caused the greatest problem for the Mexican government. The discourse of criminals killing each other, the *"ajuste de cuentas"* best translated as the settling of scores, had been the most common refrain for the Mexican government to fall back on when addressing the violence. These people were simply killing each other, and therefore it was not a matter of concern for those who were not involved in such activities.[5] With 72 migrants from Central and South America murdered execution style, their bodies lined up against the wall of an abandoned, half-finished building, there was no way to spin it as some sort of internal gang dispute. This was something much more sinister.

Rumors swirled. The initial discovery of the bodies was due to a survivor, a young man from Ecuador, shot in the head and left for dead. He was able to escape and flag down a military convoy that reported the massacre. Questions about whether he was left alive on purpose, or a member of the cartel working in collaboration, caused heated debates (sources say that his survival was neither intentional nor was he a member of the Zetas). Certainly, the fact that no steps were taken to dispose of the bodies, as had become customary in the region, raised further suspicions. Those suspicions grew as almost two hundred bodies were found buried in mass graves in the same area the following year, many of them having been dissolved in acid and burned beyond recognition. Why leave such a devastating trail of violence? For Juanito, a young man who was kidnapped and held in San Fernando two years after the massacre, the answer lay in the complicated relationship between organized crime and the Mexican government. He believed it was a cynical action by organized crime to embarrass the beleaguered Mexican government and destabilize their legitimacy by questioning their ability to protect foreigners on national soil, thereby exacerbating the international debate about whether or not Mexico was becoming a failed state.[6] By selecting only foreign migrants to murder, it applied international pressure on the administration as the governments of Guatemala, Honduras, El Salvador, Ecuador, and Brazil all joined to denounce Mexico's failure to protect migrants. In this way the Zetas hoped to force cooperation from the government, and specifically its enforcement apparatus, to turn a blind eye to the drug trafficking, extortion, and kidnapping that has plagued Mexico's Northeast.

This leads us to one of the main questions driving this research: How does enforcement shape the types of activities carried out by criminal organizations? For one, the overreliance on the military, following the arrest and elimination of local police as occurred in cities such as Nuevo Laredo during my fieldwork, led to an increase in violence targeted at local residents. Militaries are not designed to police civilian populations, especially not their own nationals. They are trained to kill enemies, not to investigate crimes, not to make arrests and get convictions in court. They are trained to confront and engage. This has caused a great deal of institutional confusion as the army and navy begin to receive training in police tactics and the police receive more and more training in military tactics and materials such as the Black Hawk helicopters provided by the United States. Life on the ground, however, shows that this has resulted in nothing but chaos and confusion.

On one of my first trips to Nuevo Laredo, I headed to the convenience store with my hosts to buy some beer for the *carne asada*. We walked into the ubiquitous OXXO, similar to the one on nearly every corner in Mexico. The young woman behind the counter was shaking. "I can't sell you anything. I have no change. They just came in here and robbed me," she said. "They put a knife to my throat." My host Fernando[7] pulled out his wallet to check. "That's okay. We have correct change for the beer." We paid and walked out as if it were the most normal thing in the world.[8] The banality of violence and turmoil caused by efforts to root out corruption was itself shocking and completely unremarkable as people averted their attention and normalized the things that were out of their control.

This is just one example of how national-level policy changes influence the nature and character of violence. But what about international policies such as border and immigration enforcement? How do the policies and even the individual decisions made by immigration officers at the U.S.-Mexico border influence the nature of violence along the border? I argue that immigration enforcement practices have been one of the major drivers of kidnapping and violence against migrants in Mexico. This occurs through the complicated geography of detention and repatriation that shuffles people all along the two-thousand-mile border, as well as the steady process of criminalization that has produced a stigma that transcends borders and has permeated Mexican society as well.

With more and more immigrants being arrested, incarcerated for greater periods of time, and sentenced for crimes that for decades were generally treated as administrative violations and not criminal acts, it has promoted higher levels of violence around undocumented migration and deportation.[9] The costs to cross, the stakes of getting caught, and the intermingling of migrants and drug traffickers in prison have all converged along the border. This, along with the uniquely situated vulnerability and exposure of clandestine migrants, has led to the complex and shifting exploitation, abuse, and even massacres of migrants in Mexico such as in San Fernando but also in Cadereyta, Nuevo León. The lack of understanding and questions about the true scope of this violence present a unique challenge for research, advocacy, and especially for asylum seekers in their quest to stay in the United States. Neither I nor anyone else can answer seemingly simple questions about what happens to people whose asylum applications are rejected. How many are killed? Where do they go? Do they hide or run? How many are conscripted into organized crime? How many are kidnapped, tortured, and exploited? This book addresses some of these questions, but arriving at a definitive answer to such hidden and violent processes will require additional research and perhaps decades of diligent work by scholars, advocates, and activists.

Furthermore, no other place along the border has generated as many unanswered questions as the northeastern state of Tamaulipas. With so little information coming out of this area, it is difficult to know for sure the levels of violence. How frequent are killings like the massacre in San Fernando? What has driven the explosion of drug cartel–related violence against migrants and deportees in recent years? One thing is for sure; this violence has drastically reshaped migration, adding new layers of violence to what was already a treacherous and often deadly journey.

The severity of the situation has left migrant rights advocates and service providers desperately unprepared and without the necessary resources. Across the Northeast, migrant rights centers were forced to close, often sending those running these programs into hiding, leaving the region or country as a whole. This lack of services correlates to the diminishing power of the press to report on crime or operate freely. In Nuevo Laredo where I worked, one could not buy a national newspaper or *Proceso* (a renowned news magazine published in Mexico City) at the local OXXO. Even the man who delivered papers from Laredo, Texas, was threatened and, as a result, stopped bringing papers across the river.

Survival became the primary organizing principle of social life. I remember walking around Ciudad Juárez in 2010, the year more than three thousand people were murdered in that city.[10] People looked curiously at me, almost tripping over themselves due to the novelty of the out-of-place gringo. However, in Nuevo Laredo, no one looked at me. They were too busy watching who might be following them. Conversations took on an eerie cadence as we chatted freely in cars or offices, but everyone became immediately silent as they passed through public spaces, concerned about who might overhear them.

Migrant shelters were particularly vulnerable and, despite assurances, had to take matters into their own hands. The cost of protection— usually manifest in security cameras that only sometimes worked or a peephole in barred doors to talk to potential visitors before allowing them entrance—was born almost entirely by these organizations. Some shelters were given a police escort during particularly intense periods when threats had been registered against shelter owners. Suspicions of being watched, as well as of people working for the drug cartels having been planted inside shelters, led to a flurry of rules, such as no cell phones (to prevent coordination with the outside) and the mandatory locking of doors that, in one nearly catastrophic instance, could have led to migrants burning to death, as a fire forced them to break the windows of the second-floor dormitory and jump to safety. Luckily no one was killed but two people were badly injured.

Shelter workers clung to shelter rules, even trivial ones, as they would to a lifeline; the rules were a way to organize and protect their space. To me, it felt like adding fresh paint to a burning building. Rather than concentrate on the extreme forms of violence and danger all around us, these organizations busied themselves with complicated systems to count the number of bars of soap given to migrants, or to keep track of the towels. This is not meant to undermine the work done in shelters and by other service providers who concern themselves with the day-to-day stresses of providing food and shelter for hundreds of deportees and migrants. This labor is absolutely necessary and, despite being imperfect as is the case in any situation where the needs grossly outweigh the resources, their dedication and commitment and sacrifices cannot be overstated. However, the necessity of having to work in a greatly constrained environment prevents those who provide care from being able to rise above the daily melee and advocate for change.[11]

As a researcher, both issues affected me. First, I was far from immune to these pressures and was forced to adjust my methodology due to the stress of the environment. Recording interviews was uncomfortable for the interviewees and for me. Writing in public brought unwanted attention. I had to write at nights or sometimes during the day when I could escape to my borrowed office at the Colegio de la Frontera Norte. Moreover, my attempts to intervene, particularly by helping people escape the region, were (mostly) disastrous (see chapter 5). Because of this, my goal for this book is to go beyond simply describing the horrible situation that people find themselves in, and attempt to use research as a tool for people working directly for immigration, asylum and policy reform. This book is therefore an attempt to address the security situation in Mexico, as well as the U.S. policies that have seriously exacerbated the vulnerability of migrants. These policies have placed people in extreme danger, which directly violates the U.S. commitment to asylum seekers as well as the commitment to the principle of *non-refoulement*, also known as the convention against torture. Mass deportation is creating the conditions of violence and vulnerability that should qualify many individuals for protection under the law, but this is largely being ignored.

THE VIOLENCE OF MOBILITY

Being defined by one's movement is to be defined as less than human. The immigrant and the deportee are identified as hailing from elsewhere, from someplace different. Human movement is etched with violence, and the people marked by these etchings are at the mercy of those around them. People in movement live through this violence, and the very fact of their mobility exposes them to new structures and forms of violence. Violence is both a social and a spatial process, with the radical "foreignness" of the individual inscribed on their being.

This is particularly true of the forced movement of deportation. While even the most desperate migration attempts, such as those fleeing violence, take place with the benefit of some choice (where to cross the border, how to travel, whom to go with), deportation is mobility rejected. It is failure. Every day, thousands of people find themselves marooned in unfamiliar, sometimes dangerous border cities all along the two-thousand-mile U.S.-Mexico divide. They struggle to decide what comes next. Return to a former home? Cross the border? Stay at the border? But the challenges of the first few days and hours are often much more dire. How will I eat? Where will I sleep? Is it safe here? How will I survive?

These questions have become paramount as the drug-related violence that has rocked Mexico for the past decade drastically changed the social order. Nowhere is this more profound and visible than along the border. Migrants and deportees are thrust into complex situations of local power-struggles, militarized policing, and brutal open conflict with no social safety net to rely on. Their movement, being away from both destination and origin, places them in a uniquely precarious situation. They arrive under scrutiny, stigmatized by the same mechanisms of criminalization that have led to ever increasing numbers of incarcerated migrants. During the same time period that over two hundred thousand people lost their lives in the "drug war," several million people were deported to the border zone. The impact of this violence on people in movement demonstrates not only the seismic impact of the "drug war" on Mexico, but the deep connections between mobility and violence as a whole.

This violence, however, does not exist in a vacuum, and the neighboring countries of Mexico and the United States influence one another in a deep and profound way. Border enforcement policies and priorities in the United States have the power to radically change the atmosphere on the border, and have often led to complete reversals of Mexico's treatment of Central American *transmigrantes*. The United States' heightened immigration enforcement apparatus, driven by the blending of local law enforcement and federal immigration enforcement, has intensified the image of the criminal alien, stigmatizing hundreds of thousands of immigrants. In many ways this is a direct extension of the same apparatus that has been criminalizing communities of color since the abolition of slavery.[12] Gang injunctions, racial profiling, for-profit prisons and their subsidiaries, mandatory minimums, and a growing list of felony eligible crimes—all tools used to lock up record numbers of people—have affected immigrants, but with the added caveat that they can be expelled afterward. The additional punishment of removal has become the dream of law enforcement agencies. Imagine not just locking people up but removing them to another country once their time is served. Not only does this make it possible to completely ignore the dire consequences of mass incarceration, especially solitary confinement,[13] but those "problematic" individuals then become the sole responsibility of another country. The social ramifications of incarceration and the consequences of institutionalization have been removed to the white space on the map: beyond our borders.

Throughout this process, the criminalization of immigration has succeeded in merging the figure of the immigrant with the criminal, not only in the United States but abroad as well. Mexican officials often laud migrants as heroes who support their families by suffering abroad, but periodically attack deportees as criminals, responsible for the violence along the border.[14] This is not to say there are not social problems created by mass removal along the U.S.-Mexico border. For example in 2007, there were 129,330 removals[15] to Nogales, Sonora, a city with an official population of only 220,000. When close to half of the population of a city is dumped on the streets over the course of a year, most with no place to sleep, no money, no contacts, and almost no government support, it is bound to have repercussions.

Combine the Obama administration's mass, criminalized removals of over 2 million people, most of whom were sent to Mexico, with the extremely volatile drug war that began in 2007 and it is easy to see how this situation exploded. The heavy death toll in cities such as Ciudad Juárez, where more than ten thousand murders took place between 2007 and 2012, completely destroyed social life on the border. People fled, stores shut down, and a de facto curfew was in place for years. This was not isolated to high-profile hot-spots like Juárez but occurred almost everywhere along the border, especially in rural zones far from the cameras and reporters who, even at the height of the violence, documented much of the carnage in cities. For the first time, the conflicts among drug traffickers became a daily concern for everyone living on the border. Fear, suspicion, and self-preservation changed people's habits. It is not surprising that narratives about the hundreds of "criminals" deported each day provoked such a visceral backlash.

This was particularly pronounced when then-mayor of Ciudad Juárez Hector "Teto" Murgia blamed deportees for the violence and urged the border patrol to stop repatriations to the city.[16] His strategy worked and removals slowed to a trickle. Contrast this with a letter-writing campaign from a group of migrants detained in a New Mexico facility who pleaded that they not be sent to Tamaulipas, home to the infamous migrant massacre in 2010.[17] Their requests went unfulfilled, as have dozens of similar attempts, such as hunger strikes and activist campaigns to stem the flow of migrants into the most dangerous region along the border. The migrant as a threat will always have traction within the current approach to border enforcement, whereas any attempt to protect migrants and thereby reduce violence along the border has been met with extreme resistance.

By examining the ways people must negotiate the border, and the violence that has become commonplace, we can better understand the impacts of mass criminalization. This helps expose those changes to border enforcement that have succeeded in putting people directly in harm's way, while simultaneously exacerbating the already tenuous security situation in Mexican border cities.

Through ethnographic research with deportees along the entire U.S.-Mexico border from 2007–18, this book chronicles how drug-related violence has reshaped migration and deportation in Mexico. Tracing the twin phenomena of migration and drug violence through the distinct border regions demonstrates the importance of movement, both vertical movement north and south, as well as lateral movement along the border. Successful northward movement is aided by previous experiences, social contacts, and knowledge of the border. Southward movement, at least for everyone in this book, is forced movement, an expulsion mandated and controlled by the U.S. state. East–west movement is far more complicated. On the southern side of the border, there is generally a concerted effort to avoid the punitive state apparatuses of both the United States and Mexico, as well as a desire to avoid criminals and kidnapping. On the northern side of the border, people travel throughout the country in search of family, work, and a safe place to live. However, once apprehended, lateral movement is used as a punishment, to further disrupt people from geographies of migration that have become familiar.[18]

This occurs through two mechanisms. The first is the confusing geography of U.S. county and federal prisons, as well as immigration detention centers that leave migrants confused and disoriented.[19] People may spend months or years incarcerated and then are removed to Mexico in a completely unfamiliar region where they know no one, and may be thousands of miles from family or friends. The second are lateral repatriation programs such as the Alien Transfer and Exit Program (ATEP) that send people to different regions of the border, in a nominal attempt to "break the smuggling cycle."[20] This is part of the fantasy that smugglers are forcing people to cross the border rather than providing an agreed-upon service. The end goal, of course, is to increase the hardship for migrants. It is unclear whether or not officials actually believe that sending people to different regions will make it harder for smugglers; however, it is obvious that this is an undeniable hardship, making the migratory experience more difficult and unpleasant.

The Consequence Delivery System (CDS)—the strategic plan of the U.S. Border Patrol, formalized in 2011, but existing in pieces for much of the previous decade and even longer as a loose series of practices[21]—marks a significant change in border and immigration enforcement. It employs a government strategy that seeks to punish individuals in escalating ways based on previous migration infractions. Rather than relying primarily on the dangers of the desert to dissuade potential immigrants, this new system evokes the full brunt of the U.S. justice system to prosecute and punish undocumented migrants. This coincides with the worldwide push to fortify borders, which, in turn, leads to greater and greater levels of violence associated with political boundaries.[22]

While most people are charged and incarcerated and removed in a matter of days and weeks, those who fear removal or have valid chances to fight removal must face the long and complex world of immigration courts. The immigration courts operate in a parallel legal universe.[23] Gone are the protections of innocence until proven guilty, gone is the right to counsel, and basically nonexistent is the right to a speedy trial, with some people spending years in immigration detention without parole awaiting a decision. Wait times stretch into the years in some federal court districts for asylum seekers. The choke point of immigration reform is therefore not policing, but the court system, an underfunded backwater of our massive enforcement apparatus. With only minutes devoted to each case, judges must decide whether or not to separate families and expel people to unfamiliar and often dangerous parts of the world. With wildly varying rates of asylum being granted by different judges and court circuits, as well as the significant role of U.S. geopolitics in shaping which citizens from which countries we choose to grant asylum, this has become a roll of the dice.[24] Dana Leigh Marks, an immigration judge in the Ninth Circuit, famously described it as "death penalty cases heard in traffic court settings."[25]

While these issues have taken center stage in U.S. and Mexican politics, my arrival at this topic was the result of a series of experiences throughout years of living and working on the border. The evolution of violence was particularly jarring and created its own needs and directions for my work that would not necessarily have emerged otherwise. I watched as fewer and fewer people would venture into the streets as dusk approached, as stores closed and restaurants sat empty. I would fall asleep to gunfire in Nogales. As an elderly woman who ran one of the shelters where I work joked, "I never thought I would learn how to tell the difference between fireworks and gunfire at my age."

And here I was, somehow a million miles from these conflicts, and yet often confronted by their realities, which I read about every day on sites like Blog del Narco and Michel Marizco's Border Reporter. The bloody videos, graphic photos, and macabre tales all served as a reminder about the reality of death and violence in Mexico. I soon began to expand my research out of Nogales, Sonora, and into Tijuana, Ciudad Juárez, and Nuevo Laredo. Going to new places without the years of contacts and built-in social support that I had in Sonora brought new methodological challenges.

METHODOLOGY: MIXED METHODS
AND MULTI-SITED RESEARCH

While there is a sprawling literature about the border, a limited amount of research on migration is actually conducted on the U.S.-Mexico border, much of it taking place instead in sending or receiving communities. Furthermore, still fewer works take place in multiple research sites along the U.S.-Mexico border. This project was an attempt to trace the twin phenomena of drug trafficking and deportation through the various settings and contexts of different border towns. The complicated movements through the carceral state, as well as lateral movements like ATEP, make the connections between places ever more intricate and harder to study, requiring a more holistic, mixed methods approach. The concept of multi-sited ethnography[26] allows us to better understand that we are not simply comparing two points on a map; rather, we are attempting to understand the different contexts and relationships between places. This book draws primarily from research with people in Nuevo Laredo, Tamaulipas, Nogales, Sonora, and Tijuana, Baja California, although research was conducted in other cities as well such as Matamoros, Reynosa, Ciudad Juárez, Altar, and Mexicali. This ethnographic work, conducted largely in migrant shelters, was a way to expand upon a large-scale survey project with deportees, asking questions about the subtle ways in which crime and violence intertwine with human mobility. These questions could not be answered through survey questions written in black and white for the world to see without additional, nuanced qualitative work.

I was one of the PIs for a binational team of sixty researchers[27] who conducted surveys with deportees in Tijuana and Mexicali, Baja California; Nogales, Sonora; Ciudad Juárez, Chihuahua; Nuevo Laredo, Tamaulipas; and Mexico City during aerial repatriations (see Map 1). Overall, we conducted 1,110 surveys with recent deportees in 2010–12,[28] each questionnaire containing 250 questions and lasting about an hour

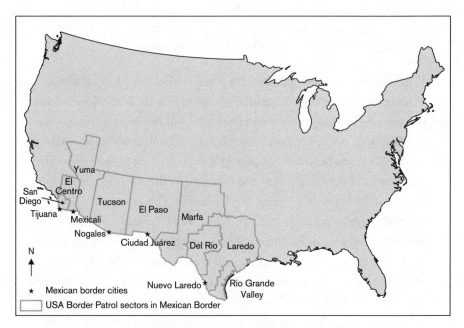

Map 1. MBCS survey locations. Source: Rolando Díaz.

per interview.[29] These surveys focused on the violence people experience while crossing the border, being apprehended, processed, and deported to Mexico. In order to participate, individuals must have crossed without papers within the last decade (to coincide with the creation of the Department of Homeland Security) and been deported to Mexico within the last month. This project, known as the Migrant Border Crossing Study (MBCS), is the first attempt to understand how peoples' experiences of being deported diverge from stated due process. However, not every question can be asked on a survey.

This is where ethnographic work becomes invaluable. In many ways the survey research led me to the ethnographic questions that form the basis of this book. The subtle interactions between people and places, the nuanced rules dictating behavior, and the undercurrent of fear associated with the brutality of organized crime and of the state are only apparent through in-depth qualitative research. However, there is always an uneven nature to this knowledge. The work in Tamaulipas was conducted in fits and starts with trips in 2011, 2012, and a five-month intensive research period in 2013, with two follow-up visits in 2016. This was to account both for time, balancing multiple research sites, but also due to the unique security situation in the region. Because of this complicated research process, readers will notice significant jumps in time and space; however, none of the characters in this book are composites.

Additionally, one constant throughout this work was engaging in migrant shelters as an important space where the violence of the drug war collides with immigration enforcement. Lázaro, who narrated the opening vignette for this book, knows the history of that violence and its impact on migration as well as anyone. His unique background informed his particular perspective. Born in the Zapotec city of Pochutla, Oaxaca, Lázaro spent more time directly on the front lines of the Zetas's reign of terror over migrants than anyone else I encountered in my fieldwork. He worked at the front door of a shelter in Tamaulipas, deciding who can enter and who cannot for over seven years from 2009–17. Lázaro, although barely five feet tall, had a presence few could claim.

He was soft-spoken but firm, relying on short noncommittal sentences. He wore a vest, and several rosaries under his bearded chin and thick spiky black hair. Lázaro developed a rare bone disease when he was a child that caused the cartilage in his joints to calcify, leading him to walk with a limp, but this did not affect his demeanor and strength. "I have no limits," he said. "I was dedicated to the farm, taking care of goats and sheep. My father is a *campesino*. It was a nice life, but at six years old I had to deal with my illness ... it is an impediment for certain movements, but it does not limit me. *A todo lo que da!*—I keep going! I am a normal person. What I have is not a limit. God gave me an open mind and I am happy." He arrived at the shelter because of his brother, who was in the seminary to be a priest. "Before, for example, I sold pirated goods, movies, CDs, cloths, T-shirts. Even back when I was in high school I started to distribute drugs. I have done a little bit of everything. That same experience that I lived in Oaxaca helped me do good things in

Nuevo Laredo. How did I detect the people who were smoking marijuana, well, before, I smoked a lot of marijuana!" laughed Lázaro.

He was well aware of the dual nature of providing services to migrants. The fact of the matter is that this is not a simple homogenous group of people. Neither the anti-immigrant right, hoping to demonize every immigrant as a criminal, nor the pro-immigrant left with a "pure" victim narrative would be wholly satisfied. People are complex and nuanced and not everyone has pure motives, and while it is factually correct that the vast majority of deportees and immigrants are not violent criminals, one needs to be aware of the potential presence of violent criminals when working in these spaces.

Many of the stories I collected depict important insights and devastating consequences of violence. Navigating this world and conducting interviews without causing potential harm to people was always in my mind. One incident was typical of this challenge:

> I had interviewed Javier, a 45-year-old man originally from Jalisco who had married a U.S. citizen and had two children in the United States. At the end of the night, as I was leaving, he stopped me. He was reading a Bible alone by the kitchen, on the one indoor step. Javier was red in the face with tears in his eyes. He told me, "I don't know who you are and what you will do with this stuff. Everyone here told you a lot of stuff. They all told you the truth and bad things could happen with it." I wrote down my contact information for my websites, my email and full name. I told him he could see what I have done, and the transparency helped a little bit, but not much. He said, "I told you a lot because, what can happen? It's already ruined."[30]

This served as a potent reminder of the challenges of working in migrant shelters. Not only are these complex places, filled with people who have wildly different pasts, goals, and purposes, but there is a sense of urgency and fear that often fills shelters. This presents an additional challenge as deportees attempt to navigate the obstacles of a dangerous and violent border region.

First, it has been well established that people working for the cartels or for human smugglers often infiltrate the shelters to find out information about what is happening there, who is around, and what they are doing. Javier's worry about some of the stories I had been told was something I had reflected upon before. Most shelters are located in poorer parts of town. Generally, neighbors are not sympathetic to dozens of people arriving and staying in nearby buildings and having nowhere to go. Wealthy neighbors have repeatedly called the authorities and used their influence to evict the shelters or curtail their activities, meaning that working-class or poor neighborhoods are generally the only places that allow them to operate. This also allows for surveillance by cartels from the outside as well as the inside. Despite the well-known prospect of people overhearing them, during my research the stories flowed, sometimes in a whisper, other times loudly, too loudly in fact. Sometimes I tried to slow or stop people, but most did not care, as echoed by Javier's last point: this is the lowest of low points on an already difficult journey. Deportation is the point of collapse, where devastation sets in. People feel they have little else to lose and the desire to tell their stories wins out. I hope to humanize these experiences through the lives of people, who discuss not only their victimization, but also their hopes, dreams, personal histories, and livelihoods. Hopefully, this can contextualize the human tragedy of deportation.

TOWARD A TOPOLOGY OF VIOLENCE

Around the world, the figure of the immigrant has seen a resurgence as the scapegoat of choice. From Western Europe to Australia to Donald Trump's anti-immigrant xenophobia, immigrants have come under intense scrutiny and become the object of heightened fear and the subject of harsh reprisals. Some attribute this hatred and fear as an admonishment of their foreignness, being primarily attributed to another nation, another people. However, this does not help us answer one of the key questions posed in this book, namely: Why are deportees, those returned to their supposed homeland, also abused, tortured, or killed with impunity? Following the work of Thomas Nail it is not the belonging to another nation that is primarily to blame for the seeming ease and ubiquitous demonization of migrants, but rather their movement.[31] As an immigrant, or a deportee for that matter, movement has been etched on their being. "Thus, more than any other political figure (citizen, foreigner, sovereign, etc.) the migrant is the one least defined by its being and place and more by its becoming and displacement: by its movement."[32] Migrants are essentially named for their movement, and thus inextricably out of place by definition, always in transit from or to a different place. Migrants are not a permanent fixture of anywhere; they are forever in motion.

The object of this research, however, is not migrants necessarily, but that subset of migrants who have come in contact with our growing repressive, anti-immigrant machine: deportees. While the migrant may be the stranger, the deportee is the reject, the stranger who could not cut it and has been forcibly returned in chains. The deportee is still defined by mobility, but it is the failed mobility, the bulimic expulsion[33] from a foreign state, that has come to define their mobility. Therefore not only are deportees always from somewhere else, they are also defined as coming from somewhere that rejected them, even as they return to what may nominally be their country of citizenship. Understanding the geography of people, particularly through labels that denote impermanence or a state of motion, will help us grasp why it has become so common and so easy to abuse, demonize, and even dispose of certain groups.

The very fact that migrants are not rooted in any one place means that, first and foremost, no one will speak for them; no one will look for them, and their story is easily forgotten. Imagine if a hundred people were kidnapped and murdered in one small town or city. Regardless of the power of the murderers this could create extreme social upheaval. The concentration of mortality from one place alone would make it impossible to hide. Indeed this has happened several times over the past decade in Mexico as villages such as Miguel Alemán, Tamaulipas, and Allende, Coahuila, were almost completely wiped out.[34] However, this is a difficult, costly, and dangerous activity, one that, barring

Figure 1. A man being deported to Nogales, Sonora, at night. Photo by Murphy Woodhouse.

immense corruption from the top levels of government, cannot go unanswered.

Now, imagine that a similar massacre happens, as it did in 2010 in San Fernando, Tamaulipas, with subsequent mass graves found containing hundreds more over the years, but this time, instead of being all from one village, the people come from all over the hemisphere. These are now people who simply disappear along the migrant trail. Reconstructing their journeys is difficult, finding answers nearly impossible. One kidnapping victim explained it to me succinctly, "If they did this to the locals, there would be a revolt!" Violence, therefore, easily concentrates on those in movement. Tyner and Inwood "contend that violence must be approached from this same vantage point: that violence must be theorized as not having a universal quality—but as being produced by, and producing" the space and society around us.[35] Individuals whose geography is defined as transient can be taken, extorted, tortured, and murdered, in the same way they can easily be demonized, criminalized, and blamed. As societies have become more and more diverse in terms of religion, race, and ethnicity (often requiring us to rethink these categories entirely), the immigrant will continue to dominate as one of the preferred objects of hate, scorn, and at the very least, indifference.

Some have questioned why Central Americans have borne so much of the brunt of the violence in Mexico, questioning if Mexicans hate Central Americans. I contend that this question is misguided. It is their movement and the distance from the social safety nets of home that exposes them to violence. Jorge Bustamante has argued that distance is the key to this violence (i.e., the farther away, the easier it is to violate people's rights),[36] but I contend it is the relationships produced through movement to issues such as the border and enforcement measures. Those who are engaged with and often labeled through the concept of "illegality"[37] face a significant degeneration of their basic human rights. For Tim Cresswell, the law is one of the principal sites of conflict through which mobilities are produced.[38] Add to this the international legal dimensions that shape who moves, and how certain mobilities, namely transmigration and deportation, place someone at the mercy of criminal organizations. While undocumented immigrants from Mexico can blend in during (most) of their travels through Mexico, Central Americans cannot. For Mexicans, deportation exposes them as foreign in their own land, as engaging with the dangerous activity of migration.

Some scholars have attempted to remake the discourse around migration, finding new words to describe this population such as autonomous migrants, or *resistencia hormiga* (ant resistance).[39] However, this fails to recognize the slippery nature of language as well as the materiality of violence. Neither can we name the forces of hate and violence, nor can we reconstruct a new identity that wards off the violence of mobility. The fact of the matter is, because of these migratory journeys, people's geography has been broken. Rather than rename migration, we must instead concentrate on how to buttress their protections, how to challenge the forced movement of deportation, and how to protect this important social group.

People in movement (particularly through the forced movement of removal) become the target of violence. Deportation in all of its forms is an act of violence, and carries with it a slew of other consequences. The question becomes: how should we protect them? There are numerous ways that this could happen: greater support during and after migration from their country of citizenship; greater public safety in the border region and other areas where deportees concentrate; humane removal policies that limit people's exposure to violence by ensuring they are not separated from their belongings or sent to unfamiliar areas of the border; fair treatment in custody and being returned at a decent hour that allows them to find safe passage home. However, these are Band-Aids. We must seek to curb the root causes of violence against migrants. This involves disrupting mass deportation.

Deportation, as the centerpiece of this book, is easier to mitigate than migration. Without downplaying the difficulty of affecting change against either of these phenomena, the law requires numerous burdens to be met before removal and, moreover, these legal benchmarks can and have been changed many times. We as a society must recognize the protections for migrants that are written into the law. Migration is determined by economic and social factors around the world, by hotspots of violence that periodically explode, and most of all, by the increasingly complex web of family ties that exist between states. Deportation *is* the state. It is the repressive state apparatus. For that reason I focus more on deportation than on migration as a whole. Migration—its routes, goals, and destinations—is shaped by millions of different people with millions of individual constraints and opportunities. Attempting to reformulate these approaches and dissuade people from crossing has been the goal of enforcement activities for decades and, after billions of dollars and thousands of lives lost, these activities have been only moderately successful at influencing people to cross in particular areas.[40]

Directly challenging the state is no simple task, but there are legal avenues that not only provide relief for individuals, but also cause problems for the internal workings of the state. These problems, usually bureaucratic and procedural, often slow down the deportation process. Without speedy, cheap, and efficient removals, the system cannot handle the volume of migration. At peak years (e.g., 2005), there were almost 1.5 million apprehensions along the southern border of the United States. Rapid removal, therefore, was generally a welcome solution both for border officials who were constrained by the lack of space to accommodate thousands of people each day, and the costs of detention, combined with migrants who were anxious to return to Mexico and either try to cross again or return home.[41] However, as the state has become more and more punitive in its approach to dealing with migration, this arrangement has broken down. Now, it makes sense (particularly for migrants with deep roots in the United States) to fight charges, hire lawyers, and demand the full protections of the law.

IMMIGRATION AND BORDER ENFORCEMENT

At the heart of this problem is the strategic plan of the U.S. Border Patrol—the Consequence Delivery System (CDS). This was in response to the much-maligned (albeit convenient) practice of returning people to Mexico after they signed a voluntary return. This was a purely administrative process and migrants were free to cross the border again and again without facing prison time, although it would cause problems for future legal migration. This had been referred to as the "voluntary departure complex"[42] or the "cat and mouse" game between border guards and migrants.[43]

Mike Fisher, former director of the U.S. Border Patrol, officially announced the CDS in October 2011. In an address to the House Committee on Homeland Security he stated how the CDS "guides management and agents through a process designed to uniquely evaluate each subject and identify the ideal consequences to impede and deter further illegal activity."[44] By applying the full weight of the punitive, carceral state against immigration offenders, the border patrol and other U.S. immigration enforcement agencies—Customs and Border

Protection (CBP) and Immigration and Customs Enforcement (ICE)—
are able to realize their long-standing dream of punishing people for
immigration violations. Unfortunately, scholars have been slow to study
the CDS, most still approaching undocumented migration through
the lens of "prevention through deterrence," which is a very limited
framework for understanding contemporary immigration enforcement.
While scholars have focused on the ills of using the desert as a deter-
rent for almost twenty years now, a formidable apparatus of punishment and criminalization has been developing under our noses that has
significantly changed the experiences of migrants.

The CDS involves a suite of programs that represent unique punishments such as lateral repatriation through the Alien Transfer and Exit
Program (ATEP), which moves people from one region of the border to
another; OASSIS, an anti–human smuggler program; and the most high-
profile and controversial of all, Operation Streamline. Streamline is a
mass trial system whereupon about seventy people are tried and convicted of illegal entry (8 U.S. Code § 1325) or illegal reentry (8 U.S. Code
§ 1326) in about a half-hour. A few migrants may try to fight their cases,
finding themselves shuffled back into the larger, full-to-bursting criminal
court system, followed by the immigration court system, waiting months
or even years, generally in detention, to contest the charges before a
judge. The rest plead "culpable—guilty" in groups of five before the
judge and their lawyers.[45]

This has been one of the main mechanisms for increasing the
number of so-called "criminal aliens." Until Operation Streamline
began in 2006, section 1325 and 1326 cases were rarely prosecuted.[46]
Although technically entry to the United States without inspection has
been a crime for decades, presence in the United States without proper
authorization is not a crime.[47] Daniel Kanstroom has masterfully outlined the development of immigration law as a parallel judiciary system
that does not provide the right to an attorney, does not place the burden
of proof on the state, and is almost entirely based on the assumption
that deportation—formal removal—is not a punishment.[48] This book

challenges that assumption. First, the strategic plan of CBP has woven punishment into the removal process by escalating the negative consequences of crossing the border. Even without these direct policies linked to punishment, deportation has never been a benign process of returning people to their homes; it is an act of violence. It destroys families and, sometimes, costs people their lives. The system of removal is a complex one, whereupon deportees are taken to various ports of entry and dumped at the border, often thousands of miles from familiar cities. They must contend with the complex geography of organized crime, avoiding corrupt police officers, kidnappers, and cartel recruiters in their attempt to make it to safety. For some, that safety only exists in the United States because, after a lifetime of living in Chicago or Los Angeles or Houston, it is the only place they know. In fact, the biggest factor in who will attempt another crossing after being removed is if the person states that they consider their home to be in the United States and not Mexico.[49] This group of people, whose home as well as their economic and social life is in the United States, is disproportionately affected by policies that punish repeat border crossers, exposing them to escalating levels of danger, in addition to harsher penalties and prison sentences. People whose home is the United States and not Mexico have been called Unauthorized Permanent Residents (UPRs) because they have all the social and cultural characteristics and ties of Lawful Permanent Residents (LPRs), but lack the formal authorization.[50] They will cross again and again to be reunited with their families and the land they know as home.

Moreover, questions about why deportees end up in certain border cities have been particularly hard to answer. The aforementioned programs of the CDS; lateral repatriation from one region to another; the connections between local and county jails and private detention and removal services—all of these complicate the geography of detention and deportation.[51] This becomes particularly problematic for those individuals who are moved between regions of Mexico that are actively engaged in an intercartel war. For example, the Sinaloa Cartel and the

Zetas have been engaged in brutal and bloody struggles since as early as 2003.[52] Those moving between these regions are in extreme danger, simply by virtue of being born in enemy territory. Others who have been engaged with drugs in different regions are in even more acute danger because they will quickly be perceived as attempting to infiltrate the region on behalf of a rival criminal organization.

The geography of removal interacts directly with the highly volatile, shifting map of criminal control over territory in Mexico. As regional power structures change and alliances and enemies change, where people wind up in Mexico upon their return directly impacts their safety. Felipe, a deportee from Oaxaca, and his friend were kidnapped and interrogated by police in Coahuila. They looked at his federal electoral ID, which shows where he and his companion were born. They let him go, but his comrade from Michoacán was not so lucky. He was never heard from again. This violence, as well as the hidden, yet pervasive presence of death and disappearance, plague migration throughout the border region.

DEATH AND DEPORTATION

While death is finite and absolute for those individuals who are gone, it is intimately connected to the social world through relationships, meaning, and grief. To fully understand how violence is intrinsic to deportation, we have to examine the ways that death has changed the migratory process. For instance, death often plays an important role in deportation since the grief for lost loved ones in Mexico frequently precipitates the return to their country of birth. This can lead to people getting caught in the back-and-forth of migration during the age of enhanced border enforcement. Many individuals who have been living in the United States for decades return home for a funeral or to say goodbye to a sick relative or parent, on the assumption that crossing back will be the same as it was in previous decades. However, this is not the case and many find themselves stuck in the criminalizing apparatus of Operation Streamline—crossing, being deported, getting charged with illegal entry and illegal reentry. The death of a loved one is, therefore, an important factor that leads people into the cycle of deportation, criminalization, and violence on the border. Furthermore, the crossing itself is so dangerous that each time people attempt to cross back, they are placing themselves in danger.

The lethality of migration increased drastically during the 1990s as the border patrol's strategic plan pushed people into the dangerous desert, which became the only viable access point to the U.S. labor market.[53] This has led to about five thousand known migrant deaths along the U.S.-Mexico border,[54] and despite the recent decreases in migration, the journey has continued to be highly lethal, with the rate of death remaining high.[55] Scholars began to study migrant deaths beginning in the late 1990s, such as Espenshade in 1995, and Eschbach et al. in their seminal 1999 publication.[56] A large literature has developed around migrant deaths that includes studies demonstrating that migrants with indigenous ancestry are identified at lower rates,[57] as well as studies of the material culture surrounding migration and the length of time it takes for bodies to decompose, among others.[58] Jason de León has used archaeological methods alongside cultural anthropology to explore the possessions people take and the evidence left behind of the arduous journey across the border.[59]

Data on migrant deaths are generally presented as "known" deaths, simply because it is impossible to know the true number of people who have perished in the vast desert.[60] The consequences of immigration enforcement on the U.S. side have well-known impacts; the connections between removal and death is less understood. While the painstaking efforts taken by NGOs, medical examiner's offices, and activists to document migrant deaths along the border should not be diminished,[61] there has been decidedly less attention given to people who die on the other side of the line. This includes people who may die while attempting to migrate but have yet to cross the international boundary, as well as the more complex task of separating out those who die in cities and those left in the numerous mass graves that have been linked to the drug war.

For groups working on identifying the dead and missing in Mexico, this has been a Sisyphean task, having identified almost no one at the time of writing. Some of the dead identified in mass graves in Mexico, especially in Tamaulipas, Durango, and Veracruz have been linked to migration and even deportation, suggesting that there is significant cross-over between the death toll of migration and the death toll of the drug war. These efforts to sort, quantify, and explain the lethality of migration are incredibly useful for families attempting to find loved ones and gain the closure and finality necessary to fully grieve these losses.[62] At the same time, we must seek to understand the deeper meanings, challenges, and significance of the way death is treated and understood from multiple perspectives.

THREE DEATHS OF DEPORTATION
Ambiguous Death

Ambiguous death surrounds migration and deportation on the border. The very nature of doing research there (or providing services for that matter) is the extreme mobility of the population. Goodbyes are rarely spoken. Personal (contact) information is rarely shared, and the repetitious process of witnessing hundreds of new people appear and disappear daily reduces individual faces to a nearly indistinguishable blur. Stories circulate of death and danger, but it is hard to investigate or verify them. One man discussed how his friend had been deported to Coahuila and someone had opened fire on the deportees, killing several of them. Despite my best efforts I was never able to confirm or contradict his story. Others spoke of escaping or being let go after having been kidnapped and of witnessing dozens of murders while detained.[63] I saw people being forced into vans for loitering in front of the shelter, a forbidden place for deportees during the day, or at key points such as informal bus stops outside of Reynosa. We never heard from any of them again. Others arrive at the shelters scared, often telling convoluted, half-finished stories before jumping into taxis or running off into the night.

Even when we know that someone has died, it is often a challenge to know who it was. In November of 2013, the body of a young Honduran man was found in the Rio Bravo on the Nuevo Laredo side. There had been 65 deaths in the river that year, but counting was still a problem as it depended on which side of the river people washed up on to determine whether they were counted as part of the Mexican or the U.S. death toll. I was originally told it was a young man named Wilson who had been staying at the shelter, but there was quite a bit of disagreement about whether or not he was the one who died. According to the other Hondurans it was Wilson, whom I had interviewed the night before. He was barely 18 years old,[64] and had been working in a *tianguis* (flea market) selling clothes in Monterrey for about six months. He and his friend were debating whether to cross or go back to Monterrey as they stared at the various maps on the wall. Neither of them knew how to swim and debated whether the risk was worth it.

This death provoked some rather heated debates among the shelter staff, who assured me that it was not Wilson, and that he had left for Monterrey and called later. The Hondurans staying at the shelter were positive that it was this young man who died. I tried to get more information from the newspapers, but there was no follow-up and no definitive answer. Unfortunately this is the reality of death on the border; it is often contested, disagreed upon, and ultimately forgotten. As a place of transience, with thousands coming and going each day, it is hard to find and understand the circumstances of those who die along the way.

Dead Bodies over Dying People

Other deaths have the power to expose the hypocrisy of movement and immigration enforcement. On April 21, 2014, Hector Barrios died. He was 70 years old and a veteran of Vietnam. He was also a deportee. His heart had given out. A group gathered to commemorate his life a few days later at a funeral parlor in Colonia Juarez, near downtown Tijuana. The other deported veterans stood guard at the casket, one at each end, commemorating their friend and fallen brother. The sadness was palpable, the loss of life compounded by the tragic realization that many of them may not live to return home. There had been a lot of talk about sending his body back because he had the right to a military burial in the United States. The family decided against it. "If they wouldn't accept him in life, what right do they have once he dies?" said his niece. The deported vets decided to carry out their own military sendoff. One friend read off the thirteen folds of the flag as two others, in dress military attire, marched and folded the flag. Afterward, his friends stood and said words about him. A young Navy veteran, also a deportee, was particularly moving. He broke down, saying that Barrios never asked for anything. He was always there for everybody and never took anything in return.[65]

Only upon death could he cross back to the United States. His military service allows him to be buried in a military cemetery. Even though he was banished while alive, and forbidden from returning, his body, the empty husk, is now permitted to return. Ultimately, his family decided not to send him back. His failing health was not enough to grant him a reprieve and allow him access to healthcare in the United States despite his veterans' benefits. His living, and even his dying, body was forbidden entry, but upon death, his body could cross the border. The hypocrisy was too damning, too severe to accept the "honor" of burial after the betrayal of removal, and his family refused.

The plight of deported veterans is a unique one, and although there is currently no way of knowing how many veterans have been removed since the increasing ease with which noncitizens can be deported after the 1996 reforms, it represents the depths of the hypocrisy of deportation.[66] Veterans with legal permanent residence were allowed to serve in the armed forces for decades, generally with the promise of citizenship, but many failed to fully naturalize. Now, even a series of mild criminal infractions can lead to deportation and the removal of legal status. The banishment is acutely painful for those who have taken an oath to defend the United States with their lives against all other nations, including their former homes. In this sense, the forced expulsion of veterans is an annihilation of their identity and self-worth.

Indeed, for others this dynamic, whereupon the dead body has rights that the living did not, has been replicated along the border. The relatives of those who have died while crossing the border are often granted humanitarian parole to come to the United States and arrange to repatriate the body or search for their loved one's remains. While this is of course necessary, one cannot help but feel the hypocrisy in allowing people to come legally to search for a loved one who died because he or she was not legally allowed to enter. It is only after people die that they deserve to be recognized. Life is excluded and death is acceptable under our current immigration policies.

Deportation and Social Death

Social death therefore is the culmination of the immigration system. In addition to punitive, anti-immigrant plans such as the CDS, the immigration court system is essentially a parallel legal world. Defendants are not guaranteed counsel and therefore must pay thousands of dollars for representation. The burden is not on the state as in criminal charges, meaning that immigrants who claim that they face persecution or even torture and death should they be deported have to prove not only that this is a well-founded fear (rather than the state proving that it is not well founded), but also that they could not safely relocate within Mexico. It is no wonder that this profoundly difficult interpretation taken by many judges and court circuits means only a small percentage of individuals receive asylum each year. The crowded courts are constantly trying to get rid of cases, leading to limits on time to present evidence or experts or other testimony.

However, the very fact that the law is applied in a profoundly different manner for citizens and noncitizens is the heart of this matter. Lisa Marie Cacho writes about social death, the presumed rightlessness that has been ingrained into our racialized legal system. She explains that "to be ineligible for personhood is a form of social death; it not only defines who does not matter, it also makes mattering meaningful."[67] To be an immigrant and to be undocumented is to not matter in the United States.

The 1996 passage of the Illegal Immigration Reform and Immigrant Responsibility Act (IIRAIRA) accelerated the criminalization of immigrants by creating new categories of crimes that would result in deportation. Namely, it created expedited removal, which is a formal removal that does not require review by a judge, and the "aggravated felony," various combinations of misdemeanors or felonies that lead to a prison sentence of up to a year.[68] Therefore, the aggravated felony is often far less severe than a regular felony, contrary to the name. To reiterate, under the law deportation is not a punishment but an administrative process, which is why immigration courts and proceedings do not need to follow the same guidelines as criminal trials.

These processes of criminalization, enacted through a labyrinthine, Kafkaesque bureaucracy, give the appearance of legitimacy and justice to people on the outside, which serves to normalize the severe harm done by removal. This veneer of justice has seeped into Mexico as well, leading to a widespread stigma that is, in some ways, a holdover of the popular view that once people make it into the United States, they will not be removed unless they commit some heinous act. The assumption that deportees "*andaban de vago*"—were acting like bums—is a commonplace assertion that is at once the negation of the humanity of suffering enacted through unjust, albeit legal processes, while simultaneously a result of the construction of "good migrants" and "bad deportees." The efforts to lionize migrants are understandable considering the forces that we have previously discussed that demonize migrants; however, it is fundamentally misguided.

Scholars have critiqued the romantic, populist constructions of the migrant. For the pro-migrant Left, there is the heteronormative image of undocumented migrants as long-suffering workers, and family *men*, doing jobs that citizens will not touch, providing for their loved ones, living in substandard conditions and suffering abuses. There is no greater exemplar within this narrative than the campaign by the Dreamers, undocumented youth who came to the United States "through no fault of their own," immediately implying the culpability of adults. The coalition for Dreamers (regularized under President Obama's executive order Deferred Action for Childhood Arrivals [DACA] that was recently repealed by President Trump, although the repeal remains in legal limbo) has built support by noting the near-superhuman prowess of these young people, valedictorians with sparkling credentials, better than perfect grades, all while working in a family business and serving in the military. Arguments to keep them in the country too often hinge on the economic impact they have and the cost to the country for removing them, rather than the simple fact that they belong here. This is not to criticize the young people who accomplish amazing things while dealing with the crushing pressure of living with a precarious status; rather, it is to point out that this narrative reinforces the perspective that removal is a deserved and natural outcome for the unworthy. Only a select few, those who are truly extraordinary, should therefore be worthy to stay.

This is why removal marks social death. All of these tropes of deservedness reinforce the undeservedness of the deported. While the immigrant is already unworthy of the same protections as the citizen, the deported is already guilty. This racialized rightlessness drives the U.S. enforcement machinery and converts migrants into the convenient object of violence, even as they return to a country that, at least nominally, is their home. For some, especially those who struggle to adapt to Mexico, this state of limbo can become permanent. People often start living as deportees along the border, unable to extricate themselves from migrant shelters, soup kitchens, and the precarious jobs offered to migrants such as selling newspapers on street corners. This is especially true of addicts, and, while I would caution against blaming any single thing for debilitating addiction, the trauma of deportation can exacerbate addictive tendencies.

Jorge[69] was 43 and had spent the last 12 years as a deportee, floating between rooming houses, rehab, and sleeping on the streets of Tijuana in the infamous Bordo,[70] an open-air drug market in the paved river beside the border wall. He had gotten addicted to crack in the 1980s and was deported after he graduated high school. We sat on the access road on the top of the canal, out of earshot of the tunnels filled with people shooting heroin just beyond the view of the motorists passing by. Jorge was a slight man. He walked with a limp and was missing a few teeth. He had a couple of bags and a big backpack with him, clutched at his feet.

At 20, Jorge gave a fake name to the police after being arrested for drugs and he had his residency revoked. Jorge had crossed back and been deported at least five times. "I want to go but it is dangerous because it is my third strike and will be lots of jail time. When I first got here it was easier, but after the twin towers came down..." He had tried going back to see family in Sinaloa, but could not handle the small town and returned to Tijuana. "Tomorrow my mother is coming to spend the day with me. You know May 10 is Mother's Day? She comes here on the 9th [to celebrate] and for the 10th she will go back [to Los Angeles]." His mother pays his bills and helps keep him off the street, but it gets hard. She had transferred him two hundred dollars so he could rent an apartment, but he got beaten up and robbed in downtown Tijuana. "After, the police grabbed me to fill their quota (*llenar el punto*), but luckily the judge let me go because I had my teeth knocked out, and one was just hanging by a thread."

Jorge's plan was to get checked into rehab. That was his mother's goal, in addition to seeing her other son around Mother's Day. She used to come more, and so did his siblings, but they got tired and stayed away. "*Todo se regresa*—it all comes back," he explained, switching into English, "Payback." His drug habits had changed since he got deported. "I like crystal," he said, referring to methamphetamines. "But it isn't so much the addiction as not having a place to live. I can't cross the line and get out of here (the Bordo) because the police grabs you. Drugs have their priorities, but it is still secondary. When I can't rent a place and I have nowhere to sleep, well, I will party (*andar de vago*), buy crystal," he explained. "I feel like a nomad right now with all these backpacks," Jorge said, switching back to perfect English.

The family ties that have helped him navigate his addiction in a foreign land are notably frayed. Even though he was excited to see his

Figure 2. Tijuana, Baja California, Mexico. Homeless deportees sleep in an underpass on top of the canal known as "el Bordo." A busy freeway passes in the background, mostly commuters crossing back and forth to the United States. Photo by Murphy Woodhouse.

mother, he noted that she used to come more and it is hard on her to see him like this. These cycles of addiction, incarceration, removal, and then the despair of being banished are a never-ending nightmare for those who cannot adjust to their new country. For Jorge, who had spent three and half years at the rehab center last time, this was another attempt to change his story. The Bordo, of all places, attracted these individuals, now stuck in the limbo of deportation. However, Jorge was quick to defend the area as well. For migrants and other desperate people, "It is a gold mine of food. Don't say the Bordo is just drugs, do you understand? ... At night, yes, it is drugs, but during the day, there are families and migrants." I agreed with Jorge, explaining that I had been volunteering at the Desayunador Salesiano where more than a thousand people got breakfast every day. "*Con razon!* I recognized you," he exclaimed. In some ways, the prevalence of services, breakfast, sandwiches, and clothing giveaways attracts people here—sometimes it provides a needed respite, at other times it is a trap. The police watch who comes and goes, often arresting or extorting them, which can start people down a dangerous path, leading to somewhere far worse than where they had been before.

BOOK OUTLINE

In order to understand the social and spatial processes of violence against deportees that lead to the extreme precarity on the border, we follow several distinct moments of the migratory journey. Chapter 2 outlines the journey across the border and the influence of organized crime and drug trafficking on clandestine migration. The explosion of violence that occurred as alliances between drug cartels splintered had a drastic impact on the border, and this chapter explores the micro-level outbursts that affected Sonora as well as the rest of the border. These changes shaped the migrant experience during much of my fieldwork in surprising ways. While questions as to whether human smugglers (known as coyotes) are part of drug cartels abound, I assert that such questions are short-sighted. Rather, we must look more closely at the ways that drug trafficking, undocumented migration, and human smuggling interact in the shared clandestine zone of the border, producing unique outcomes for people attempting to access the United States.

Chapter 3 explores how the controls on movement that exist for migrants living without status in the United States are replicated upon removal to Mexico, creating a distinct set of rules that govern movement for deportees as they navigate highly contested border spaces. Chapter 4 focuses on the consequences of failing to abide by these restrictions in the form of kidnapping. By asking why has the kidnapping of relatively poor individuals proliferated to such a terrifying extent, we can move past the ransom narrative into an understanding of how possessing people's bodies is also about accessing their labor. This often occurs through recruitment into drug trafficking activities. This chapter also explores the policies and practices of deportation that are actively exacerbating the situation and putting people in harm's way.

Chapter 5 centers on the issue of drug cartels actively, often forcibly, recruiting migrants and deportees into organized crime. This chapter focuses on the extreme way that these two geopolitical phenomena—prohibitions on the sale of drugs and the movement of labor—collide. Deportees who have criminal records are concentrated in the northeastern and northwestern edges of the border, and they have become convenient fodder for the seemingly endless violence of inter- and intra-cartel struggles. For the Northeast, recruitment generally involves guarding the river from potential migrants who do not have approval from organized crime and, therefore, involves a role reversal from potential migrant to someone actively trying to stop or extort money from would-be border crossers.

Chapter 6 delves into the overlap between the death toll of drug war violence and deaths related to migration. As bodies have piled up in morgues along the border, so too have migrants been found in clandestine graves along migrant routes through Mexico. How have processes of disappearance, loss, and suffering related to migration become intertwined with the death toll from Mexico's so-called "drug war"? To truly understand the linkages between deportation and death we need to take note of the difficulty of counting and classifying deaths, especially those that take place outside of traditional border-crossing points such as Arizona and south Texas.

In chapter 7, I visit the important ways relationships among deportees provide a potential to safeguard them from the dangers they face during migration. While stories of betrayal abound, so too do heroic acts of kindness and support. By understanding the support people offer one another, we can also see the detrimental ways through which border enforcement policies often drive wedges between people, pitting them against one another instead of helping them unite. Moreover, this leads us to question the limits of state and nonstate violence. Where will it end and how are people already resisting this social order?

Chapter 8 explores our complex Kafkaesque asylum system, whereupon the validity of a person's life and death is determined based on a set of subjective and confusing criteria. This process of determining which deaths are valid for protection under the law is the heart of our asylum system. In addition to exploring these legal hurdles, this chapter calls upon other scholars to participate in court proceedings, offering their expertise as evidence. This often will present academics with some uncomfortable realities, namely, the gulf between legal definitions of expertise and contemporary scholarship. However, addressing and developing a framework for academics to participate in these venues will increase the impact of scholarship and the valuable knowledge we often already possess.

To conclude this book I return to many of the people we will meet throughout these pages, leaving us to question the long-term implications of removal on peoples' lives. We still do not know the social implications of deportations, especially when discussing why some people successfully readapt to life in their former country, while others seemingly cannot. This leads to a push to reimagine deportation, not as the administrative process of sending people home, but a profoundly violent process of forced movement, one that has intense ramifications for both Mexican and U.S. society. This is not to say that some people are not able to escape, move on, cross again, or return to a previous life. Certainly, there are many thousands who move on fairly easily; however, those without contacts in Mexico are often stuck and unable to make their next move, or are often forced to cross in unsafe and dangerous situations without the forethought and planning that is necessary to successfully cross the border. We must push back on removals, not just for the physical violence and persecution that they so often precipitate, a clear violation of U.S. law, but through deeper challenges to our fidelity to place and the pain caused by separation from families and homes, on both sides of the border.

CHAPTER TWO

I Want to Cross with a Backpack

It's hot. My mouth is so dry my lips stick together. I awake after a few hours' sleep in the shelter in Altar, Sonora. It's late May, and summer has hit the region. It is 110 degrees and the desert air ripples in the distance. Earlier that day I caught a ride to Sásabe with some protestors who were walking the migrant trail, an annual march through the desert to protest migrant deaths. There, I met up with Padre Maximiliano, two parts Sonoran cowboy and one part priest. With his quintessential northern Mexican style, cowboy boots, hats, and a northern-inflected accent, he is tall and, like most Sonorans, fair-skinned. We had known each other for the better part of a decade. He is jovial, well spoken, and approaches his work with the typical sense of humor that has become a nationwide defense mechanism in Mexico. As a protector of migrant rights his unique approach is unparalleled, and he is regarded as a pillar of the local community because of his ability to directly intervene in support of kidnapped migrants. His oversized personality and Sonoran taste in horses, trucks, and cowboy hats set him apart from many of the more subdued, migrant rights activists. I rode with him, one of the nuns, and the shelter worker from Sásabe to Altar, Sonora, in their Ford F-150 truck.

Altar, once a sleepy town whose mayor debated a journalist in *El Imparcial* about whether or not his town had garbage pickup and was not

Figure 3. Sásabe, Sonora, Mexico. The small town of Sásabe sits on the border with Lukeville, Arizona. Migrants cross through this harsh terrain on their journey north that can last anywhere from three days to a week. Photo by Jeremy Slack.

in fact "forgotten by modernity" in the early 1990s, had become the epicenter of undocumented migration by the mid-2000s. It is nestled deep in the Sonoran desert where the starkness of the saguaro and cholla cactuses and the ocotillos contrast with the red rocks, sand, and the jagged edges of the purple mountains in the distance. It is a landscape that is both majestic and terrifying, like being lost in a dry ocean. At this time of the year, even though it was only May, the heat itself feels alive.

We had taken the infamous backbreaking road from Sásabe, its washboard corrugation on the sand and dirt creating nonstop vibrations in the priest's truck. I had driven this road a handful of times in previous years, but it had been a while. A colleague had been held at gunpoint during a fieldtrip for teachers, which caused all of us border researchers to avoid the area for a few years. However, the road was still a mess, with dunes whipped by the wind now scattered across the roadway, ready and willing to send any car into a fishtail. There were fewer broken-down vans than on my prior trips. This road was once littered with abandoned vehicles that were no longer able to handle the constant pounding of being overloaded with 20–30 people (the seats having been removed) and then driven like mad through the desert dozens of times a day. Some flipped over, others simply broke down, and no one thought it worth the time or effort to recover and repair them.

The route had been the main access point for clandestine migration into the United States for almost 20 years. It emerged after Operation Hold the Line and Operation Gatekeeper, as enforcement efforts began to concentrate in urban zones, pushing migrants deeper and deeper into the desert beginning in the mid-1990s. Altar, Sonora, is essentially as deep as you can get. With only the mountain ranges for orientation, skilled smugglers guide groups through this unforgiving terrain, often successfully, sometimes unsuccessfully. This has been the hotspot for migrant deaths throughout the 2000s, when one in every three border patrol apprehensions occurred in the Tucson sector.[1] Despite increases in migration through South Texas, due in part to the increase in Central American migration, increased enforcement in the Tucson sector, and growing knowledge of the potential danger of the desert, this small town remains one of the key entrance points for migrants and, now, marijuana.

Typically, each region has one or more favored migrant and drug smuggling corridors, each located away from urban areas. For Tijuana, people cross to the east through areas known as El Hongo or La Rumorsa, a mountainous and hilly area where people and drugs can pass undetected. For those in Ciudad Juárez, the town of Anapra to the west and through the Valley of Juarez to the east remain favored smuggling routes. In South Texas, the area around Rio Bravo, outside of Reynosa, was a favorite location. Each of these areas develops a specific economy based on their unique situation along the border: close enough to cities where migrants and deportees congregate, but remote enough to make smuggling easier. However, none of these areas occupy as prominent of place in the geography of migration as Altar, Sonora. Its evolution into the most important hub for drug and human smuggling also marks a significant change in the presence, power, and violence of organized crime along the border.

RESEARCH ON THE BORDER AS THE "DRUG WAR" UNFOLDS

I began conducting research on the border in Nogales, Sonora, in 2003 as an undergraduate intern with Diane Austin at the University of Arizona. I spent several years working on issues related to reforestation, green technologies, and housing, developing an understanding of this often misunderstood place. The continuous laments that people mistreat Nogales because no one sees it as their true home, while thousands in fact continue to make it their home, spoke to the fly-by-night nature of the border. For some it is home, but for others it is simply one leg of a journey. Nestled high above the Sonoran desert, too high for the characteristic saguaro cactus to grow, Nogales was founded due to the railroad that runs along the valley between the hills and mountains.[2] Later, with the establishment of the Border Industrialization Program and then the *maquiladora* industry, Nogales grew from a tiny town to a more significant manufacturing and shipping hub. With it came its share of problems such as haphazard urbanization, lack of infrastructure, crime, and environmental degradation.

And yet, during my time working there in the early 2000s it seemed similar to most other cities in terms of drugs and violence. Sure, there were signs of drug trafficking like the gaudy mansions that popped up amid the humble shacks on the outskirts of town or the stickers and tattoos of the *Santa Muerte* (Saint Death)[3] and Jesus Malverde, a dapper folk saint for narcos, but nothing too out of the ordinary.[4] In 2006 a young woman was brutally murdered in the community where I worked, and it was treated as it deserved to be—as an extraordinary, tragic, and heartbreaking event. People debated who did it and why such a tragedy could

Figure 4. Nogales, Sonora, Mexico. On the southern edge of the city altars to the Santa Muerte have spread. This place of worship began in the early 2000s, but the number of altars quickly grew to over twenty. Many have offerings of flowers, candles, alcohol, cigarettes, and marijuana. Photo by Jeremy Slack.

have happened. This murder still divides people to this day, as many do not believe that the 17-year-old boy who was convicted of the murder was guilty, or that he acted alone.[5] However, this response to a tragic act of violence, an understandable reaction one would expect, became nearly nonexistent in 2008 with the arrival of the "drug war." The change in peoples' reactions to violence and grief is what truly shocked me.

While the bloodshed was already reaching record levels in Ciudad Juarez, Culiacan, and Tijuana in 2006 and 2007, Nogales and particularly Sonora had remained relatively untouched. August 29, 2008, however, had a drastic impact on the city. The severed heads of three teenagers were found downtown, near the international border in a Styrofoam cooler from a convenience store. The boys, later identified as two 19-year-olds and one 16-year-old from a poor neighborhood on the outskirts of town, had been kidnapped several days before, according to sources who knew relatives of the boys. Their bodies were found in a white Dodge RAM double cab, with Arizona plates two days later.[6]

The killings represented, more than anything else, a message: there was a new force in town. This new presence was announced yet again on October 23, 2008, with a high profile shootout during the day on a busy street that left 10 dead,[7] and then on November 3 of that same year with the assassination of Juan Manuel Pavón, the police chief of the state of Sonora (Policia Estatal Investigadora—PEI), in a highly coordinated attack.[8]

These events sent shockwaves through the city. People refrained from venturing out in public. Once busy streets were empty as soon as dark approached. The violence also brought an onslaught of state and federal police, as well as the military. Roadblocks became more frequent, upsetting the local balance between residents and the police. Frequent clashes between authorities and gangs left neighbors scared to leave their homes and the fear of getting caught up in the violence led to a notable silence on the part of the residents.

Juan Pablo, who lived at the shelter for migrants where I was working, had recently been deported from the United States and was selling newspapers as a way to save some cash for his next move. He was caught in a shootout one afternoon. A man was murdered leaving a nearby gym. Juan Pablo said that he just froze, terrified when the bullets started flying. He showed me the photos of the dead body that he took with his cell phone. I was taken aback by his voyeurism and asked him why the cops did not try to stop him. "The police yelled at me and told me to get out of there and they tried to take my phone. It was crazy, but at least it is a good time to sell newspapers," he added glibly. "People stop and ask, 'What? No shootouts yesterday?' and then they won't buy a paper!"[9]

At first, these were high-profile events and people would talk end-lessly about who did it, why, if it was an accident or an instance of mis-taken identity by the assassins (often the case). The gory photos that adorned the covers of newspapers were a constant reminder, not of the tragedy of death but of its otherworldly, grotesque, nonhuman dimen-sions. These images produced a distance between the living and the dead through their portrayal of horrors as a spectacle rather than a tragic loss.[10] The violence in Mexico became simply too vicious to relate to on a personal level. It was an exhibition, a show, and a horror movie, rolled into real life.[11]

CARTEL DRAMA HITS NOGALES

The conflict in Nogales was the result of an internal split in the Sinaloa Cartel as the Beltrán Leyva brothers began fighting with their former subordinate, Joaquin "El Chapo" Guzmán.[12] El Chapo controlled the east side of town and Los Beltrán Leyva controlled the west side. Massacres to the west in Caborca and Tubutama had created no-go spaces, off-lim-its to the government as well as the casual observer. Around the country a similar pattern emerged as the conflict between groups heated up and intensified, all with the backdrop of increased military operations aimed at killing (or capturing) drug traffickers. These clashes simply augmented the terror.

In 2009 Mexican Marines engaged in a firefight for hours in an upscale apartment building in Cuernavaca, a city known for its beautiful churches and plazas, the farthest thing from the industrial sprawl of Ciudad Juárez. Apartment 201 was filled with bullet holes and by the time the shooting ended, Arturo Beltrán Leyva, "El Barbas," was dead, his body riddled by more than a hundred bullets.[13] A national uproar was sparked when his body was displayed, disfigured by bullet wounds, covered in blood-soaked pesos and other documents, with the soldiers standing over him like a trophy. Then President Calderón publicly thanked the lone fallen Marine by naming him and his sacrifice. Hit men went to the fallen soldier's family's house and killed them all.[14] Similarly, there was an eight-hour shootout in Matamoros to kill Antonio "Tony Tormenta" Cardenas Guillén that involved grenade launchers and closed down three international bridges to the United States.[15] These are simply two examples of the chaos and disruption brought on by heavy-handed military operations. However, what followed these targeted killings was often worse, as internal strife led people within the drug cartels to fight over the newly vacant throne.

Throughout the country, fractures to previously consolidated and cooperative power structures led to intense conflicts, as the Sinaloa Cartel expanded into Ciudad Juárez and other parts of the country. The Zetas broke from their onetime bosses, the Gulf Cartel, and set the northeast ablaze with their tactics as a paramilitary cartel.[16] In Michoacán, La Familia, followed by their rebranded name, the Knights Templar, created a pseudo-religious cult around their leader, El Chayo, demanding devotion and spouting Christian faith and family values.[17]

The panorama of violence erupting in these cities along the border and deeper into Mexico had their own unique characteristics, and for Sonora, a state long tied to drug trafficking, it was peculiar how (relatively) little violence actually occurred. Often, corruption has acted as a buffer, with clear ties between drug traffickers and politicians serving to lessen the public nature of violence, as targeting the population at large is avoided in return for being allowed to traffic drugs openly and with impunity.

Figure 5. Altar, Sonora, Mexico. The church in Altar, Sonora, sits in front of the plaza that was once packed with people preparing for their journey north. Photo by Jeremy Slack.

ALTAR'S MARIJUANA HIGHWAY

On that day in May 2014, gone was the constant flow of vans stuffed with people. As mentioned above, there were only a few of the broken-down vehicles that I had seen in earlier years littering the side of the dirt road. Instead we passed no more than a handful of vehicles, most carrying marijuana. In recent years, there has been an inversion of power. When migration ruled, particularly in peak years such as 2005, the main plaza of Altar was packed with people. Shops appeared selling goods aimed exclusively at migrants: black clothes, thick black-plastic water bottles (locally made to resist cactus needles and not to reflect light), strips of carpet that people strapped to their feet to avoid making footprints,

Zippo lighters (the American flag design being the most popular), repel-
lent for snakes and scorpions (usually garlic based), and a panoply of
cheaply made jeans and sneakers. However, this open-air bazaar was not
a welcome sight to all, and pressure to pull people indoors slowly grew.
This was the result of political pressure, but also a consolidation of power
in the region. Altar is primarily controlled by coyotes who live here.
While most of the businesses are owned and operated by people from
Sinaloa (not uncommon in other parts of Sonora as well), it is this intense
local regulation of illegal activity that makes Altar such an important
place for understanding the ties between drug trafficking and migration.
Using data collected in the first wave of the Migrant Border Crossing
Study, Daniel Martínez found that most migrants crossed with a coyote
they met at the border, rather than one from their hometown.[18] The slow
process of monopolization had taken hold, leading to a greater concentration of power, greater coordination, and, in turn, to the primacy of drug
trafficking over human smuggling in the region. Those structures of
power that govern the region, especially as it relates to the relationships
between different types of illegal activities, set the rules for interaction,
economic activity, and life in general here in the desert. Debates about
whether or not human smugglers are members of drug cartels often miss
the nuanced forms of power that have risen along the border, drastically
changing people's experiences.

Statistics from the Center for Investigative Reporting show the massive disparity in terms of marijuana apprehensions between ports of
entry.[19] While apprehensions of illegal drugs at ports of entry remain
large (and fairly uniform throughout the borderlands), marijuana in
particular has shifted to the Arizona Sonora desert (followed by south
Texas). This is partly because it is a bulky product, especially when
compared to other drugs. Even compressed into bricks it is much more
voluminous than methamphetamines, cocaine, and especially heroin.
These products are also much more valuable, and therefore greater
care is taken to avoid interdiction such as modified engine compart-
ments, or clever ways to mix them in with legal cargo in addition to the

always popular corrupted officials who wave them through for a fee. Marijuana, on the other hand, is cheap to produce, cheap to replace, and still profitable to sell in the United States, sometimes by mixing it in with higher-quality U. S. product.

Most of the marijuana here comes from the so-called "golden triangle," the region bordering the states of Sinaloa, Durango, and Chihuahua, an agriculturally rich zone where marijuana grows with little or no labor, fertilizer, or inputs. The numbers can often be unclear, but the vast majority of the product can be lost and still be profitable. This has led to tactics that throw large quantities of marijuana at the border with the knowledge that most of it will not make it across, assuming that even the small percentage that arrives will be more than enough to turn a profit.

Driving down to Altar that day, I counted eight vehicles carrying drugs, two of which were flatbed pickup trucks. During research over the previous years, I had begun to hear more and more stories about groups of migrants being coordinated so as to hide the shipment of marijuana. Groups of 20 migrants, staggered in 30-minute intervals, would strike out into the desert, and behind them would come the drugs. This became evident when stragglers could not keep up or they had to scatter to avoid detection by the border patrol.

> After being robbed by *bajadores* (rip-crews or bandits), and losing all his money, and even food and water, Ramon and his group turned around and headed back toward Mexico. Soon, they ran into a group of narcos. The backpackers *(burreros)* were carrying AR-15s, which they pointed at Ramon and his group instructing them that they had to keep walking into the U. S. Ramon said that they were using the migrants as a shield so the burreros can cross marijuana. "Si regresas, te mato!" (If you go back, I'll kill you!), said one narco.[20]

Ramon and his group were decoys to the more profitable (and more powerful) drug trafficking interests. The greater control over the region led to strict hierarchies and rules dictating that groups of migrants not cross at certain times, so as not to cause a shipment of marijuana to be lost. Repercussions for those who broke these rules were swift and harsh, as recounted by one migrant.

> "They [the Sinaloa Cartel] kidnapped our group and tortured the guide for *calentando el terreno*—attracting too much attention. They tortured the guides, tying them and hanging them upside-down while hitting them with cactus pads for having crossed at the wrong time and without permission," explained Jose.[21] [He and his group had been held on a ranch where "massive" amounts of drugs and guns were being stored.] "There were about 300 captives in all. The men told me, 'We have the right to kill you.'"[22]

Order imposed by drug cartels has reshuffled the geography of the border, creating a distinct pattern of movement through the desert. Whereas migration was once the main economic activity in between ports of entry on the border, drugs, the ultimate in profitable commodities, took over the Sonoran desert. Drug smuggling became so prevalent that people started to traffic drugs, not simply as a one-off activity on their way to the United States, but professionally and full time. While many still engaged in drug smuggling to supplement income from seasonal agricultural work, these committed burreros became a part of the community. However, trafficking marijuana through the desert is not an easy task and often has hidden catches that people are not aware of when they start. The following interview shows how easy it is to get stuck in the drug trade:

> Jose, a short man with baggy clothes and a shaved head, was originally from Veracruz but had been living in Ciudad Juarez, the epicenter of the drug violence in recent years. Despite having originally crossed as a migrant to work in Los Angeles ten years ago, he had crossed the border several times with backpacks filled with marijuana. His first trip was through Magdalena, Sonora, a town about 40 miles south of the border. Jose had run into some friends and they started talking about crossing into the U.S. They got into a truck, filled with oranges covering the packages of marijuana, that, unbeknownst to Jose, were hidden underneath. After some gentle coercion from his friends they struck out for the U.S.

Under the weight of the 50 pounds of marijuana and the supplies for the journey, they could only walk for short stretches because of the weight. Jose explained that there were ten people carrying the drugs, as well as a guide and the "encargado." They refer to the leaders as "guia" or guide and "encargado" or leader. It is important that no one know anyone else's name, for safety. The leaders are in charge of the safety of the shipment. The guide was carrying two handguns.

Jose informed me that the real boss is the encargado. He knows the "dueños" personally. Only his word will save you if you lose a shipment of drugs. The encargado has to tell them that it was the "migra" [border patrol] or soldiers or bajadores who took the drugs. This is to insure that no one runs off with the drugs. They walked for three days and nights, hiding and sleeping in the day, walking at night. They diverged from the traditional migrant paths after the first day and went really high up in the "sierra," where the migra rarely goes. No one goes there because it is so high, and so difficult to climb. Jose said that all the ranchers are working with the drug traffickers. They coordinate shipments, give signals that the coast is clear, and give rides to people. A van picked them up and they waited for a series of signals from the ranchers, lights, and radio communication and following GPS units that they all carry.

Upon arrival in Tucson, Arizona, they were driven to the Tufesa bus station and sent back to Mexico. He said that they were supposed to pay him $1,300 there, but they didn't. Jose said he was going to go back to see them in Mexico and collect his money. He shrugged and said, "No me pagaron, Esta vez, no me pagaron." (They didn't pay me. This time they didn't pay me).[23]

Failure to collect payment was a constant problem for drug smugglers. So much so that a group of burreros began to organize and demand better pay and treatment. It had become common to refuse payment to burreros and simply keep sending them back and forth across the border until they were arrested. This led to a strike, as people demanded backpay for the promised payment (about 1,500–3,000 USD per trip).[24] The fact that drug smugglers attempted to unionize makes it abundantly clear that this is not your average town. Not only are there enough people who work as burreros to demand fair treatment, but that they do so openly and publicly make it clear who is actually regulating the economy of the region.

As we entered Altar, we passed a small, makeshift tollbooth. Two men sat outside, lounging in the desert heat. Maximiliano, Max for short, took off his cowboy hat, stuck his head out of the truck, and waved. They motioned us through. "He is one of the top *sicarios* (hit men) here," explained Max, referring to the younger man at the checkpoint. "They are watching who comes and goes. *Te mata!* He will kill you!," he said making his fingers into a pistol and pointing at me. "But I have known them since they were kids. They just ignore me." The toll here is open and brazen, a small cinderblock cubicle, no bigger than a shed with a few cones in front, always staffed with people charging all the migrants who pass. Everyone knows about it and who runs it. When we were first conducting research in 2008 they would charge migrants about 500 pesos, but the toll steadily rose and by 2011 people were paying an average of 1,500 pesos (about 150 USD) for the opportunity to get near the border.[25] By 2014, this price has continued to rise to a reported 6,000 pesos (429 USD).[26] This control of movement is not unique to Altar, and has steadily developed over the years in other locations, alongside consolidation of illicit power.[27] The "big dogs," usually the cartels, set up checkpoints, send lookouts to guard the river, and generally scrutinize everything to make sure that everyone who accesses the border space pays them a cut. Needless to say this has had a huge impact on migrants, and for those who work guiding migrants through the treacherous desert terrain.

This leads us back to the question of whether human smugglers should be regarded as part of a larger criminal enterprise. Some scholars have asserted that coyotes should be considered good-faith actors whose business relies almost entirely on word-of-mouth recommendations.[28] However, there are a whole range of activities that dictate interactions between migrants and their guides. For instance, people must determine who will in fact take them across, versus others who may simply want to trick them into a safe house where they will be forced to pay ransom. Still others may want to rob them or find out personal information in order to execute a "virtual kidnapping"—that is, where extorting phone calls are made to the migrants' family members from people who claim to have kidnapped them or who claim to have successfully crossed them into the United States, demanding money as though one of those premises were true. With 17 percent of migrants reporting this experience it is a constant threat, and has caused people to guard personal information carefully.[29] Nicknames based on where people are from (Michoacán, Guanajuato, Oaxaca) have become the common monikers of migrants and deportees. This presents a challenge when attempting to identify those who die during the journey across the border, since many refuse to carry identifying documents or contact information. Extortion has become a fact of life for migrants, but also for residents of the border who receive threatening phone calls frequently.

While I do not contend that all coyotes are engaged in extortion, it certainly has become such a prominent part of the migratory experience that it is hard to excise it from migrant / coyote interactions. In fact, it becomes unproductive to simply blame one group or another for these abuses, rather than attempting to develop an understanding of the underlying causes. In this case, migrants are worried about being extorted, with family nervously awaiting instructions for payment and frequently being duped. Coyotes on the other hand do not want to be apprehended by the border patrol and want to ensure they are paid. Do coyotes sometimes attempt to extract payment without taking the risk of crossing through the desert? Of course! However, migrants also sometimes attempt to escape without paying their guides. By understanding the types of relationships, hierarchies, and rules that have developed along the border, it gives us more insight into the ways that cartels and other criminal actors behave.

The concept of the illicit regime is integral to understanding the argument set forth in this book. Nonstate structures of power frequently dictate the rules, patterns, and intensity of violence for those crossing through the borderlands. These are separate from the state in name, but cling to the government's punitive apparatus (police, military) as a parasitic organism through bribery and corruption. The most powerful organizations, in this case the drug cartels, create regulations that will favor their activities and profit above all else. For coyotes and migrants this results in rent-seeking behavior, collecting taxes in the form of the tollbooth checkpoint, but also through payments made by everyone else operating an illegal business such as human smuggling. The control over movement, and the interest taken in deportees and migrants by organized crime, is a direct symptom of this power and control over territory. As cartels have become more entrenched, violent, and engaged with other industries through extortion and control (as opposed to simply producing and exporting drugs), more and more people are sucked into their orbit. The cartels' power solidifies and becomes sedentary, attached to place, with rules, and structures. The parasite on the state apparatus begins to become the de facto state.

While cartels do engage sporadically in beneficence, making a show of toy giveaways, or handing out turkeys at Christmas, or simply by sponsoring over-the-top parties, it would be wrong to think that these illicit regimes seek to co-opt the full functioning of the state (schools, infrastructure, health and welfare, etc.). Rather, they mimic much of the clientelistic, populist activities of the Mexican state such as handouts and direct giveaways, but their interests fall well short of providing the full range of activities that a state engages in. Moreover, these altruistic acts are really a prestige-seeking mechanism, aiming to highlight not only the magnificence of the bosses, the *capos,* but also their power and wealth. Violence, however, is central to this power. For these border zones, the control of legitimate violence, long theorized to be one of the defining characteristics of the state,[30] belongs to the cartels who can kill, kidnap, and maim without fear of reprisal, except from other cartels. They also often take the place of the justice system, frequently lynching robbers, rapists, and pedophiles.[31]

For migrants this has had mixed results. It has led to issues such as kidnappings, beatings, and murders for people who cross when they are not supposed to, but it also has led to drug cartels killing off the more unpredictable and violent ripoff crews known as *bajadores.*[32] Small groups of two or three armed young men camp out in the desert on the outskirts of cities such as Nogales, or Altar, Sonora, and rob migrants and burreros carrying drugs, taking food and clothes as a way of prolonging their time in the desert. A 25-year-old man from Zacatecas recounted that his group was once confronted by armed men with bandanas covering their faces who ordered them to hand over everything. "If you hide money, we are going to shoot you in the foot and leave you here to die."[33] Bajadores are extremely violent and often responsible for rape and assault. One woman I interviewed reported that bajadores raped a different woman in her group. Two men had tried to intervene, and they were shot and killed.[34] An older woman named Marla said that bajadores raped a young girl in her group.[35] The men held a pistol to her boyfriend's head and told him that if he moves, he is going to die right now. After they had gone, the young girl that had been raped said she wished they had killed her.[36]

While it is doubtful that drug traffickers were particularly concerned over the plight of undocumented migrants, the bajadores, by robbing drug traffickers, were essentially challenging the illicit regime and had to be dealt with. On the morning of April 24, 2009, a man was found murdered in the border city of Nogales, Sonora, with a message, commonly referred to as a *narcomanta*, attached to the body. It read: "This will happen to all bajadores, or *ratas* as well as the people who help them by letting them use their ranches, we know where and who they are, you are screwed."[37] In the following three months the same newspaper noted 30 similar killings in the area. Robberies by bajadores decreased rapidly, from about one in three reporting robberies in the first wave of the MBCS (2007–09)[38] to 12 percent in the second wave (2011–12). In this sense the slew of murders by the cartels actually increased safety for migrants. Not only does this highlight the power of cartels to control clandestine activity, but also reflects the supreme absence of the state. This inversion of who has the right to kill and punish, as well as which rules must be followed, is at the core of the chaotic terrain of the border.

The knowledge of how to navigate these illicit regimes takes years to develop. The ultimate example of this is Maximiliano. He knows how to navigate the rules and norms, but is able to bend them to his advantage in ways I have never seen outside of Altar. Having spent most of his life here, Max describes his relationship to the narcos as functional because he "marries them and buries them." When living in Altar, or many other regions of Mexico, the distinction between legal and illegal becomes meaningless. Narco power is the real state power in many regions, often indistinguishable from the police or military and generally more present than the formal state. He told me a story about being stopped by fake soldiers in masks. He was with a group of kids, and when the *narcosoldados* started interrogating him, one of the kids looked around back and asked innocently, "Desde cuando se hizo Chalo un soldado?" (When did Chalo become a soldier?) The guy who was interrogating Max tried not to laugh, but Max could see the smile under the mask. It was obvious that there was recognition between the local kids and the narcos but no one wanted to say anything. This tacit recognition, as well as the blurred boundaries and even accepted nature of drug-related activity, puts the region in perspective. As a priest, as a local, as someone who has a clear mission in the region, Maximiliano is allowed to act in ways that few can. He has consistently interceded on behalf of kidnapped migrants. "The first time I knocked on a door and demanded that they let the migrants go, I was terrified," he explained. Somehow they let the migrants go and it became common for Max to intercede on behalf of the migrants.

He explained that he has been able to maintain a good relationship with the narcos because Altar has remained fairly locally controlled. However, "when they are *madreaando* (beating) someone (to death), they tell me, this isn't a migrant. It is not your fight." And yet he continues intervening, knowing full well the fine and extremely dangerous line he is walking.

LEAVING ALTAR: WHAT NOW?

The next morning I wandered out into the streets of Altar, following a group of migrants I had met the night before. They arrived late after a

35-hour bus ride from Nuevo Laredo, Tamaulipas. They were afraid of that city and the Zetas, but were second-guessing their choice as the temperature was already well above 100 degrees at 7:30 in the morning.

One man used the nickname "Torreón" (from Coahuila), even though he was actually from Michoácan, an enemy territory of the Zetas.[39] He had previously been kidnapped in 2010, after being deported to Nuevo Laredo. While trying to cross the river, he and a friend were stopped for not paying the toll.

> A group of kids, 13–14 year olds, came up to them with guns and said, "What are you doing? Who are you? Where are you going?" They had no money so the kids said, "Let's go," and a van came and picked them up. The hit-boys shoved Torreon and his friend into the van roughly, pistol whipping them on the way in. One of the kids called his boss and explained, "We got some people but they don't have any money, *Le damos piso?* Do we kill them?" The silence on the other end of the line almost killed him. "I thought I was going to die," explained Torreon. The boss just said, "Nel, they are nobody. Just let them go." The hit-boys kicked them out of the van, beaten, bloody, and shaken up. Since then, Torreon has avoided Nuevo Laredo at all costs. He had been deported there again the week before, but he was willing to go all the way to Altar because one of the friends he met in detention knew the route. Even though he was just going to Corpus Christi, which is only four or five hours from Nuevo Laredo, he took a three-day bus ride to Altar, Sonora, instead. Torreon and the others were upset that the toll to cross was 6,000 pesos each. The price to cross had increased and they could no longer simply find their own way out of the town and through the desert as they had before.

In the heat of the day, I started chatting with an older man named Kiki who was sweeping the fallen leaves and sand after cutting the bushes in the plaza on the steps of the church. I gave him some of the Pepsi I bought for the guys from Nuevo Laredo. He had come from Tijuana to Altar, looking to cross or make some money. Kiki had spent a few years living in the Bordo de Tijuana, the community of homeless addicts. His English was excellent, and he had lived in the United States through high school, but was deported as an adult, now unfamiliar with

Mexico. Kiki came to Altar a few months back to cross but he didn't have the money. He said rather bluntly, "I want to cross with a backpack." I looked at him skeptically. I didn't think he could make it. He was small, well past 40, and weak looking ... maybe an addict. I may have guessed this due to my own prejudices, having come from Tijuana and knowing El Bordo all too well. The open-air drug market of the Bordo attracts drug addicts and deportees who have little or no contacts to any community in Mexico. With the risks and rewards of crossing the border largely the same with or without drugs, some people seek out the "backpack" option. However, achieving this goal is not an easy task. Kiki had already been here a month, and was desperate for money. I doubted his ability to become a burrero because he simply did not fit the general profile of all the burreros I have interviewed. José, who I had interviewed at the border a few years back, was short but strong, physically fit, and could be intimidating when he wanted to be. Burreros are generally strong and around their physical prime. While some of them are in their forties, they are often agricultural workers, fieldhands, people whose lifetime of manual labor has made them tough as nails.[40] While it is accepted that some marijuana will be lost, not just anyone can carry the 80 lbs of marijuana on their backs for five days through the desert.[41]

The lucrative nature of drug trafficking, which outweighs all other forms of illegal activity by many orders of magnitude, makes it by far the most powerful and profitable enterprise along the border. In this illicit regime, violence is standard fare. It takes brutality to make sure fees are paid, and that the cartel gets its share. While the violence associated with regulating the formal economy is outsourced to the state in the form of fines, sanctions, or even incarceration for fraudulent businesses, the violence of regulation is outsourced to the most powerful actors in the illegal world: the cartels. This is the fundamental challenge of the cartel member / noncartel member binary. Are you a part of the cartel if you pay protection to them, even in the form of extortion? All illegal activity in these heavily controlled regions must pay a portion of their income to the bosses or they will be punished. Does this make an individual a cartel member? Not as such. However, what if one were to use the dispute resolution services of a cartel—an alternate-universe version of filing a claim with the Better Business Bureau, small claims court, or the police, except with far more lethal results? Still, this is unclear. With the loose structure of many drug trafficking organizations, these murky hierarchies and indirect ties are the norm. Therefore it is better to understand the complex ways these interactions shape the experiences of people crossing the border. Migrants passing through the borderlands are particularly vulnerable to these forces and often unaware of the rules.

At the peak of undocumented migration in 2000, there were 616,386 apprehensions in the Tucson sector alone and most had begun their journey from Altar, Sonora.[42] However, by the late 2000s, with the housing crisis in the United States in full swing and construction jobs almost nonexistent, these apprehensions declined drastically. The teeming masses of people milling about in the plaza as they emptied from rickety buses with the names of obscure towns in Chiapas, Oaxaca, and Guerrero painted on the sides had disappeared. The shops selling their migration-focused wares were empty, dusty, and often shuttered. Now, upon leaving these buses, rather than explore the plaza and the various guides or shopkeepers looking to provide services, people were whisked away to so-called *casas de huespedes*—guesthouses. These guesthouses provide people with a place to stay and sleep (for a fee), while their guides decide when to cross the border. The casas de huespedes varied widely in quality—some were similar to low-cost hotels, while others packed people in, dozens to a bunk, renting each scrap of padding and cloth for an additional charge. By moving people indoors, into these controlled environments, it made it easier to manage which guides were taking which people across the border. It also made it easier to know which guides belonged where. This served to sharply deter outside competition, as it was now harder to find people intent on crossing the border by themselves or with the aid of a local from their hometown; instead, migrants essentially had to stay in hotels with ties to smugglers. Even people who are able to avoid these casas de huespedes, like Torreon and his friends who were staying in the migrant shelter, find additional barriers to attempting an independent crossing. Moreover, moving people indoors, and out of sight, makes it harder to study abuse, mistreatment, kidnapping, and extortion:

> One migrant named Esmeralda was held at a casa de huesped for two days before being transferred to an even more remote location outside of Altar, known as the *ladrillera* (brick factory). The guides demanded money, so she gave one man 8,000 pesos, about 800 dollars at the time, but they demanded more. She explained the coyotes' behavior as follows: "The first one, the one who tells you things and arranges travel is always nice, but the ones who walk with people are *groseros* (rude, uncouth). They are on drugs, so they can keep walking," she explained.[43]

While the people holding her may or may not have officially been part of a drug cartel, this activity was certainly happening under their purview, with a portion of the profits from her extortion going up to the most powerful people. This is the only explanation for why powerful and profitable drug traffickers would care about migration, which pales in comparison as far as profitability. Why police migrants and deportees at all? Why care about who they are and where they move? By being a body in movement, the protections and safeties that arise from knowledge of a place and its people are removed and migrants can be brutalized, extorted, and sometimes forced into organized crime. These patterns and controls shape the movement of migrants near the border area and provide important insights into how and why cartels have begun to scrutinize migrants with such intensity.

CONCLUSIONS

As I waited for a bus to take me back to Nogales the next day, I thought about the changes that had occurred. It was certainly different from Tamaulipas, with an uneasy balance established between drug traffickers, human smugglers, and those with more mundane lives, such as the ranchers, field workers, and people selling beers at the *expendio* or knickknacks in the plaza. The walk around town with Torreon and his friends was decidedly different from experiences I had wandering around in Tamaulipas. I don't know if this is the result of more or less control, of less interest in extorting, recruiting, or protecting territory or, simply put, the confidence of hegemony, of complete power over a territory. I have always found it easiest to work somewhere where narco-power goes uncontested, where there is no reason to doubt the dominance of the illicit regime, as opposed to a place where others are attempting to wrest control from whomever currently holds it.

On Highway 2, just outside of Altar, the bus I was riding passed through the government toll, erected as part of a private / public partnership. It had angered residents because it was so expensive, so an arrangement was reached. They lowered the price for the "locals," allowing them to travel back and forth to ranches and fields outside of town. This seemingly natural compromise is similar to those that happen in the illegal world: the need to find a balance between overtly oppressive policies and the needs of the population. Mexico's political system has often been referred to as the "perfect dictatorship," because the one-party system was able to remain in power for almost seven decades. The subtle forms of oppression, intermixing extreme violence and corruption with government handouts, a populist front, and media-savvy politicians—all combine for a particularly sophisticated form of pseudo-authoritarianism. This unique form of governance is partially responsible for the immense power and influence of drug cartels throughout Mexico. Local control by *caciques* (local bosses / strongmen or -women) has long been a hallmark of Mexican governance, with regional power brokers also typifying the fragmented cartel landscape.

While these local brokers will occasionally reach out to the community in order to increase their favorability by giving away goods or throwing lavish parties, the mobile population enjoys no such perks. Both the state and organized crime must find a balance between oppression and assistance for citizens, and yet, the migrant is afforded no such deference, however slight. People in movement are always excluded as their lack of belonging (coming from somewhere else) and their transience (they will soon leave) have subsumed their identities.

It is clear how the figure of the migrant then becomes the most opportune scapegoat for both criminal organizations and the state. Migrants have no ability to organize, put pressure on, or create a backlash against abuse. Even once they settle permanently in towns and cities across the United States, their irregular statuses keep them forever out of this negotiation between oppression and protections. The violence experienced while in transit, however, is perhaps at its most intense in such spaces because they are designed for anonymity, and have conveniently become places where people disappear and no one ever hears from them again. In order for deportees and migrants to survive these threats they must learn and follow unique and complex sets of rules for movement and activities along the border, something that not everyone is equipped to master.

CHAPTER THREE

Te Van a Levantar—They Will Kidnap You

Deportation and Mobility on the Border

I decided to follow the group of migrants staying at the shelter on their day in the streets, similar to the way I often did in Sonora. However, I soon learned that in Tamaulipas, this was a different proposition. The shelter worker looked at me incredulously and shrugged when I told him my plan. As soon as we exited the shelter two coyotes and a man running another "shelter" looking for tenants to pay for rooms approached us. The other shelter owner tried to find out who was getting kicked out here and might be interested in paying for a room. The coyotes asked us if we wanted to cross. Everyone said no, at which point one looked at me and asked incredulously in his thick northern accent, "A poco tu güero, no tienes como cruzar?" (Really blondie / gringo, you don't have a way to cross?) Everyone thought this was funny and started laughing.

An elderly woman dressed in her bathrobe and slippers approached and began telling us how dangerous it is in this neighborhood. "See that house there?" she asked, pointing across the street. "They killed them all. Their son got mixed up in some bad stuff and was hiding weapons. 'They' came and killed everyone, mother, father, children." I looked across the street at an abandoned building, which I had not paid much attention to before, although it was occupied during my previous trips here. At first I thought this to be a simple random interaction with a senior citizen, but later realized it was a clear warning that there is a hidden, violent geography to this city. Deaths linger in abandoned houses, and in places that this group of recent arrivals cannot possibly know. It was essentially an admonition: "Don't linger here. If you step out of line, there will be consequences." However, the migrants simply shrugged at this gruesome story, already eager to get away from the shelter and into the plazas downtown.

As soon as the last straggler from our group hurried out the shelter door with a half-eaten *pan dulce* pastry in his hand, we headed on our way. We walked toward downtown, parallel to the river. Monterrey and Zacatecas became my guides that day and for much of my fieldwork in Tamaulipas. This inseparable pair were my comrades and confidants in Nuevo Laredo. They arrived as deportees and adopted the traditional naming custom of deportees. People began introducing themselves with place names in shelters because of the prevalence of so-called cyber or "virtual" kidnappings where people call family members and extort money on the pretext that someone has been kidnapped. Real names and any other personal information can be used against you. This was more common in the Northeast as the level of violence and insecurity was much greater, leading to increased caution as well as mistrust. These two, however, were consummate hustlers. Monterrey, short, pugnacious, and friendly, talked so fast that I often wondered how he ever caught a breath between streams of words. His shaved head and round face always sported a wide grin. He always had a scheme and became the unofficial wire-transfer collector for the shelter. Deportees would have money wired to Nuevo Laredo in his name when they did not have any valid forms of identification, a frequent occurrence. He would take a cut and pass them the money. Zacatecas, however, was taller, lighter-skinned, and handsome with thick short-cropped dark hair and a thin mustache. His cynical attitude caused him to constantly dissect and critique the people and the world around him. He would sit back watching while Monterrey ran around meeting people and talking. When he did speak, the insights flowed. Zacatecas's grassroots philosophy with respect to migration and deportation cast a revealing light onto the dynamics of the region. Both of them break from traditional narratives of migrants as saints who only work and support families. Neither had solid relationships with their families, which was why they stayed at the border rather than returning home. And yet, they are charming, vivacious, generally harmless, and chaotic, providing a vivid lens through which to study what it takes to navigate the border landscape.

Monterrey began telling me his nicknames for all of the dogs on the walk downtown. "That's Chato, and Gordo, and Rambo. Rambo acts tough but won't bite," he explained. I thought it was odd or impressive (or a joke) that after only a week here, he had such a well-developed understanding of the inhabitants of this particular road. After about twenty minutes we arrived at the first plaza. It was small, but had a library and a movie theatre. People chatted about topics related to theology and drug addiction. "Maldita piedra!" (Damn crack!) exclaimed Zacatecas. He openly chastised a few of the deportees for smoking crack, particularly a young kid (19 years old) from Chiapas, separated from his family for the first time. Soon we moved to the next plaza closer to the border. There were four guys walking around asking people if they wanted to cross, all were in their mid-forties, or fifties, a contrast from the younger, mostly teenage *halcones*—the lookouts who watch over the city.

The first coyote, with small, round, Lennon-esque sunglasses, walked by me and asked, "Want to make a deal to take people across?" I began to explain my role as a student and volunteer but he didn't stick around for my answer, vanishing as I began the labored explanation of my purpose. I was unsettled by this interaction. I already knew enough to realize that a question asked without waiting for an answer is a threat, or at the very least, a strong suggestion that I reconsider what I was doing there. Zacatecas, ever watchful, was also nervous about our interaction and suggested we move to the next plaza. "That wasn't good. Let's go somewhere else," he said in a whisper.

We were only a stone's throw from the port of entry now, but there was a lot more movement here. People were milling about. Young men were standing on the street corners and military convoys, Humvees, and trucks with armed men in the back zoomed by frequently. I lent my phone to a man from Honduras who was trying to get in touch with his family in Houston, taking advantage of the U.S. cell service near the line. He began speaking in an exaggerated, loud voice about where to get picked up. Zacatecas looked at me disapprovingly, "This isn't good. *Te van a levantar* (They will kidnap you) ... They are going to think you are a coyote and are stealing their business." I knew it was bad before he said that, but it sent a chill down my spine. "They probably won't do anything today, but if you do it again, they will definitely pick you up," added Monterrey. "Seguro que va a haber tablazos!" (Of course they will paddle you!), Zacatecas said laughing. I didn't find this funny.

We walked back to the first plaza that was calmer, with less people. Geraldo, a middle-aged man who worked as an informal vet for livestock at a feed store in Central Texas, ran into us in the plaza and started talking to me about his situation. He was staying at the shelter last week but his time ran out and he found another shelter nearby. We were talking about his immigration case when a heavy-set man wearing a track jacket and a baseball cap pulled low over his face came and sat next to us. He was leaning in to hear our conversation and he had one earphone in and the other one dangling into his lap. I was immediately on edge and I offered to buy the group some Cokes as an excuse to get out of there. When we got up to walk, Zacatecas whispered to me, "Did you see him? There was a man who was very interested in you." I nodded. "Let's go to another plaza," he suggested.

We sat high up on some steps that looked like a public amphitheater, ate a bag of *Ruffles Queso* and drank a two-liter Coke from thin plastic glasses we bought at the OXXO convenience store. About a half hour later the same guy showed up and sat on a bench right below us. I pointed him out to Zacatecas and he looked worried. "Let's go to the hospital. There is a lot of military there. I doubt they will try anything." We walked a few blocks away and waited next to a military checkpoint until it was time to return to the shelter.[1]

Every day migrants repeat this routine. They bounce from one plaza to the next, down one road until it becomes dangerous and then they move to the next one. People were constrained to a very specific route that they walked again and again, memorizing its smallest detail. *Halcones*, literally falcons, or lookouts, are a fixture of the landscape. In typical dark humor an ex-cop told me a joke that the military likes to arrest them and take them up in the helicopters. They ask, "What do halcones do?" and the kids respond by explaining how they look out for people coming and going. "No, halcones fly!" respond the soldiers, pushing them out of the helicopters.

Teenage males decked out with Aeropostal, and Ed Hardy several sizes too big, hold their radio phones in front of their faces to signify their constant state of being in contact. They report back to unnamed voices on the other end about the comings and goings of the border: the closer to the bridge, the closer to the river, and the greater the intensity of surveillance. The beep of Nextel radios sets people on edge. From the first moment I arrived here, that sound immediately shut down any conversation. The secure radios were a favorite of the lookouts, monitoring public spaces for anything out of the ordinary.

My presence was not welcome and I did not repeat this experiment here again (at least not in the same form). There are strict rules for movement that are highly contingent upon who you are. For deportees, there are specific places where they are allowed to be. This was demonstrated by the fact that Monterrey had already given names to all the dogs on the street. It was the only street he was allowed to be on. While I met up with Zacatecas, Monterrey, and other deportees at different periods during fieldwork, I never again followed them the whole day. In all my time there, I rarely moved around on my own. Safety of movement was always a concern. Whenever we had to do something out of the ordinary that required breaking away from those plazas, it prompted a debate, concern, and careful planning. "Not that street!" or "Two more blocks, then we can turn right" were common refrains as they negotiated the complicated terrain, ironically superimposed on a simple grid of streets. Picking up on the subtle clues takes diligence. Someone standing on the corner on an otherwise empty street can signal a *safe house*, a place where drugs, migrants, or kidnapping victims are held. People on roofs or terraces almost always mean surveillance, as I became aware as soon as I arrived at the shelter. My first approach to scope out this research in the spring of 2011 was far more disturbing, as a terrace overlooking the shelter and the house immediately across the street from the door were firmly occupied by the Zetas. I had had to convince a taxicab to take me there, since no one who lived in Nuevo Laredo would go anywhere near the shelter. Researchers had recently been threatened and it was shortly after a volunteer who was also a journalist and blogger was brutally murdered.[2] I rang the buzzer and waited, watching in the mirror-plated glass as armed men trickled into the street behind me to supervise my arrival.

Construction in front of the shelter, which coincided with the demolition of some of the lookouts' houses, had led to a slightly calmer moment to work there in 2013, but I was still under no illusions that this was a safe place. The unique patterns of movement, timed with the opening and closing of the shelter, show the level of narco control, but also the position of deportees within this hierarchy. At first, I struggled to understand exactly why such effort was taken to monitor, corral, control, or even entrap migrants and deportees along the border. General explanations—such as that it is simply a case of exploiting poor migrants—fail to capture the full extent of these often highly organized and coordinated efforts. For the Zetas, intelligence is key. Knowing who is coming and going is paramount. Who are these transient individuals? Where are they from? Who has ties to enemy gangs or cartels? Who may have useful skills, meaning that they would make good recruits? And, perhaps most importantly, who are the key individuals to kidnap and exploit, usually because of perceived wealth and strong ties to the United States? In this sense, deportees are seen as both threat and resource, a source of anxiety and a potential boon for any criminal organization.

This is yet another parallel of the ways that the state often switches back and forth between discourses that laud migrants and discourses that blame and fear them as criminals and intruders. The symbolic malleability of those individuals in motion, the Central Americans dislocated between home country and destination, as well as the deportees, can be appropriated for whatever violent purpose is needed. The concentration of deportees along the border serves a unique purpose because it allows for surveillance, as people must stay in specific locations, such as the plazas in Nuevo Laredo, in front of government offices, a basketball court and a church in Nogales, or the Bordo in Tijuana. Mixed in with this floating population are spies and lookouts, sent to get an idea of who has arrived or is leaving, making it imperative that shelter workers have a good memory for faces, as repeat visitors are deemed suspicious and sometimes expelled (if they give different names, for example). With the population contained, as opposed to spread throughout the border cities, all of those "who, what, where, and why" questions are easily answered.

Simon Izcara's work with coyotes / *polleros* in Tamaulipas outlines the importance of profiling migrants to kidnap and extort them.[3] The guides are skilled in discerning who can and who cannot afford a guide, and, therefore, who would also be able to pay a ransom. One coyote explained that the guides who are recruited are forced to plan the kidnappings, locating the victims. "Otherwise, how do they come to know how to do the job? And how do they know how to distinguish between those who can be kidnapped and those who aren't worth it because they are worthless?"[4] It is extremely likely that the guides who asked me nosy questions, insinuating that I too was a coyote, were involved in these activities. The savvier migrants at the shelter would never talk to them, only contacting guides through personal recommendations, and never in anonymous public spaces.[5]

This was particularly true of Reynosa, long considered the most dangerous place for migrants. I spent very little time there due to the level of conflict and fear expressed by everyone working with migrants. When I did finally visit I was met by Ricardo, who as soon as he saw me in the

Reynosa bus station said, "You look like a cop."[6] Ricardo was a jack-of-all-trades who had worked in everything from the government to journalism to law enforcement. He immediately quizzed me on my knowledge of Reynosa's narco-conflict, stressing multiple times how dangerous it was here. He had been threatened about ten times; the last one scared him and caused him to lay low. Soldiers had stopped him and even though they were wearing uniforms, they were not actually soldiers. "They had the wrong shoes on and used handguns instead of rifles," Ricardo explained. "Four of the [fake] soldiers got into my car and put their guns on me. They were young and nervous. They interrogated me for what seemed like hours. They kept asking me to do things and contradicting themselves: "Give us your wallet! DON'T MOVE! How do we know you are who you say you are? Lift up your head. DON'T LIFT UP YOUR HEAD OR I'LL KILL YOU!" they would scream.

Ricardo took me around the city, pointing out the halcones watching the street corners, the spots where people get abducted, and the military checkpoints. He pointed out what looked like a stolen silver Mercedes S-Class careening over the rough road at breakneck speeds, and tried to follow it, but (fortunately) we lost them. We came upon one of the main spots for migrants to get picked up, a taco stand next to a Waldo's, Mexico's version of a dollar store. A bus had pulled up right before we arrived and a guy with a green hoodie stepped off, followed by two skinny teenagers who were completely underdressed for the biting cold. Immediately, I could tell they were *catrachos*, from Honduras, due to their dark skin and close-cropped haircuts. "Let's follow them to see what car he puts them in," said Ricardo. "This is what happens. If you are a migrant and you come to this city, they take them off the bus either here, or by the Soriana [supermarket]. Did you stop there [on your ride in]?"

"Yes," I replied. I had been half-asleep but awoke when we stopped at a random street, rather than the bus station. Someone had stuck his head in and looked around, but no one got off.

"I am going to go there and park and ask if they sell Christmas tree lights. You stay in the car and don't look suspicious, and DON'T take any pictures," Ricardo said, jumping out of the car before I could interject.

I got a better look at the *enganchador* (recruiter) in the green hoodie. He was just a kid too, probably 17 or 18. The two Hondurans were eating some tacos while the enganchador was on his radio. "This is how it works. Everything seems nice. Someone jumps on the bus and tells anyone who looks like a migrant who is not already claimed by a coyote that they have to get off the bus here. They hand over IDs and take them to a safe house and that is where the negotiations begin." I asked if they actually take people across or is it just extortion. "They do, but only for a lot of money, usually it is just kidnapping." These hotspots, as well as the networks of young men locating and abducting migrants— either through trickery, convincing people that they will take them across or even offering them work, or violently if that fails—make it extremely dangerous for anyone attempting to navigate the border.

These enganchadores are trained to spot and locate the best targets for kidnapping. The criterion most used for encountering the ideal victims for kidnapping and extortion are ties to the United States. However, it does not always go as planned and sometimes ill-planned kidnappings end in some sort of theatre of the absurd.

> Fernando, a 31-year-old man from Cunduacán, Tabasco, who had been kidnapped in 2005 on his first try to get to the United States, explained the almost comical experience of being abducted. He was coming up from Tabasco with a small group of friends, one of whom, Fernando's girlfriend's uncle, knew the way. The uncle had crossed through Altar several times. He had disappeared to make arrangements when a van pulled up and told the remaining group of *tabasqueños* that "your family is looking for you." "We had no experience, so we didn't think it was suspicious and we got into the van," he laughed. The kidnappers interrogated us and wanted us to pay $1,800 apiece!" said Fernando. This price is suspiciously close to the amount of money most migrants would have access to in order to pay for their guide. "However, none of us actually knew where we were going, or had any contacts in the United States to call, so after a day of frustration, they just let us go."[7]

Without knowledge of who to kidnap, valuable time can be wasted on first-time crossers without a previous history in the United States. Fernando's story coincides with the rise of migrant kidnappings in Sonora and most likely would have had a different result later or in another region. The increased brutality in recent years has become shocking and ubiquitous, with torture frequently employed as a method of getting access to the contact information for migrants' families. Kidnappers have become increasingly sophisticated, using trickery and intelligence gathering. Some of their approaches include monitoring pay phones, cloning cell phones, or the simpler tactic of posing as a friend and lending a cell phone only to record the number and call back for virtual kidnappings and extortion purposes.

Because of this, linguistic markers such as Anglicized Spanish, brands of clothes from the United States, and even haircuts have become important to hide upon arrival at the border. For deportees with no or limited Spanish, striking up a conversation, especially in linguistically puritanical Mexico, can be an extremely dangerous activity. With the repeal of Deferred Action for Childhood Arrivals (DACA), Obama's executive order that created temporary status and work visas for people who arrived in the United States as children, mass removal of individuals tied to the United States will dramatically increase this violence. The bulk of the research for this book was carried out before DACA, therefore we would frequently interview people who would have qualified for DACA if they had not been deported. These individuals routinely struggled to adapt to Mexico, unaware of the bureaucratic machinery in Mexico, as well as its geography, language, and other practical issues such as the exchange rate. "I think I was born in someplace called Jalisco, is that close?" asked a deportee named Rafael.[8] Another, upon being denied access to social services because of his lack of a birth certificate, stated, "It's like I don't exist anywhere!"[9] For organized crime, these floating, dislocated, nonexistent individuals are prime targets. Much as Central Americans are viewed as foreigners, Dreamers are viewed as gringos, with all the resources and wealth implied by that identity. Fearful Dreamers often attempt to talk their way through the port of entry. While some are undoubtedly successful at chatting their way through the border because of their fluency in English and cultural Americanization (i.e., "I played basketball or football in the high school right up the road..." "Our mascot was..."), particularly in the biometric era with fingerprint identification almost ubiquitous, most are not. For those caught making a false declaration, the consequences are severe: a permanent bar. Even those individuals with serious violent crimes have a better chance of legally returning to the United States than people who make false declarations.

Not all deportees are perceived as a source of fast cash, however. Some are viewed as a threat or a potential recruit, a condition that usually coincides. For example, if a deportee is suspected of belonging to a street or prison gang from the United States, or another part of Mexico, they are abducted, interrogated, and often strip-searched to look for tattoos signifying membership in a criminal organization. They are often given the choice of joining, or death. I will further explore migrant recruitment by drug cartels in chapter 5, but it is worth noting that the daily flow of hundreds of people into these border cities provides a desperate, often disenchanted group of young men who will almost always take the nonfatal option. However, not everyone who is presented with this option actually has had some former affiliation with a criminal organization. One of the most pressing problems for deportees is actually birthplace. Being born in enemy territory places one's life in significant danger. Upon arrival to Tamaulipas, people from Sinaloa/Sonora and Michoacán were frequently kidnapped, interrogated, and tortured either by police (state) or gang members.

> Lázaro, the Oaxacan shelter worker, explained one of the worst things he saw over the years in Tamaulipas. "What sticks out in my mind was one deportee, a deportee who was from Sinaloa and his crime, the only crime, was telling people he was from Sinaloa. It was about two meters from the migrant shelter and they were beating him. They beat him horribly. They stripped him naked, put him facedown and were standing on his hands.

They hit him in the butt with the paddle. I stopped in front of them and one of the kids *(chavos)* told me, "There is enough for you too! Come over here, there is enough for you too!' I tried to call the police. It was 2010 and the municipal police were totally corrupt *(bien metido)*. We saw the police stopped right in front, laughing at the spectacle happening in front of us." When they stopped beating the deportee, Lázaro went to him. "We dragged him a little bit, and then got him inside. We gave him clothes because he was naked and wrapped him in some sheets. We immediately took him to the Red Cross but they left him so bad, man: ribs, fractures, black eye. They said he was probably going to lose his eye. His butt *(pompis)* super bad. I swear, I cried from rage. I had those images in my mind of what happened right in front of me. I was even more angry that it happened right in front of the police."[10]

The narco-geography of Mexico often clashes with migration and deportation patterns from southern and central Mexico to and through the border regions, sucking people into a conflict that they never expected. One example was Jonathan, a 46-year-old *campesino* from Hermosillo, Sonora, who was wearing the trademark pale gray sweatpants, sweater, and navy blue slip-on shoes that they give you when you leave federal prison. He had spent six months incarcerated for smuggling marijuana through the Arizona desert.

"I needed some extra money because I am taking care of my son. He is older, your age," he said, pointing at me, "but he can't work. He is not right in the head." He had walked for six days with 80 pounds of marijuana on his back. They were going to pay him $1,600 but he got caught. Now he was in Tamaulipas, land of the Zetas, who are also fighting the Sinaloa Cartel that controls Sonora. "Everything is very controlled here and I don't want them to look at me like the enemy," he said, nervously clenching his fists.[11]

Jonathan, apprehended in Arizona, had been spit out of the complicated geography of the U.S. prison system, with its network of county and federal prisons, as well as immigration detention centers and border patrol processing centers, into enemy territory. Data obtained by the American Immigration Council through a Freedom of Information Lawsuit shows that 29 percent of deportees in Tamaulipas were being deported due to the Criminal Alien Program, meaning that they were deported due to run-ins with the police.[12] In our post-deportation survey the police apprehended 40 percent of the people deported to Nuevo Laredo versus 22 percent border-wide, showing that those who are sent to the Northeast seemed to be disproportionately the product of the criminal justice system rather than border enforcement. This leads us to question whether or not the concentration here is intentional. If the strategic plan for border enforcement means escalating the consequences for migration, then would being expelled to Tamaulipas, home to migrant massacres, be the ultimate punishment?

The increase in people with criminal records, concentrated in this violent region, means that not only is there an influx of desperate and sometimes angry people, but that local criminals are suspicious and fearful that deportees are in fact members of rival cartels. Those born in enemy territories, people with visible tattoos and other markers of having been in prison such as clothing, are subject to additional scrutiny and interrogation. The intensity of local conflicts created a particularly treacherous dynamic as Reynosa, controlled by the Gulf Cartel, and Nuevo Laredo, the Zetas's home base, were at war with each other during my research. It became customary for migrants to take a bus three hours south to Monterrey, and then back four hours north to Reynosa to cross, simply to avoid the strip of road known as the Ribereña that connects the two. The shelter would receive calls from relatives desperately seeking news about their loved ones who had embarked on their journey to Reynosa along this road.[13] Lázaro, the doorman at the shelter, assured me that this is a nightly occurrence. "It's best not to think about what might have happened," he explained. Rules of movement such as this can have devastating consequences for people unfamiliar with the border or a particular region. Aside from the geography of warring drug cartels, deportees must learn the subtle cues that govern movement and activity along the border.

The consequences of missing these cues can be dire. No threats are ever uttered out loud. They are communicated through a glance, a whisper, a question without interest in the response. When I first arrived at the shelter, Chiapas, a small mustachioed man with curly hair, showed up with his backside beaten to a pulp by the infamous *tablazo*. The ubiquitous paddling, usually with a board with holes bored in it or roofing tacks stuck to it, was the common penalty for being "out of place." As deportees and migrants arrive to the city, there is a steep learning curve that almost always involves one or all of them receiving a beating as a warning.

The problem of mobility posed particular challenges for simple tasks, even for people who had spent several weeks navigating the border. For instance I bought a cell phone for Monterrey at an OXXO, but it didn't work so we had to return it. I had trouble remembering which store I had originally purchased the phone from, but eventually we found it. Two young men, wearing baggy clothes and baseball caps, took notice though and followed us to the OXXO. I tried to get them to exchange the phone but they went through a whole song and dance, checking it and calling managers. They were really hesitant to give me a refund because Monterrey had opened the chip. We waited a long time because they were trying to get someone on the phone. The two young men were still hanging out front and they seemed interested in us. Zacatecas went outside to sit on the steps and see what was going on. He always got quiet and serious when the situation was tense. We walked out and there was one of the guys with his Ed Hardy hat and headphones in one ear sitting on the stoop to my right. He was chatting with a woman who was walking into the OXXO.

"I don't know the guys down here, closer to the river. We need to get out of here," explained Zacatecas under his breath. Having spent a few months at the border, he explained, they began to know who was who, slowly moving out of the topology of migrants and deportees and becoming established residents of the border. "It is easy to get stuck in this lifestyle. You know how to get cheap food. It is cheap to live here. Work is sparse, but you can get what you need," said Monterrey. I heard this sentiment echoed along the border, but with particular frequency

Figure 6. Tijuana, Baja California, Mexico. A man bent over in the Bordo. The U.S.-Mexico border is in the background. Many people who live here are heroin addicts and open-air drug use is common. Photo by Murphy Woodhouse.

in Tijuana where the proliferation of humanitarian organizations made it much easier to live off of handouts.[14] Over a thousand people eat breakfast every day at the *Comedor Salesiano,* located right next to the Bordo. Other border towns have scarcer options, but local churches and government programs offer a few benefits. Once people learn to negotiate these complicated geographies, they often stay longer than anticipated. The boundaries to exit are daunting, as the costs increase to travel to some distant, former home in the interior of Mexico or the risks of crossing the border become precariously high.

In many ways the movement of people through the streets and plazas along the border directly mimics the controls for passing through the border and living without documents on the other side. There are areas where people, marked by their journeys as migrants, can go and other places where they cannot. They are monitored and, at times, brutalized or exploited; at other times they are ignored. The fact that they do not belong, that they are from elsewhere, makes them into permanent foreign strangers. They are defined by their movement, and therefore, their mobility is distinctly altered. Not only do organized criminal groups take a specific interest in where they go and why, but so does the state. After years of living in the United States, with its proliferation of checkpoints, and the *polimigra,* a term used to denote the blending of local law enforcement and immigration officials, this restriction of movement has been well engrained into their behavior. Scholars have discussed the problem of mobility under the deportation regime,[15] but none have explored how this movement is shaped after removal. Even after people leave the structures of enforcement in the United States, whereupon their illegality has been constructed through notions of a foreign threat, they return to yet another configuration, where they are once again a feared, controlled, and victimized group.

The bus stations were almost always the most dangerous places since they were highly controlled with surveillance constantly looking for people to kidnap or who may be suspicious and represent a threat. Particular care was taken to try and improve this situation by either installing the military directly at the bus station or circumventing it entirely and having all deportees taken directly to Monterrey from the border with a military escort. However, for some people who just want to go on their own and get away from this police escort, the consequences can be dire. Lázaro, the shelter worker, shared a particularly extreme example:

> One kid surprised me. This kid, Israel, was very interactive and talkative. It was nine in the morning and the Instituto Tamaulipeco was supposed to come pick them up, which they normally do at about ten. But Israel was impatient and wanted to go. He asked us to get him a taxi. I tried to tell him to calm down, and that all sorts of bad things can happen and for security they should wait for the Instituto. [Israel replied,] "No, no, don't worry. Thanks for your help but I am going to go." He was with three others. I said that if you take a taxi it is your responsibility and the taxi will get you to

the bus station, but the danger is in the bus station, the central. They were adamant and I can't keep anyone here by force so I got them the taxi. About a half hour later, Israel came back. He had no shoes and his socks were torn and bloody ... He arrived desperate, banging on the door. I opened it up and gave him some water, but he was in shock. He could not talk. He didn't talk for almost a month. The kid was super affected. The psychologist would work with him and try to get him to talk, but he wouldn't. He had been kidnapped, but was able to escape. The three guys who were with him did not get away. He was from Reynosa! [about three hours away] They had to come for him and pick him up.

Once he was able to speak again they contacted his family who came for him. "He went from someone who was very interactive to a very calm person who would not get involved with anything. He would just walk back and forth, back and forth," said Lázaro.[16] This trauma and violence can leave scars, and furthermore creates more questions about what happened and the ultimate fate of Israel's comrades. Issues like this have led to the need for more safety at points of transit.

However, the bubbles of safety such as shelters, plazas, or bus stations often create their own problems. For instance in Matamoros, Tamaulipas, there were problems with criminals kidnapping, intimidating, and threatening people at the bus station. The Mexican government decided to install the Marines permanently at the bus station to protect employees, travelers, and migrants. This, along with a module for migrant aid run by the state government and the local shelter, made a huge difference for migrants. However, the safety and availability of support created a new problem. People who did not immediately have resources with which to buy a bus ticket and get out of the region would get stuck in the station. With no showers, and limited options for food, it took its toll on deportees who often spent days or even weeks living there. Moreover, they became a captive population inside the relative safety of the terminal. Once they would venture out, usually a block and a half to the *Soriana* supermarket where the Moneygram kiosk allowed them to receive a wire transfer, people knew exactly why and what resources they now carried. The trip back from the supermarket to the bus station was a dangerous one, as people were frequently robbed or kidnapped. These bubbles of safety develop hard edges, because they allow people to be easily identified once they decide to leave, exacerbating their vulnerability.

This phenomenon was not unique to the Northeast, although it was greatly heightened and more violent. Anti-migrant sentiment is prevalent throughout Mexico. A mural painted in Oaxaca circulated around the internet as an example of people telling migrants not to stop, not to get off the train, and to move on or there would be consequences.[17] In Tijuana, at the opposite end of the border, the fear and restrictions on mobility stemmed directly from the police. For migrants staying at one of the shelters on the eastern side of downtown, the walk back up the hill, along a busy street after a hard day's work, would almost certainly lead to a police shakedown. As the shelters open in the evening, the police would watch for people coming back after working all day, begging in the streets, or often receiving a wire transfer from family members. Those who could not pay a bribe to the police would go to jail for 36 hours for not having any identification or some other trumped-up charge. "Why work if I am going to lose it all anyway?" asked one young man. This lack of mobility often trapped people near their refuge, particularly the street in front of the shelter where the cops would not dare to hassle migrants. As a result, migrants would congregate out front, washing cars or begging for change, which in turn led to increased tensions with neighbors.

For Jorge, whose situation we discussed in chapter 1, the most dangerous place was entering and exiting the Bordo. "The police yell, 'Hey, where are you going?' and you know they got you." Jorge avoids sleeping in the Bordo for this reason and just visits to get his fix of meth and the free food or donations that were frequent there. For many recent deportees to Tijuana this aid industry actually attracted them to the Bordo for the first time. There were sandwich giveaways in the afternoons, groups donating clothes on the weekends, and, of course, breakfast in the mornings. This had a pernicious effect, attracting migrants and deportees into what is essentially a dangerous area simply because of the large aid industry using the stark visuals as a photo opportunity. While I do not want to blame the aid industry for bringing people there, it is always important to reflect on the unintended consequences of aid. As Jorge waited for his mother to help him check into rehab, he noted that the Bordo is not just drugs anymore, but a place for people to get sustenance.

Jorge did, however, have some safe places that he used to sleep or beg for change, as an escape from the dangers of the Bordo. One was near the border, "by the yellow taxi station. When there is a (long) line I can ask for change. I feel safe there. I can hide from the police quick. Two times, I have been caught, but they let me go quick." The other place was a small park that he would sleep in near some soccer fields.[18]

The restrictions on movement lead to micro-level barriers. Many Central Americans, particularly people from El Salvador where the gang presence is so extensive and suffocating, discuss the first step of migration as sneaking out of their homes. "I had to leave in the middle of the night and jump over a fence behind my house so they wouldn't see me." Others got into the trunk of a car, or acted like they were going to work and simply never returned, leaving all of their worldly possessions, except for a backpack donated by a friend or relative.[19]

This same dynamic occurred in the shelter as well. One evening a young man from Honduras asked me if I could help him sneak out. He didn't want the rest of the shelter to know that he was leaving. Shelter workers let the four of them quietly sneak out of the shelter after dinner and I never heard from them again. Exactly why this happens is hard to say. Maybe they had arranged for only a few of them to cross and not everyone could come. Maybe they were afraid of someone in the shelter and did not want them to know that they had arranged to cross and therefore would be better to kidnap.[20] What is clear is that the movement between places becomes a commodity, something to be prized, nurtured, understood, and controlled. This commodity is not only sought after by organized crime, but often involved a negotiation between the police or military and criminals. Lázaro said:

> One time, it was about 9 am, and there were seven Central Americans, they [Zetas] had them pushed up against the wall outside the shelter, and were going through their stuff, their backpacks and the little they had with them. I called a number we had for the army, and sure enough, they arrived and grabbed [the gang members]. Then, from the window I heard the *comandante*, I think he was the *comandante*, call someone from organized crime, he told them, "We have your boys. They are bothering the people at the migrant shelter. What should we do with them?" "No, let them go, give them to me. I will tell them not to bother the *casa del migrante*," said the voice over the radio. They were talking on Nextel radios so I could hear both voices easily. The commander said, "Okay, but tell them not to cause any more trouble because they will call us for help."[21]

However, the desire to bother migrants did not go away. The focus on migrants is most visible among the population of ex-prisoners who are concentrated in the eastern and western edges of the border. Incarceration produces a kind of stunted mobility, as a prisoner must ask permission to go anywhere, as well as the trauma and isolation associated with solitary confinement. Such impacts cannot be understated. After years of incarceration, many struggle to adjust to the outside world in a familiar place, let alone a now unfamiliar country.

> Don Gerardo had been in the United States since 1962 when his parents brought him over as a two-year-old. He told people that he was born in Mexico City, but no one was able to find a birth certificate or any other record of his existence. He knew of no family in Mexico. Gerardo had just spent 25 years locked up in a supermax facility in California for multiple robberies. He was short and stocky, with eyes that bulged and darted around the room. He was unkempt and usually wore a stocking cap and a scraggly beard. He immediately gravitated toward me because I spoke English. He spoke almost no Spanish and even speaking to him in English was difficult because of his severe stutter.
>
> "I don't sleep at night," he explained. "Too many people in the dorms. During the day I go find abandoned houses to sleep in." "That's dangerous,"

I cautioned, knowing that people use abandoned houses as stash houses or for torture and the disposal of bodies. "No it's not," he said. "I go upstairs and hide in a closet." One day he returned to the shelter happy because he found a culvert to sleep in.

These symptoms are textbook after-effects of institutionalization. Solitary confinement creates severe mental disorders, such as this type of agoraphobia, making people feel exposed and vulnerable unless they are alone and in tight spaces.[22]

Over the next few weeks we discussed his plans. No one had the heart to kick him out of the shelter when he passed the one-week limit. First he wanted to try and talk his way through the port of entry like many native speakers of English. I tried to explain that he would most certainly wind up back in jail with a permanent ban for migration, but that might not be a bad option for him. It would be unlikely that he could ever legally enter the United States again in his life. However, he did not understand my point and decided against it. Later he settled on going to Tijuana.

One day I returned late to the shelter and found out he was leaving. An administrator decided to buy him a bus ticket to Mexico City. The rumor was that this was just their way of getting rid of him. They didn't have the heart to turn him away and he had already stayed well past the allotted week. Gerardo still assured me he was going to Tijuana but I confirmed that the ticket was for Mexico City. "That's on the way, right?" he asked me. "No," I told him, but he was not deterred.[23]

A priest took him off to the bus station late that night. I never heard from him again, although I often looked for him in Tijuana, in the canal, known as El Bordo, where homeless deportees congregate. Gerardo and people like him are wiped off the map, expelled from the boundaries of the United States and returned to a country where they also do not exist. His institutionalization made his movement through even the relatively benign geography of the migrant shelter into an arduous task, not to mention the much more complicated and dangerous terrain outside those walls. His case was one of extreme mental disability. He had obviously hurt a great deal of people in his life, but after so much time as a prisoner in the United States, where does he belong?

There are thousands of others who struggle to adapt to Mexico. The stigmas of crime, of deportation and migration itself, leave them in a particularly vulnerable situation along the border. Add to this the tensions between the United States and Mexico, and deportees with a lifetime in the United States take on an imputed "American" identity that further ostracizes them. The sheer violence and brutality of the rules dictating movement and access along the border make research difficult. Most people, like Don Gerardo, simply disappear and I never hear from them again. Others I can follow, such as Monterrey and Zacatecas, more tech-savvy operatives always looking to chat (or looking for help out of a jam). And still others show up dead, washed up in the river or somewhere worse. For people who violate the unspoken rules of mobility after deportation, they face a dire set of consequences, sometimes a beating, sometimes extortion, and other times, worse. The ultimate manifestation of control over movement comes in the form of kidnapping. The process of taking possession of people's bodies is a disturbing, brutal, and complicated phenomenon about which we understand very little.

CHAPTER FOUR

They Torture You to Make You Lose Feeling

The massive vat at the edge of the compound gave off a faint, acidic smell. When the bodies came out, they were little more than lumpy white balls, which were then spread around in nearby fields. Juanito, a survivor who spent seven months kidnapped and held by Mexico's infamous Zetas cartel, said there was nothing recognizably human about the remains.[1]

"They were like dirt," he said in Spanish. "It was as if they were salt."

Juanito lost count of how many fellow-kidnapping victims ended up in the vat, but he said the killing was a daily occurrence.

"Maybe a hundred? No, I believe it was many more. Yeah ... two hundred, or less, I don't know," he said. "One or two daily. Imagine it! It was a lot."

The horrors he witnessed at the Zetas compound raise complicated questions about the motives behind the epidemic of migrant kidnapping that has drawn international attention to Mexico. As Juanito himself said, only those who have gone through it can truly understand the experience. His story is without a doubt an extreme vision of migrant kidnapping; however, journalists and scholars have generally studied this phenomenon indirectly, hearing snippets of first- and secondhand accounts of torture, murder, and recruitment. With more than 37,000 people having disappeared in Mexico during the past decade,[2] the well-documented practice of dissolving bodies in acid has confounded investigators and families in search of answers. There are particularly egregious cases, such as Santiago Meza López, better known as the *Pozolero,* or the "stew maker," who has admitted to dissolving over three hundred bodies in acid.[3] However, these disappearances are often framed statically as the result of the drug war, and are rarely tied to violence against migrants, and the kidnapping epidemic that has been viewed as a parallel issue. Add to this the general danger of working in these regions and it is easy to understand why so little research and so few answers have been produced.

To further complicate these issues, many of the kidnapping victims I interviewed[4] frequently escape or are let go, leaving us to question what is happening with the thousands of other people kidnapped each year. Moreover, beyond a rare look at the inner workings of the Zetas, Juanito's testimony is also a grisly account of the most extreme consequences of mass deportation from the United States.[5] We are left to wonder, Why commit such atrocities? Why kidnap relatively impoverished people? Stories like Juanito's, as well as the surveys and interviews collected throughout the course of research, paint a more complicated picture of migrant kidnapping, one that extends far beyond the ransom narrative. Namely, kidnapping is about the control of people's bodies, their labor and participation in illegal activities, and therefore it plays an important part in the preservation of criminal organizations, especially during times of conflict when the death toll from inter- and intra-cartel wars is so high. The constricted labor supply that is the result of decades of fighting has led criminal organizations to find new ways to attract and control an expendable labor force.

Migrants become an important resource as manual labor (working in the fields, growing, producing, packaging, shipping drugs, etc.), or often under duress as active members of criminal organizations such as assassins, drug traffickers, and even kidnappers themselves. Through post-deportation surveys,[6] MBCS data found that seven percent of deportees (n = 83) had a previous experience of being held against their will. This may not appear significant, but kidnappings are considered extremely rare, generally measured in events per 500,000 inhabitants for countrywide data.[7] To have a measureable percentage appear in a random sample is indeed extreme. However, this is not to say that this is a precise estimate of the number of migrant kidnappings in Mexico. This survey only included individuals who had been deported to Mexico within the last month, and since kidnappings occur during multiple parts of the journey (travel through Mexico, in a safe house prior to crossing, during the crossing, upon arrival in the United States, etc.), our survey often missed people who had been abducted. Estimating a phenomenon such as this is a huge challenge. Mexico's national human rights commission notes that 9,758 people were kidnapped in a six-month period,[8] but they arrive at this estimate through the people who reported their abduction to authorities and then made a rough estimate of the number of people simultaneously being held in captivity. Mexico's census organization INEGI estimated 69,107 kidnappings in 2016; however, they also estimated 66,842 victims of kidnapping in the same year, causing us to question the data further.[9] This gives a better idea, but it is in no way a definitive answer to questions about the prevalence of migrant kidnapping. Take into account that Mexico's census bureau found that 98 percent of people did not report kidnappings[10] (every kidnapping victim I interviewed falls into this category), and those who are never released, and it is possible that the number is greater still.

My interest therefore lies in gaining a better understanding of why people are being taken, held, extorted, and tortured in such numbers. What interests are being served, who is behind it, and what could be changed to prevent such tragedies from occurring? About half of the kidnapping victims were held by their guide or coyote, and 36 percent were held by gangs, such as the Zetas. One in four experienced some sort of physical abuse and about half were threatened with a weapon (see Table 1). Despite these pervasive and vicious activities, U.S. depor-

TABLE 1

Kidnapping

Variable	Percent / Mean (N)
Male	88% (73)
Female	12% (10)
Age	33 years
Kidnapped by Coyote / Guide	51% (42)
Kidnapped by Gang / Bandits	36% (30)
Time in Captivity	6 days
Number of People Held Simultaneously	20
Ransom Demanded	69% (57)
Ransom Demanded (USD)	$2,800
Ransom Paid (of people asked)	58% (33)
Ransom Paid (USD)	$2,149
Reported Physical Abuse	27% (22)
Reported Verbal Abuse	72% (57)
Threatened with a Weapon	55% (44)
Reported Physical Abuse of Others	49% (38)
N = 83	

SOURCE: Migrant Border Crossing Study, Wave II

tation policies and procedures have actively exacerbated the situation, increasing the vulnerability of deportees, and concentrating them in areas with higher levels of violence.

As it currently stands, some of Mexico's most dangerous cities have also been among the largest repatriation sites. Researchers from the Washington Office on Latin America (WOLA) found that between 2009 and 2012 Mexican border states with declining homicide rates had declining deportation rates while states experiencing increases in violence were receiving more deportees.[11] In 2015 there were 92,410 repatriations to Tamaulipas and Coahuila, the neighboring state also controlled by the Zetas. This is despite the fact that only 73,939 Mexicans were apprehended in the corresponding border patrol sectors, leaving 18,471 people being electively sent here by U.S. authorities.[12] In 2013, one of the worst years for violence in northeastern Mexico, the difference was 58,980. Why have tens of thousands of people been diverted to this region, the states most known for migrant massacres?

While the top state for deportations has oscillated between Baja California and Tamaulipas during the research and writing of this book, the very fact that authorities have not taken steps to avoid returning people to the region despite its reputation should in and of itself be a damning condemnation of immigration enforcement practices. Juanito's story demonstrates the connections between U.S. immigration and deportation policies, the drug war raging in Mexico, and the use of kidnapping as a tool for extortion, recruitment, and manipulation. He agreed to share his story, both as a cry for help for the people who did not escape, and as a tool to reach out to both governments, to end impunity and change policies and practices of deportation that have led to escalated violence on the border.

INTERVIEWING JUANITO

A journalist friend and colleague named Murphy Woodhouse and I rushed down to the border as soon as I got a call from an activist at the soup kitchen for deportees.[13] Juanito had been deported and he was trying to figure out what to do next. I had met Juanito through his lawyer and interviewed him in prison in Florence, Arizona, but when he was unexpectedly released and deported to Mexico, we very much wanted to talk with him.[14]

As per Juanito's wishes we brought a video camera to record his story in the event that anything happened to him. We sat down in the migrant shelter to record his account. His leg shook uncontrollably as he recounted the gory details of his imprisonment and recruitment by the world's most feared criminal organization. His nervous twitch left an eerie background sound to the recording. Only when he reached particularly strong points of his experiences did he stop moving, punctuating the conversation with a deafening silence.

He speaks slowly, and softly, though his voice sometimes trails off into a mumbled whisper. He looks at the floor. He is good looking, and in his early twenties with a crooked smile he flashes when he's nervous. He is short and slim, not weighing more than 140 lbs soaking wet. It is hard to reconcile his soft speech and calm demeanor with his tremendous story of survival and perseverance.

Juanito's nightmare began shortly after his October 2011 deportation to Piedras Negras, Coahuila, a Mexican border city across the Rio Grande from Eagle Pass, Texas. He had just finished serving a prison sentence for running a backpack full of pot into the United States through Texas in 2010. For Juanito, like many poor, young men on the border, running drugs was one of the surest sources of income in an otherwise cash-strapped region. Juanito is up-front about his own participation, saying that he was in a tight spot and, as the only adult male in his household, decided to take the risk.

After making it home for a week to see his family, he headed to Chihuahua, the capital of Chihuahua state, where he planned to travel to Tijuana and see his older brother. There, Grupos Beta[15] agents, or at least people dressed as Beta agents, told Juanito and a large group of recent deportees that they could cover half the cost of a bus ticket to their final destination. This is a service offered in many repatriation sites along the border. This, and the promise of a free meal, was the bait. Our survey research showed that trickery, rather than brute force, was the most common way for people to be taken captive. While armed kidnappings do exist, especially for migrants riding the infamous trains through Mexico, it is generally easier to prey upon isolated, vulnerable, and often naïve migrants and deportees.

"[F]or them, it's easier to grab someone like us, people who arrived deported because a lot of us don't have money. We came without clothes and hungry. The way they get us is by tricking us into thinking that they're going to take us to eat and give us a discount on the bus ticket to where we're going," Juanito said. "You approach them looking for help, but what actually happened to us…" he trailed off. Once the group of deportees were in the truck, the men stopped acting like government agents from a migrant aid organization. "They put black bags on our heads … and they took our belongings from us … approximately 35 of us were kidnapped in that moment."

The relationship of movement and violence is clear. Juanito stressed that the Zetas could not exist if they behaved this way with the local population. "They would revolt!" he exclaimed. Migrants and deportees are rendered vulnerable by their journey through clandestine space. Their relationship to the border, as undocumented migrants, means they are no longer connected to the social fabric as citizens with identities, families, friends, and social ties; rather, they have been dislodged from the norms and protections of society as a whole. This comes on top of an already well-documented erosion of basic human rights in Mexico.[16] Being out of place, a stranger, severed from one's social ties, family, friends, and professional acquaintances, increases the ability of criminal groups to act with impunity, all while the authorities turn a blind eye. Being labeled as a migrant or deportee allows for this type of violence since they do not now, nor ever will, belong here. Combine this with the mass forced movement of over 4 million people deported back to Mexico during the Obama administration and not only do we see people risking everything for a better life, but the state contributing to people's vulnerability.

From Chihuahua, Juanito and his 35 companions spent their long drive to somewhere in Tamaulipas with their heads covered and their hands bound by zip-ties. "I don't know how long it was but it did take quite a while because I slept, woke up, and went to sleep again and the van was still going," Juanito said. "We arrived at a small, deserted town, maybe San Fernando, Tamaulipas, or San Vicente. It was one of those, but I don't remember well." San Fernando, the site of the infamous 2010 massacres of 72 would-be migrants from Central and South America, received a heavy influx of military and federal police after this tragic event. However, in the years following, several mass graves containing 193 bodies were found in the surrounding area, suggesting little had changed.[17]

The first day I met Juanito in an Arizona prison, he immediately asked if I had heard about the capture of *La Ardilla* (The Squirrel). He was referring to Salvador Alfonso Martínez Escobedo, who had been arrested the day before. I was not well aware of the rather obscure drug lord from the Zetas who became more famous upon his arrest and the maniacal face he made as he was paraded in front of the reporters. He has largely been recognized as one of the architects of the massacre. While many still speculate on the motives for the massacre, Juanito had developed his own understanding of why the Zetas committed such a gruesome crime. "To apply pressure. A part of the government wanted to stop cooperating with them. This was to make a lot of noise and put more pressure on them [to cooperate]," Juanito explained. This perceptive theory has a certain logic to it. In fact, the massacre was a huge embarrassment to Mexico and broke through the discourse that only people involved with drugs were being killed. This "guilty victim" discourse mirrors closely Melissa Wright's work on the femicides of Ciudad Juárez. She argues that this is a way to absolve the state from its responsibility to provide justice, accountability, and basic security or police services.[18] By killing migrants, particularly foreign migrants,[19] it demolished this script, leaving the state vulnerable to looming, interventionist critiques that Mexico is a failed state.[20] The murder of foreigners had a dual effect. Not only did it raise the ire of the international community, but it also served to shape public opinion on kidnapping of migrants as a distinctly non-Mexican problem. While it is certainly the case that Central Americans are kidnapped in large numbers, kidnapping of Mexican migrants, particularly deportees, remains rampant.[21]

Torture Started as Soon as They Arrived

"We got there ... and they took off our clothes and hung us from iron bars, with our hands cuffed," he said. "When they strung me up, my arm was dislocated. They bathed me naked with a high-pressure hose, hung up on a hook. Then another person came and put electrodes on my private parts, wires with electricity. After that I don't know what happened because I passed out from the pain. After a while, I don't know how long, I woke up and had three wounds on my head and was completely bald. I had no hair. I didn't have toenails either, or finger-nails. My tongue was inflamed and my lips were split open. My testicles were also very large. They didn't tell me what had happened. It was in that moment that I realized that I was in a safe house run by the organi-zation known as the Zetas, and that it was possible that I wouldn't get out of there alive."

In Juanito's recollection, this was the treatment most people received when they arrived. He and a handful of others, however, were also sub-jected to regular sexual assaults. Juanito said the purpose of the Zetas's mistreatment was simple: breaking people and, out of the remnants, forging drug mules, slaves for their pot manufacturing operation and cannon fodder for their war. This is consistent with harrowing stories collected by journalists with survivors of human trafficking.[22]

"The organization's first step, the torture, is to make one lose feeling, lose feeling for other people. They want you to feel bitterness, and to take it out on the new people arriving there day after day," he said. "They're recruiting people. After they eliminate weakness in them, they make them strong and give them guns and send them to different parts of the Mexican republic to try and take territory from other organizations."

In order to understand why kidnapping has become so prevalent in Mexico, traditional narratives of ransom and return must be set aside. Juanito was forced to contact family. They paid 5,000 USD but he was not released. This is consistent with my broader research. Survey data with the 83 kidnapped deportees in the MBCS shows that only 67 percent (n = 54) were asked for ransom and only 57 percent (n = 31) of those actually paid the ransom. Eight people were let go without pay-ing, and 12 people escaped. This points to the fact that paying ransom does not necessarily correspond to being released. If people are paying ransom and not being released, or often being released without paying, then the true motives of kidnapping must be more complicated.

In fact, for the people who are never asked for ransom, the purpose of their kidnapping is usually about information obtained through interrogation and torture. This is generally because someone is suspected of belonging to another gang, either in the United States or in Mexico. As we explored in the last chapter, the complicated geography of removal brings many people to northeastern Mexico who did not choose to cross there and directly puts them in harm's way. The Zetas immediately pick up people from rival territories and interrogate them under the suspicion of being connected to a rival cartel.[23] This practice is consistent with the rise in popularity of the term *levantón* in Mexico, meaning a kidnapping without the intent of return. These are commonly associated with how intercartel disputes are settled, but in reality, have become an important part of the complicated motives behind kidnapping in Mexico.

As we can see in our survey data, however, kidnappings by gangs are typically much more violent and brutal than those committed by guides (see Table 2). This stems from the type of torture Juanito describes, which is common throughout my research. "They cut out a young Nicaraguan guy's eye and severed two of his fingers because he didn't pay. He bled to death in two days," explained a young man who had been held in Matamoros, Tamaulipas. Others describe similar vats used to dissolve bodies, as well as the infamous *tablazo,* a paddling with a piece of wood filled with spikes. This indicates that kidnapping has become an integral part of the recruitment process. One migrant from Honduras explained his own experience being kidnapped:

> On June 20, 2011, I was near Veracruz, at about midnight. I had gotten separated from my friends so I was alone by the train tracks. A black truck with tinted windows drove up to me. They offered me a taco, but suddenly three men got out of the truck with their guns. I was in the army in Honduras so I recognized the *cuernos de chivo*, AK-47, Mini Uzis, and AR-15s. They pointed their guns at me and told me they were from the Zetas, and asked me if

TABLE 2

Comparison between People Kidnapped by Their Coyote or Guide and Those Kidnapped by Gangs

Variable	Kidnapped by Coyote (n=42)	Kidnapped by Gangs (n=30)	Difference
Held in U.S.	64%	25%	39%**
Number of People Held	17	26	9***
Drugs Present at Safe House	32%	57%	25%*
Amount Ransom Paid (USD)	$1,893	$2,534	$641**
Report Physical Abuse	17%	33%	16%
Report Verbal Abuse	59%	92%	33%**
Threatened with Weapon	30%	87%	57%***
N=83			

SOURCE: Migrant Border Crossing Study, Wave II

Note: * p< 0.05 ** p<0.01 *** p <0.001 indicate the difference is statistically significant.

I wanted to work for them as a hit man. I told them I wasn't interested, that I was heading to Mexico City for work. They chained me up by the wrists and told me they were going to kill me. They took me to a ranch near the ocean. I don't know where it was but I could hear waves. I could hear people in the other rooms. I think there were about 8 or 10 people there and two women. I spent 8 days locked up there. They practically didn't give me food. They came to interrogate me two times a day. They asked me when I was going to give up the phone numbers for my family in the north. I told them I didn't have any and I was going to DF for work, not the U.S. After beating me and yelling at me for days they said, "What the fuck are we going to do with you? Give up the phone numbers or come work for us and we will let you go." But my family doesn't even have enough to take care of themselves and I was leaving to help them, not hurt them. I am poor, I told them. I have nothing, why else would I risk this? Finally on the 28th they beat me badly. I thought they were going to kill me, but they dumped me on the street. I was dripping blood from my nose. I found a hospital where I stayed for four days. I got back on the train again and was almost kidnapped again in Lecheria [Mexico State]." When asked at the end of the interview if he would tell anyone about this, he said no. He didn't want his family to worry about him.[24]

But Juanito was not tasked with becoming a hit man. On several occasions, he assisted in one of the Zetas's most atrocious sideline businesses: harvesting and selling the organs of young children.[25] "They have this place, where there's a bed and they suffocate the people with a bag. Then they lay them down, strip them naked and drain their blood. They forced any of us who were near there to cut open the bodies. They were children, minors. Nine- to twelve-years-old," he said. "And, well, it was my misfortune to participate in several acts of that magnitude. They forced me to open up the bodies of those creatures (*criaturas*). They have coolers, the ones that smoke comes out of [with dry ice], and they throw the organs in a bag, put the bag in the cooler, and take them away."

This remains the single most traumatic aspect of Juanito's experience. The acts that he committed in the name of survival are worse than all of the torture, abuse, and rape combined. For psychologist Jonathan Shay, committing acts that are contrary to our moral understandings of the world creates a unique form of trauma he has dubbed "moral injury."[26] His work with combat veterans asserts that the suspension of one's moral compass during wartime is a key component of post-traumatic stress syndrome. Committing acts that one would never do within the context of the norms and rules we are taught in society as a whole causes extreme emotional distress. The suspension of traditional values and standards that we consider to be good, bad, or fundamentally amoral damages our psyche. This process is actually one of the Zetas's and other drug cartels' techniques for recruitment, which is apparent in their use of kidnapping, torture, and coercion. By inflicting *moral violence* upon their captives it separates them from society as a whole, from their old lives and even from who they were. This is a fundamentally life-altering technology: forcing people to engage in horrific acts such as murder to break them away from their former life. No longer captives in the physical sense, people are intimately linked to their captors, bound by their inability to reenter and partake in the world around them. Having broken the basic rules of decency and morality, it creates a loyal, malleable group of peons who bear the brunt of the brutal conflict that has raged in Mexico for the past decade.

While many have suggested that economic inequality,[27] and sometimes prestige,[28] is the main driver for participation in drug trafficking, questions arise when the level of violence becomes so great. With the costs so high and the rewards so slim in Mexico, how do drug cartels continue to recruit? The price of an assassination in Ciudad Juárez dropped to just 50 USD during the height of the violence.[29] It is reasonable to think that the years of violence and death have led to decreased willing participation in drug trafficking. However, by forcing people to tap into their basic survival instincts, it dislocates them from society as a whole. This is another example of the intimate relationship between movement and violence. As people leave their hometowns or countries, they also pass into another world, one that is dictated by different rules, norms, and morals. While not everyone is forced to make the decisions that Juanito did, the ability for a criminal organization to put people in those positions is a direct by-product of the massive clandestine migrations that occur all over the world.

"You have to do what they say. Because in moments like that, you're crying and your life ... you want to get out of there alive," he said. "But in my case I think it would have been better if they had just shot me. I think that for me that would have been more comfortable. Because they are things that I will never be able to forget ... [T]he reality is that when you go through that, it's difficult to continue being the person you once were. I don't think I'll ever be able to carry on with the life I had before because I'll always have memories of all this. I'll always see their faces."

After months of working in the fields, learning how to clone, grow, and package marijuana, Juanito was able to convince them he could help take a load of drugs across the border. Juanito attributes his survival to his passivity. He is a small man, slightly effeminate, and as a gay man he was constantly harassed but was not viewed as a threat by his captors. The people who tried to fight back, who resisted, were quickly killed and disposed of in the vats. Those who joined the Zetas "put on the hoods" and disappeared among the ranks of torturers and enforcers, explained Juanito. Then, they are sent off to one of the battlegrounds, such as the western state of Nayarit, or into Central America.

Juanito's testimony also troubles the very idea of who, exactly, is a Zeta. Was Juanito a Zeta? He worked for them, but certainly against his will. How many so-called "Zetas" are like Juanito, doing the work because to do otherwise means a bullet in the head and your body being dissolved out of existence? This is not to absolve people who participate in these heinous acts as purely victims of a monolithic edifice of unjust drug and immigration policies. We must not lose sight of the fact that there are people with real power and wealth who have actively provoked the misery and death of thousands of people because of their greed and lust for power. However, the brunt of the violence that has reshaped Mexico, and particularly, Mexico's northern border, in recent years is born by low-level operatives, mostly poor, young males. In the past, people frequently engaged in the illegal economy sporadically, as a supplement to meager wages in Mexico. However, this took a turn during recent years as the level of violence associated with the once rather innocuous activities of drug or human smuggling skyrocketed. These changes have an enormous impact on the lives and activities of people who were once only peripherally involved.

As Shaylih Muehlmann has noted, the slippery slope of involvement creates mental borders between people's self-defined roles within illegal enterprises that are far harder to distinguish in the material world than in common discourse.[30] Juanito is adamant that he is not and never was a Zeta, and likely, the Zetas would agree, but at what point does participation for survival become participation? Presenting the facade that he was passive and nonthreatening allowed Juanito to avoid recruitment as a full-fledged member of the Zetas. However, this was a ruse to mask his inner strength, which is evidenced by his will to survive.

Escape

Border patrol agents are rarely a welcome sight to migrants and smugglers crossing the desert. For Juanito, however, getting apprehended was exactly what he wanted as he walked through the Arizona desert with a backpack full of pot in the spring of 2012, while armed Zetas were nearby and quietly keeping watch. He deliberately left the most conspicuous tracks he could, and it eventually paid off: agents found him, arrested him, and unwittingly brought his nightmare with the Zetas to an end.

Before his trip to the border, his captors brought him outside. Along with the other captives he was made to stand in a line. The Zetas fired a pistol and told everyone to run. Juanito ran as fast as he could. "I thought they were going to kill us, but it was a test." Juanito won the race and proved that he could handle the trip across the border with marijuana. By skirting the line between competent and passive, tough and timid, Juanito was able to maintain the balancing act of survival.

Upon his arrest by the U.S. Border Patrol, he pleaded for them to look for the rest of the Zetas that were with him in the desert. Each person was sleeping on a different hill so as to avoid detection of the entire marijuana shipment. "I made them aware immediately that there were people there who had kidnapped us and there were different groups scattered around, but they just told me I was lying." The agent "became so bothered that he started to verbally assault me and he pushed me down the hill ... I fractured my left leg.[31] I tried to file a complaint but they ignored me," said Juanito.

A helicopter arrived to pick him up and he was immediately sent to the hospital. The examination showed the extent of his torture, the markings on his body and the physical trauma of his captivity. "I saw the marks on his body, on his back, small marks on his testicles, on his legs. He had a scar, a pretty significant scar," explained Juanito's lawyer. "I believe it was over his lip. His head had palpable bumps where he had been pistol whipped."

"For me, it was better for the immigration police to detain me, because then I would be free of those people," said Juanito. He never went to trial. Court delays meant that he had already spent twelve months in jail, making his trial a waste of time since a plea would get him out on time served. He was deported to Nogales, Sonora, in 2013. "[I] believe that since that moment until now I have not been able to keep my conscience calm, neither emotionally nor physically calm, because those people did a lot of moral damage to me," stated Juanito. His experiences with survival left him scarred. The moral violence of being put in positions where he had to choose between participation in the deaths of others and his own continued survival has done damage to his sense of right and wrong, to his ability to justify his actions as morally right. For Juanito, accepting his situation has been a constant struggle in the years and months to come.

This is one of the challenges for Mexico as it tries to recover from years of violence. While the country as a whole continues to undergo serious conflicts, individual cities have been able to stem the tide of killing. However, this is but one step. Dealing with the damage to people's moral sense of right and wrong is a more challenging process. Moreover, with the continued removal of "criminal aliens" there is a constant influx of people who struggle to adapt to life in Mexico on many levels.

Data obtained by the American Immigration Council demonstrates that the Criminal Alien Program (CAP) removes immigrants convicted of crimes in the United States into two main regions, Tamaulipas and Baja California.[32] These data show that the difference between the number of apprehensions to the northeast and the number of deportations is largely the result of criminal deportations (Map 2). With 29 percent of all removals to Tamaulipas coming from CAP, it is clear to see how people are being funneled into this region as opposed to other areas. Moreover, Tamaulipas received 126,212 deportations through the Criminal Alien Program from 2010–13, more than any other state despite the well-known issue of migrant massacres coinciding with this time period.

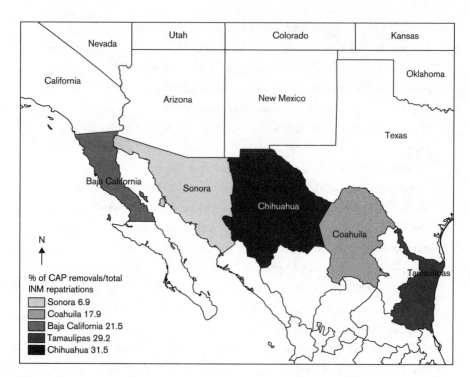

Map 2. Percentage of deportations processed through the Criminal Alien Program. Source: Rolando Díaz, Criminal Alien Program and Instituto Nacional de Migración.

The "criminal alien" deserves some scrutiny since immigrants are considerably more law-abiding than citizens,[33] and many of the people removed through the CAP have never been charged with a crime.[34] However, there are a considerable number of people who have been removed for serious crimes. This creates a whole new set of challenges. A priest, running a shelter in northeastern Mexico, confided, "Those are the vulnerable ones. Those are the ones whose bus tickets I buy. They come here and everyone knows they will be recruited." He had just paid for a bus ticket for a man with a big scar on his head that was exposed by his short shaved hair. "I want to go back to Guerrero, to Chilpancingo," he said, "but I have been in jail for five years and don't have anyone to send me money for the bus ticket." "I am worried about him," the priest told me later. "Guerrero is really bad, but I bought him a ticket because at least he will be out of the border, and has a chance to start up his life again." Deportees become expendable lives in the ongoing drug war in Mexico. With little to no connections to Mexico, especially with the stigma of deportation, possibly having assimilated culturally and linguistically to the United States and having been sent to prison, it is likely that their economic prospects in Mexico will be slim to none. Tattoos, a Chicano accent, or typical American-style baggy clothes draw attention, sometimes for kidnapping simply because they must have family and relatives in the United States who can pay a ransom, but also because they are likely recruits.

The challenges of returning to Mexico are vast and complex. Not only does kidnapping present complicated questions about why so many relatively poor individuals are abducted, but it stands in direct contradiction to the U.S. commitment to the Convention Against Torture (CAT), which prevents the removal of people when they are likely to be tortured. The shifting geography of drug-related violence in Mexico, combined with the movement of people through the maze of prisons and detention centers in the United States, places deportees directly in harm's way, while simultaneously fueling the conflict that continues to devastate parts of Mexico. The next chapter explores the processes of recruitment of deportees and migrants as they attempt to navigate dangerous border cities.

GOING HOME . . .

After we finished our interview with Juanito, Murphy and I took him downtown to eat some tacos and get him a haircut. He complained that his hair was too shaggy, and did not want to show up back home looking that way. Juanito stood at the corner with his hands in his pockets, waiting for a bus to pass before crossing the street. The U.S.-Mexico border wall, with Nogales, Arizona, beyond it, was a hundred yards to his left. His hair was fresh cut and smartly gelled now. It was a clear and warm afternoon and Juanito was walking surely through it. The scene stood in contrast to the intense, three-hour interview we had just recorded about his experiences being kidnapped and tortured by the Zetas.

We went to a *taquería* by the line and he ordered two quesadillas and a Coke. The three of us sat down and chatted in a mostly normal way about the same things everyone talks about. If not for his constant fidgeting, his sometimes inaudibly whispered voice, and his tendency to look down instead of in the eye, there would be no reason to suspect he had survived anything more or less difficult than most folks living just south of the border. It was difficult to reconcile his cheery demeanor with the angst and horror that had filled the last two years of his life.

When asked what lessons he wanted the world to know about what happened to him, Juanito replied: "More than anything, I want the [U.S.] government to understand that it's not necessary to be dropping people off, deporting them to all these places. It's possible to find a city, where it's safe, where there is assistance, like I've seen here. There are people that give you humanitarian and medical assistance ... If the government doesn't stop this, there will be no end," he added. "Fortunately, I had the luck to escape with my life." While my research has shown that these safe spaces seem to cycle in and out of waves of violence, his point is well made: more care is needed to keep deportees away from violence.

Juanito has had a difficult time since he returned to Mexico. Aside from problems finding work or a place to stay, Juanito has not been able to access medication prescribed by his therapist. Worst of all, he is not safe in Mexico. After meeting with us in Nogales, Sonora, Juanito took a bus to his hometown in the Northeast where he was kidnapped two more times, this time by a rival of the Zetas, La Linea. "They wanted to know who kidnapped me ... [and] how I got free," he explained. He was held for 15 days while they interrogated him and investigated his story, accusing him of being a spy for the Zetas. When he was able to convince them of his story, they let him go, but kept a close eye on him, accosting him on the street. "They beat me, but nothing like before," he stated nonchalantly. The first abduction occurred shortly after he had returned. He was trying to find a place to live after he was unable to stay with his sister. He was bouncing between homes and someone reported him to the cartel who picked him up and interrogated him. The practices of monitoring who comes and goes from cities throughout Mexico has reached new levels as fears of possible incursions from rivals drive paranoia and violence. I will discuss this in more depth in the next chapter. Anyone who has had a run-in with rival cartels will be regarded as suspicious and Juanito's kidnapping was no different.

He tried to report the kidnapping by the Zetas but officials from Mexico's National Human Rights Commission told him too much time had passed, despite recent legislation intended to give compensation for victims of crimes.[35] The "Ley General de las Víctimas" was passed with much fanfare, but has yet to show a real impact on protecting victims. The idea behind the law was that the state was responsible for helping victims of crimes by paying for funeral costs, medical treatment, housing, and food. However, the burden fell on the states to fund these programs and it has been uniformly criticized as nonexistent in the majority of the country. People like Juanito have been routinely turned away.[36]

These kidnappings were not nearly as brutal as the first, but contributed to his psychological and emotional decline. Juanito bounced around from different houses but the kidnappers made it very clear that he was not supposed to leave town, showing up and terrorizing him as he began to work in a local bar. Despite these warnings Juanito decided to try and escape. The fear that his kidnappers would simply not believe he was not involved with the Zetas plagued him. Knowing full well that a kernel of doubt about his allegiance would make it easier to simply kill him, erasing the slim possibility that he was a spy is often easier than living with suspicions. He called me while trying to sneak on a bus to the capital of his home state; afraid they would catch him and kill him. However, he only made it to the capital city of Chihuahua before he was found and forcibly taken back by cartel enforcers. Intense fighting the year after he arrived led to almost total destruction of the local gangs and Juanito was momentarily forgotten in the chaos. "Everyone who kidnapped me here is dead," he explained. Juanito found steady work at a pharmacy and a safe place to live; however, these seemed like small consolations after the brutality and continued persecution that arose as a survivor of cartel violence. The conflict has created a temporary respite, but who knows how long it will last. Mexico's future often feels like it rests on the hope that old feuds are forgotten and that the death toll will simply continue to mount until all debts, fears, and conflicts are forgotten.

CHAPTER FIVE

Guarding the River

Migrant Recruitment into Organized Crime

Rudi, a Salvadoran man traveling with his wife, was stopped today by the Zetas. They pointed guns at them and searched them. "I thought I was dead for sure, but they were really just looking for recruits. They said they would pay you 8,000 pesos a week to guard the river. You would get money clothes, guns, a truck, a house. And girls. The guy told me, 'We have girls between 3 years old and 15." Rudi was furious at this comment. Normally jovial and playful, he clenched his lips with anger and crumpled up his trademark red beanie. "That's sick," he said. "I wanted to fight them but they would kill me." I asked if people went with them. They said yes. Four or five people from the shelter went. Rudi said that "it's not true what they are offering." Kalangas, another man from El Salvador, spoke up and said, "Of course it isn't true. They know that too. First, no one is going to pay us that much for honest work. Second, part of your mind just clouds over when you think about the tempting offer."[1]

Several of the people I knew from the shelter joined the cartels over the course of fieldwork. They agreed to *guard the river,* which typically meant to watch for people crossing either as migrants or drug smugglers who did not have authorization from the Zetas. Guards would talk on cell phone radios, a secure form of communication and also a locally known sign of participation in organized crime. I would see some of the recent recruits around, such as an effeminate young Guatemalan man named Ramon who was barely 18 and missing his two front teeth, and Chino, a curly-haired *tapatio*.[2] However, after a few awkward encounters they simply disappeared from the streets and the areas frequented by migrants. While migrants often discussed being caught at the river and given the infamous *tablazo* (a paddling by a board with holes or nails in it), I also heard of people bribing their way through for as little as 40–50 USD. Most people thought there would be at least one warning, but it was difficult to know for sure, especially with so many people who simply disappeared.

Recruitment of migrants by drug cartels has become a polemic topic, as the anti-immigrant Right has for years conflated migration with terrorism and cartel violence spilling across the border, while the pro-immigrant Left will not touch the topic. It has become taboo among the latter to discuss migration with anything other than the stereotypical romanticized, heteronormative caricatures of immigrants as hard-working family members intent on forming part of the American melting pot. However, by understanding the complicated ways that people are drawn into organized crime during migration and deportation, it shows the negative consequences of criminalizing immigration, as well as our zero-sum worldwide war on drugs. Sometimes recruitment is completely forced and is generated through kidnapping and torture as discussed in the previous chapter. However, in other instances, it is far more nuanced, banal, and triggered by specific elements of a migrant's past life. For example, past gang membership, tattoos, and a criminal record often lead to recruitment that is predicated on a deportee proving that he or she is not a threat and is not aligned with a different criminal organization. Military service is also another factor that places deportees and migrants at risk of forced recruitment, as the skills associated with such service are highly valuable to drug cartels. In this sense recruitment is where two geopolitical phenomena collide. The patterns of movement, mobility, and family ties across the border all feed directly into the never-ending "war on drugs" and its seemingly limitless body count.

It is convenient and easy to look down from a thousand feet and compartmentalize the forces of migration and the conflict surrounding drug trafficking, but as we get closer to the ground the realities are dirty, smudged, and blurred. Poverty, the great dislocator, spurs people to strike out for a new country despite the dangers and prohibitions on labor migration. Moreover, for those who enter the world of drug trafficking, with few exceptions, it is not a decision made from a position of economic security. For many living in Mexico and Central America the only people they can relate to as having successfully changed their economic class are the migrants and the traffickers, creating a vicious cycle. This is not meant to create any equivalency between labor migration and participating in narcotics trafficking, but to show the shared roots of desperation and poverty. Furthermore, migration has been shown to be out of reach for the poorest of the poor, and only those with family or friends abroad or enough capital to pay for the journey are able to successfully cross into the United States.[3] The drug world is far more open for poor, desperate young men; however, the costs of participation are exponentially higher.

As policy is made in the capitals, far from the realities along the border, drug interdiction efforts, such as foreign aid through Plan Colombia and Plan Mérida, are seen as addressing one discrete problem: drugs. Immigration policy is regarded as another thing entirely, something to prevent through police and military actions on the border, not through strategic aid. In reality, the mass removal of individuals into zones of conflict is the policy equivalent of addressing a pollution problem by disposing of flammable chemicals in a dumpster fire. Neither effort will succeed unless serious attention is paid to the interrelated nature of these problems. For this chapter we explore just how people are enticed and recruited into organized crime upon deportation or failure to successfully cross the border. Instead of looking down from above, we must employ a ground-level, bottom-up approach to these two issues and investigate how people experience drug trafficking and migration, not as wholly separate issues, but as a mixture born out of the chaos and uncertainty of removal to the border.[4]

It should be noted that the violence in Mexico over the past decade, where over 200,000 people have lost their lives, has taken a toll on drug cartels, mostly in the form of sporadic shortages of labor. It is no longer as easy to attract the ranks of hungry, impoverished youths. Drug cartels work as a kind of pyramid scheme, with those on the streets making very little money, taking on most of the risk, and often dying quickly. Those at the top, with real power and influence, need hordes of people working for them, and replacing them can be a challenge. This has, broadly speaking, led to increased reliance on blind mules, and on those trafficking drugs under duress. Whereas before, many people along the border and in Mexico, and the United States for that matter, have viewed drugs as a victimless crime, a necessary fact of life, now, with the high death toll, people are generally less willing to engage with that world. For those who are deported to Mexico, this places them in a bind. If the conflict has been particularly brutal and there is a shortage of new members, recruitment will be more intense and violent, whereas at other times, when labor is plentiful, it will be more casual or sometimes nonexistent. The complex system of *halcones* that monitor and follow deportees who arrive at the border is a byproduct of the interest in deportees, not just as threat or economic resource, but as a potential labor supply. This attention to the who, what, where and why of deportation is precisely because this influx of unknown people into highly contested cities along the border represents potential new recruits, but also a possible threat from rival cartels.

For instance, Nuevo Laredo was one of the first places where violent incursions from the Sinaloa Cartel caused a rupture in the tenuous peace established by the dividing of Mexico into distinct drug war territories in the late 1980s.[5] In 2003 the Sinaloa Cartel sent hit men into Nuevo Laredo to try and take over the lucrative trucking route known as one of the largest landlocked ports in the world.[6] This led to organized crime quickly incorporating the local street gangs, in this case los Tejas, who would carry out street-level dealing, act as enforcers, and often most importantly, serve as lookouts to report back as to who was coming and going from the city. This intense scrutiny of outsiders ran across the spectrum, from casual observation to kidnapping and torture, often with the involvement of authorities.

For instance, one day I was chatting with a friend of my wife's in Tijuana over seafood at *El Mazateno*. He casually said that while studying in Mexico City he had driven his car up through Tamaulipas in order to cross into South Texas, but quickly the police stopped him because he had Sinaloa plates. They locked him up in jail and would not let him make a phone call or communicate with the outside world. "I was able to make friends with one of the guards who seemed sympathetic. I told him I was going to school with the governor's son and he was a friend. I begged him to let me use my phone and he passed it over to me. The friend was able to mobilize contacts and they let me go." One of the cops told him on his way out that he did not know how lucky he was. That phone call very likely saved his life.

The ability to travel between regions has deteriorated to the point that even those with money and ties to prominent figures—in other words, "those who would be missed"—are in danger. Therefore, what must it be like for the migrants and deportees who are deliberately ignored by society as a whole? Imagine the level of danger experienced by deportees who have no contacts, no ties, and no resources with which to hide from surveillance and scrutiny. The shifting geography of inter- and intra-cartel conflict makes it almost impossible to predict when and where people will become a threat. La Familia Michoacana is fighting the Zetas, who are fighting the Gulf Cartel, who are fighting La Linea, who are fighting Sinaloa, who are fighting Tijuana, Los Rojos, the Cartel Jalisco Nueva Generación and the Beltran Leyva for good measure. The Zetas have now split, creating new borders of the conflict between factions down to Ciudad Victoria, several hours south of the border. This opens up yet another zone of conflict for people to avoid as the internal struggles between factions vying for the Zetas brand have escalated the violence. One day Nayarit may be the battleground state, the next day it is Guerrero or Colima or Baja California. And people are identifiable by state or region through the federal electoral identification, as well as by their accents in this highly regional country.

Because of these divisions, as well as other signifiers, recruitment becomes a welcome trade-off for some. Cartel members (sometimes police officers) often pick people up off the street to interrogate them, whereupon they are questioned about past crimes, gang activity, and ties to other organizations.[7] Those who fall into suspicious categories may be given only one option to prove they are not a threat: join.

There are certain markers that make it much more difficult for people to escape this scrutiny. First, deportation from prison grew more and more common during the later Obama years. As mentioned in chapter 4, the concentration of people with criminal records in the Northeast leads to a particularly vicious cycle and throws fuel on the fires of violence that intermittently flare up in the region. When deportees arrive from prison they are usually wearing prison-issue clothing, blue or orange slip-on shoes, baggy light gray sweatpants and sweaters, and sometimes khaki pants. They almost never have any Mexican identifying documents and often lack the cultural and linguistic skills to blend in when they return to what was once their home country, as the aging home invader Don Gerardo from chapter 3 showed. Lookouts know that anyone wearing these clothes has likely been incarcerated for a long period of time. The shelters fill up with bags of prison clothes and shoes as people quickly try to rid themselves of these garments, often wearing ill-fitting, worn-out, or seasonally inappropriate (sandals in winter, sweaters in summer) attire simply to avoid the stigma of criminality that prison-issue clothing makes all too clear.

More problematic are the tattoos. In Mexico as a whole, tattoos are far less common and more stigmatized than in the United States. There are still medical bars on people with tattoos donating blood and a member of congress named Claudia Sanchéz Juárez from the conservative National Action Party (PAN) recently attempted to create economic sanctions against companies who have pictures of tattoos or things that appear like tattoos on their products.[8] Although she backed off, as the president of the Health Commission, her comments that tattoos are detrimental to young people's health and work opportunities are indicative of broader social attitudes. Namely, tattoos are still largely associated with crime and delinquency, a stark difference to the United States where tattoos are extremely common. For deportees, regardless of their actual affiliations in gangs, tattoos attract extra scrutiny.

When interrogated, people are immediately strip-searched to determine if they have any allegiances. One problem is that many tattoos that stem from Mexican American or Chicano culture have become associated with gangs despite being extremely common cultural products. This is largely a product of the racialization of antigang enforcement practices in the United States, which has trickled into Mexico.[9] Therefore these markings, etched on the body for a wide variety of cultural, personal, and symbolic reasons, become signifiers of criminal or dangerous individuals once they cross the border. Moreover, there is constant slippage within these images as the cultural or law enforcement definitions of an image can change and morph over time, such as the case of generic tattoos (i.e., the Virgin of Guadalupe, the Aztec calendar, and "Hecho en Mexico"—"Made in Mexico") that signify Chicano identity becoming associated with Latino street gangs.

There have been efforts to remove tattoos from ex–gang members deported to El Salvador because this problem has escalated to epic proportions, whereupon people cannot travel within different neighborhoods because of differing allegiances.[10] Moreover, members of organized crime have also began to distance themselves from the ritual practice of tattooing simply because it attracts too much attention. However, in Mexico the face tattoos of MS-13 are far less common and the issue has not attracted as much attention. For those who are deported with visible, large, and distinctive tattoos, the border is an extremely precarious space to navigate.

U.S. prison and street gangs tend to maintain loose associations with Mexican drug cartels, meaning that much of the dynamics regarding who will be viewed as an ally or an enemy is locally contingent and constantly shifting. However, for people who are affiliated with non-Mexican street gangs, it is certain that their presence along the border will not be easily accepted. For one deportee, tattooed on his whole face and body, his problem was ethnic since he had been part of the Bloods in Houston, a typically African American street gang. "I hung out with the blacks so they don't trust me here," he explained in perfect English. "I was a tattoo artist and did a lot of artwork in prison though so a lot of people respected me. Here, I am not sure what is going to happen," he explained.

However, for others, these signifiers that attract attention are less important than the simple lack of resources and employment:

> Matías was 24, originally from Tehuantepec, Oaxaca, with a Chetal-speaking mother; he had been living in Los Angeles for the last eight years.[11] He was bonded out while fighting his case, but ICE showed up while he was still fighting his removal and deported him. I interviewed him outside of the shelter in Tijuana. He had had a rough time while in county jail and got in three fights before joining the Sureños for protection. Upon deportation he struggled to find income or a way back to the United States, and was arrested by the police for not having identification (or enough money for a bribe). The police in Tijuana constantly patrol the road to the shelter, looking for deportees on their way back from work or from collecting a money order to steal their money. This leads to deportees being trapped on the actual street where the shelter is located.
>
> As I was finishing up for the day, he came up to me and asked if we could talk privately. I agreed and he burst out crying as soon as we were away from the other deportees. One of the friends came to him with a job opportunity, to watch a stash house. When the job was done, they didn't get paid. "Now my friend has disappeared and I think I am next." He started crying and said that he didn't know what to do. He pointed to another deportee I had interviewed (not eligible for the survey) and told me he was the one in charge of the drugs and he thought they had robbed their bosses and were planning on pinning the lost drugs on Matías and his friend.[12]

Perhaps the group most clearly sought by cartels are deported military veterans. Having served in the armed forces as Lawful Permanent Residents and then had their immigration status revoked because of criminal convictions, they represent an Americanized, vulnerable group, with a criminal history and the valuable training of the U.S. armed forces.[13] A former Marine explained that he had been approached twice by the Sinaloa Cartel to work for them. "I declined. They then felt slighted, I guess, and attempted to terminate my life twice already!!!!" He had to move three times to avoid their attempts.

Another Marine, Robert, explained the danger he faced when he returned to his birthplace in Acuña, Coahuila. "I was threatened to either comply with them to have my wife cross drugs across or we would get hurt. They knew I was former military and to prove that I wasn't a secret agent from the States I was told to join them. We were always being watched, and harassed by the cartel. I sent my family back to the States and later I joined them [in the United States] for fear of the cartel threats." This story shows the challenges, not only of being back in Mexico with a history of military service, which immediately draws attention from cartel members, but also of having a transnational family.

There is always an imputed assumption that deportees are no longer truly Mexican, and are somehow part of the United States, either as a secret agent like Robert or something akin to a wealthy ex-pat retiree. This lack of belonging for the deported makes them easy to kidnap, extort, or coerce. The fact that Robert's wife was sucked into the orbit of coercion is also exemplary of the way recruitment by cartels functions. The vulnerable individuals who cannot escape are used as leverage for others and make it easy to gain compliance. For everyone who has been removed but chooses to try and relocate their entire mixed-status families to Mexico, the risk that their Americanized children and spouses could become another point of leverage increases. Forced to engage in dangerous criminal activities to protect their Mexico-bound family members, it pushes even U.S. citizen family members into the orbit of the conflict. Engaging in drug trafficking frequently results in arrest or death. For example, if drugs are lost, and it cannot be confirmed whether drugs were lost to law enforcement or simply stolen, there will be reprisals. While there are certainly some people who openly seek out a career as drug traffickers, it is rare that this happens without some degree of outside pressure, whether it is structural in the form of poverty, hunger, and survival, or through more direct forms of coercion and threats.

As Shaylih Muehlmann has noted, the line between participant, narco, and someone who is simply dabbling around the edges of criminal activities is blurry and confusing.[14] For many migrants, the temporary employment and money offered by organized crime is simply one option for getting enough resources to try the crossing again or head back to wherever in Mexico that they had come from. In fact, most of the *burreros* I have met would not consider themselves migrants at all, even though they cross the border. As one deportee explained bluntly, "No soy migrante, soy burrero" (I am not a migrant, I am a drug mule). This is because their time in the United States is completely inconsequential and temporary. They walk across simply to drop off their load of drugs and head back in order to get paid. The journey is one long loop from Mexico to the United States and back without stopping. Most of the people I interviewed who had crossed drugs through Sonora were in fact seasonal agricultural workers and just engaged in drug trafficking to supplement the meager wages in Mexico. Moreover, farmworkers made excellent mules due to their hard work ethic and the strength required to survive a summer picking grapes or melons in the desert sun.

However, in other regions, activities vary with significantly more direct ties to serious criminal activities. Guarding the river, for example, served as the nominal activity for a recruit in Tamaulipas, something that appeared benign and easy, but actually encompassed other activities. As Kalangas explained in the opening vignette of this chapter, "no one pays that much for honest work." In reality, they are tasked with kidnapping fellow migrants who dare to try and cross without approval.

This process of incorporating migrants into organized crime precisely to persecute other migrants leads us to question how people negotiate the violence they are exposed to upon deportation or during the migratory journey. When the readily visible structures of power clearly show how little value is placed on migrant life, this life defined by its spatial temporality and nonbelonging, how long does it take to consider leaving this position and becoming a more powerful narco? Jumping between identities may lead to some protections from kidnapping, extortion, and the general powerlessness of the scores of people moving through the border, but in the end, it is far more lethal. Low-level drug traffickers or enforcers, especially those who join as unknown migrants, are little more than fodder in the drug war. These expendable ranks must constantly be purged and replenished. In order to amass the wealth and power that the top drug lords possess, there must be hundreds of people working below them with little chance to become wealthy or powerful themselves. For many of the people who are being recruited, such as Rudi's experience at the beginning of this chapter, they will not be aware if they are working for the Zetas or someone else.[15]

While I was at the shelter, the group leading an incursion into Nuevo Laredo was led by a trans woman. She would stop and try and recruit migrants as they sat in the plazas. While some people asserted, "They were nice to me. They just asked if I wanted a job and I told them no thank you and they left me alone,"[16] others reported more aggressive tactics. The presence of two competing groups recruiting from the migrants led to confusion and the police or local cartel members began interrogating the migrants about the trans woman and her activities. "They asked me who went with her, how many, what they looked like and wanted to know why I didn't go with them," explained Rudi. Essentially, the migrants were caught between two nebulously powerful, dangerous forces, and no one knew for sure who was from the Zetas and who the other people were (Gulf Cartel, Sinaloa, or simply another faction of the Zetas). Rudi grew increasingly agitated, every day receiving more intense interrogations followed by threats. "They said they would kill me if they see me again," he explained. The people attempting to recruit him assumed he had ties to gangs in El Salvador. While I never confirmed this to be true or false, that he had grown up on the streets without a family increased the likelihood of some form of involvement. Moreover, as an Afro-Latino, his dark skin attracted extra attention in

Mexico. The recruitment became more and more heated, and his options began to decrease. Vanda, his wife, was too weak to walk across the border. We decided that they needed to get out of the region. Due to some complicated coincidences, we were able to get financial support from an aid organization to send them to Sonora, where legal aid was available to help them apply for asylum.

ESCAPE FROM RECRUITMENT

When the day came to send them out of town, Rudi told me, "I don't think I will make it another day out there." I had arranged a ride from a local colleague named Regina, who was willing to be seen with us, a risky proposition for Laredenses who needed to avoid attracting attention. She was running a little late and a group of migrants had decided to sit on the jersey wall in front of the shelter, a dangerous spot that most people know is forbidden for migrants. Paranoia got the better of me as I checked on them out of the slot in the door every few seconds. If they were sitting there, then they were either in danger or acting as lookouts; either way, it was not a great time to be seen picking up migrants carrying their luggage. Regina arrived around ten, visibly nervous; once we were in the car she shot the wrong way down a one-way street to make sure no one was following. Regina was also concerned about the three men outside. "Are they trustworthy (*de confianza*)?" "They slept here last night," I said, a wholly unsatisfactory response.

We dropped off Vanda and Rudi at Regina's office, leaving them with the security guard. We made them coffee and sat them in the kitchen to wait. A white Chevy Tahoe drove by with a man talking on a radio. Regina asked the guard to keep a watch out for that SUV. We went to collect the money that had been wired in my name, switching into a company car, and again driving the wrong way out of her office building so that the halcones on the corner would not see us enter and leave. On our way to pick up the money, there was a problem. It was a holiday and a lot of the money transfer places were closed. We went to the Farmacia

Guadalajara, then *Salinas and Rocha,* waiting in line for what seemed like hours only to find out that we could not collect the money because it was more than 6,000 pesos, a little more than 450 USD at the time. Anti-money laundering measures made it harder to complete this small task.

We had to go back to the office building and wait while I tried to get them to rewire the money to somewhere that we could pick it up. Rudi's migraines, along with nerves, had laid him out, and he needed some food and sugar. We ordered some tacos and a few Cokes. After we ate, Rudi showed us his handicraft skills making flowers out of Coke cans. The security guard told us that a woman had been standing out front with a baby, talking or pretending to talk on a cell phone. I tried to project calm, but the atmosphere was tense. When guards are afraid of women with babies acting as spies and of every car that rolls by slowly, it becomes painfully obviously the level of fear that people here live with every day.

After several failed attempts to get prepaid bus tickets, arrange a hotel, and find out how to get the cash to get them out,[17] we were able to pick up the funds at Moneygram. I ran into one of the deportees at the transfer place, the one with the full-face tattoos who used to be a member of the Bloods. He was friendly and said hello, but I was feeling too paranoid to be glad to see him. I knew he had also been threatened because of his gang ties, so it was likely that he had made some arrangement with the local powers to be able to stay here safely, probably by joining up.

Regina drove even faster after we were holding the money, knowing full well that money transfer spots like Moneygram have plenty of keen, prying eyes in them, often the tellers themselves. I didn't mention the backstory of the man who said hi to me, but she noticed. That's the problem with full-face tattoos. We snuck into the back entrance of the bus station to buy Rudi and Vanda the tickets so they would not have to walk around the terminal. They had to go to Monterrey, spend the night, and then transfer to Nogales, Sonora. A trusted taxi driver showed up to take them separately to the bus station, so they would not be associated with our frantic attempts to collect money all over the city. When I got word that they had checked into their hotel in Monterrey I felt a huge sigh of relief. Regina commented how good it felt to actually do something, no matter how small, in the face of all the danger.

Upon arrival in Nogales, the lawyers were troubled by the fact that Rudi and Vanda had been granted asylum in Mexico, which effectively eliminated their chances of seeking relief in the United States because it wipes out their claims of persecution in their home country of El Salvador.[18] Essentially, once an individual has been granted asylum in a second country, all claims made must relate to the country where they have been given refuge. Talk of making Mexico officially a safe third country will require anyone who passes through Mexico to apply there first, essentially closing the door on Central American asylum seekers headed to the United States.

This problem has already had a significant impact on Central American asylum seekers who apply for and are sometimes granted asylum through NGOs working in Mexico. However, their final destination is still the United States, and upon arrival at the border they are often surprised to find that they can no longer apply for protection in the United States. The issue is a complex one since many groups began aiding Central American asylum claims in Mexico with the express intent of protecting them from extortion and kidnapping along the migrant route. People with asylum no longer need to ride the *bestia,* and yet, those people are now excluded from the United States where many have friends and family waiting for them.

Stranded in legal limbo, Vanda and Rudi began living in Nogales, Sonora. I found a friend who could put them up for a few weeks, but the situation deteriorated as they had trouble finding work or other opportunities. The weeks stretched into months. Vanda, in particular, was unable to cope with past traumas and would call me at night with stories about how people were after her and how someone was following them. One evening a group of people came over to a party at the house where they were staying and she was convinced that one of them was staring at her and was going to attack her. Having lived through assaults and rape and attacks against her children it is no wonder that danger is omnipresent for Vanda. One of the aid workers from Nogales described it best: "She needs a full-time social worker and mental health support."

The line between past violence and present threat became a constant balance throughout my work, making it difficult to distinguish how valid or real a threat may be. As an ethnographer, I am careful not to present people's fears as concrete truths, but I also will never write off these fears as simply a fantasy. For those who have already escaped death multiple times, the threats are always real. The only thing that has kept them alive this long has been their uncompromising treatment of the entire world as dangerous. In my experiences doing this research over the past decade it is often when people slow down and stop running that the real trauma shows. The scars are buried deep, and so is the resilience, but there is no telling how profound the impacts are. The trauma of seeking asylum is no different, especially for those who cannot speak, who fear that they will be targeted and whose lives are forever altered by violence, be it in their former homes or on the migrant path.

In the years since this experience, after testifying in dozens of asylum cases in the United States, often for people who were forced into organized crime or kidnapped, I think of the horror awaiting all of those who are denied. If Vanda and Rudi, with financial assistance from a major international human rights organization and the aid of a gringo researcher with ties to a local support structure and legal advocacy organizations, have so much trouble, then imagine the rest. How will they run and hide? Will they live on the move, locked away from the world? How will they survive, knowing that people want to kill them, and thinking that every parked car, every sideways glance could signal their impending death?

Eventually we raised money to get Vanda and Rudi to Mexico City. However, the last that I had heard they had gone to Guatemala in search of Vanda's missing daughter. Things did not go well and she became stranded. Rudi stole her identification and was renting it to migrants trying to cross Mexico's southern border. He began working for the Zetas and had threatened to kill Vanda if she filed a complaint. After all that time of resisting being recruited, I was never able to find out exactly why Rudi decided to join.[19] Perhaps he was threatened with violence against himself or his family. Maybe he was kidnapped like Juanito, or maybe he simply got tired of being pushed around. Many migrants tire of their position as the most vulnerable, the perennially exploitable, kidnappable and killable subjects of the border. For some, the desire to become the hammer and not the nail is a direct result of this frustration. Neither Rudi, nor Chino or Ramon, the Guatemalan kid, were what anyone would describe as intimidating.

However, to be clear, not everyone takes this bargain, and why some people such as Chino and Ramon choose to engage directly with a group of criminals like the Zetas is hard to explain. Ramon in particular was the butt of a lot of jokes in the shelter, for his slight stature, the lisp brought on by his missing teeth, and his generally effeminate mannerisms. Others referred to him as *el jotito,* a diminutive version of a common antigay slur. This is why it was surprising to me at the time that he would take such a violent step to change his circumstances, but in retrospect perhaps it was not. Now, he is in charge of the river. He is armed. He is the one demanding money and not the other way around. The difficulty of finding out what happens in the end makes it an incomplete story to tell, but it is unlikely that he would survive long—the overall level of violence is far greater for those involved in the cartel than for those they prey upon. The consensus has always been that this recruitment is simply about replenishing the bodies. How can drug cartels maintain their ranks of low-level, expendable people? The answer lies in recruitment, both forced as we saw in the last chapter and voluntarily, albeit through false promises to highly vulnerable individuals.

One particular case caused divisions at the shelter.

Lázaro explained the moral dilemma of dealing with migrants who join the Zetas. "One time there was this kid from Honduras, 16 years old. He stayed here for six days but after he would come back and look for people to work with him in the Zetas, to watch the river or watch safe houses. He would tell them enormous sums of money. One time he said they would make 15,000 pesos (about 1,000 USD at the time) a week. I told him, "You are not allowed in here anymore," but outside, once people left the casa, he would grab people there. One day he showed up without any teeth and his eye all swollen, beaten up, really beaten. He was looking around desperately. They beat his ass (*paliza*) because he got high, he got drunk with two others when he was supposed to be guarding a safe house and the people escaped." I asked, "You mean he was watching a safe house where people were kidnapped and being held captive?" "Yup! Exactly! I felt a lot of resentment toward him because he was very disrespectful to me. Now he needed help?" They ended up helping him, calling a doctor to come to the shelter in order to treat him so that the mafia would not see him in the city. They kept him downstairs in the private rooms they rarely used. "He told us that inside the shelter there were many people from organized crime. The shelter is a business for them. That's where the merchandise is! For organized crime migrants are money, if they have it or they don't there is someone in the United States who will respond to them."[20]

Eventually they were able to get him back to Honduras, but it was a challenge since he had no identification and the Mexican authorities did not want to take him. However, people like this who are tempted by the promises of money and power often find themselves at the mercy of the same violent groups that employ them. They are disposable and easily disappeared with the knowledge that no one will look for yet another low-level gang member who falls from sight in the perennial struggle over control of drug trafficking routes.

One of the reasons for the proliferation in family connections at the top of drug trafficking organizations is the fundamental issue of trust. Damien Zaitch has explored notions of trust among Colombian cocaine dealers in the Netherlands. In general, knowledge about an individual is considered power, therefore having close ties and intimate knowledge about one's inner circle is highly important.[21] Trust, or rather distrust, is a commodity and therefore knowledge about people becomes highly valuable. Family then becomes a commodity, limiting who is allowed to be close to the highly lucrative centers of power. In order for this to work, there must be a lot of fodder— replaceable, expendable people who can be recruited to do menial tasks such as guard the river, watch a safe house, report on movements in the city, and hold a gun if need be. Much as blind mules have become popular methods of transporting drugs across the U.S.-Mexico border, since they are unaware they are carrying illegal substances and therefore calm, but also have no information to give to authorities, recruiting low-level, expendable labor has its benefits.

Recruitment, especially forced recruitment, follows highly regionally specific patterns. For example, in Sonora it was rare for people to be forced to backpack drugs across the desert. It was viewed as too difficult of an activity to entrust to a random migrant. Coercion for migrants in the Arizona desert is more often tied to using people as decoys. Agricultural workers from the fields around Caborca and Altar, on the other hand, were often targeted since they are used to working long hours in the heat. Deportees in urban centers such as Nogales, Tijuana, and Mexicali are brought to the fields thinking it will be a normal job, only to be presented with backpacks to cross. The same happens in the Valle de Juárez and the agricultural fields along the South Texas border. Moreover, trickery is employed more often than brute force. Violence is implied and once someone accepts a nondescript "job," and they have traveled to a remote location, it is too late to say no.

The problem with all of these arrangements is ensuring that terms are met. For many, this manifests in not being paid, but for others it essentially results in being bound to one's employer. Upon joining a gang or cartel people are immediately unable to make their own decisions about what to do and what not to do, where to go and where not to go. When I was doing fieldwork in Tamaulipas recruits who made it a few weeks would be shipped out for training and then to the "war," which, at that point meant going to Nayarit in western Mexico to fight against the Sinaloa Cartel.[22]

For the burreros who traffic marijuana, the game is much different. "They are my friends so they always pay me," said one smuggler from

Oaxaca. For others, it is less certain. As we explored in chapter 2, the problem for many is that they take one load across and must come back to Mexico to collect their fee, but once they arrive, they are informed that they need to take another load, and another and so on until they are caught and sent to jail, at which point they are no longer useful. Smugglers are given amphetamines, usually cocaine or meth, to keep them moving through these harsh conditions. However, these drugs actually make it much easier to become dehydrated and die.[23] Moreover, people usually take about 80 pounds of marijuana, careful to keep the whole load under 800 pounds so that the federal prosecutor will not treat it as a serious case. These bales of marijuana, pressed, sprayed with bleach and insect repellant to prevent infestation during the weeks in the desert, are tied with twine or rope, sometimes secured onto a regular school backpack, other times just using the rope itself as a makeshift carrier.

Neither of these are ideal working conditions and essentially derail any and all plans for future life. In fact whether it is the grueling trek through the harsh conditions of the desert, or the near certain death as a foot soldier in Mexico's drug conflict, those who join are not entertaining a wide array of options. One day while visiting one of the guest houses by the river in Nuevo Laredo, Monterrey asked me about the marijuana trade in Sonora. "They say you get good money working for El Chapo.[24] Do you think it is true?" I told him a lot of people I know were not getting paid after the journey and he soured on the idea. He and Zacatecas had been living in Nuevo Laredo for a few months now, struggling to find work to buy food and pay the 20 peso (about 1.50 USD at the time) daily charge for their room.

These "guest houses" work as a secondary or tertiary system of shelters all along the border, offering extremely cheap room and board in a rather dilapidated setting. From Tijuana to Matamoros they cater to a mix of the deported, migrants stuck waiting to cross, and the homeless or addicted. *La Choza*, as they called it, was better than most. It was open, next to the river, and had a big courtyard with scattered palm and banana trees, giving it a slightly tropical vibe even though the winter months were bone-chillingly cold. There was even a view looking out over the Rio Grande winding its way through the tall brush that separates the river from the twin cities. The rooms were small but private, although the gaps in the doors and under the walls let in the cold wind during the night. There were maybe a dozen rooms, constructed out of a mixture of shipping pallets and scraps of plywood, but at least it was all painted with a uniform, though fading whitewash. I would meet up with them in front of the shelter and we would stop in an *abarrotes* (corner store) to grab some food to cook on their makeshift grill that consisted of two cinder blocks and a bent oven rack.

The other flophouses were a good deal more dilapidated, usually in a semi-abandoned building, where people would grab a scrap of fabric and sleep in the corner of a big room. Generally there was no privacy, and one needed a keen eye watching over any possessions. These living situations are particularly draining and only those with truly limited options stick around. Migration creates a unique set of pressures that have consequences for people such as Monterrey and Zacatecas. Neither of them felt comfortable returning to their hometowns, even though Monterrey's family lived only a few hours away. For the people who migrate to the United States, there is an expectation of working, sending remittances, and maintaining a connection to family, friends, and hometown. However, the difficulty of the journey has led more and more people to permanently settle in the United States, either by accident after years of working, or deliberately as they may bring spouses and children to live with them. Those who stay and perhaps start a second family, or fail to send money back to Mexico, often burn their social ties at home.[25] The pressures of being a worker, the gendered, heteronormative expectations of being a family "man," often conflict with the difficulties and stresses of finding work as an undocumented migrant in the increasingly punitive anti-immigrant atmosphere of the United States.[26]

Monterrey had a long history of working in the United States, often bouncing between different cities and states seemingly at random. He worked sporadically, but also found himself getting stiffed by employers or laid off unexpectedly. There is a reason that so many migrants follow their friends and family to specific cities. Once migrants have set up particular industries and businesses there is a degree of protection against unscrupulous employers. Overall, however, in our surveys, 24 percent of people reported working for less than minimum wage and 15 percent were not paid what they were owed.[27] While we may be aware of the consequences for anyone working a manual job or not being paid, migrant labor often has the added pressures of social responsibilities usually tied to the financing needed for their trip. The debt that people accrue paying for the coyotes who guide them across the border usually comes from others, especially family members. If someone fails to pay this money back, they usually choose simply to never return rather than face the stigma of failure.[28]

However, if they have burned their family ties, once deported the situation can be dire. Family support is vital for deportees attempting to escape the chaos of the border. If goodwill has been eroded by their time in the United States, this aid may be scarce. Moreover, simply being removed can result in a stigma that may decrease the willingness of family members to help. While it has become easier and easier for people to be removed for even minor criminal infractions,[29] many people in Mexico still maintain the attitude that deportees must have committed a serious crime or were, simply put, *"andando de vago*—acting like a bum" in order to get deported. This stigma further compounds a general lack of concern or respect for deportees, as opposed to migrants. As prison sentences have increased for simply crossing the border due to the proliferation of illegal reentry charges, more people are deported after serving a criminal sentence. Combining people who are charged with immigration violations with those who have more serious criminal violations can produce unexpected consequences. Namely, people are being incarcerated and introduced to gang culture, and once removed may only know other individuals who were incarcerated, increasing the likelihood of criminal involvement. Other times, the hatred and anger between rival groups can unexpectedly erupt in violence. This has had a significant impact on the situation in shelters and along the border.

The anger and violence that people experienced in their journeys even culminated in a murder at one of the shelters, showing how thin and tenuous the rule of law is in the region.

A group of 20 deportees arrived one night and officials informed the shelter staff that there was some bad blood in the group. "One man had severe mental problems, I'm not sure if it was delusions of persecution or what.... The official told us that there was a problem at the port (of entry) and he had jumped on top of another deportee. The military had to intervene," said Tonatiuh, the shelter manager. "My decision was not to let him in and send him somewhere where he could get psychiatric help, but the director intervened and let him stay. However, he seemed calmed. I made a mistake, I thought. The man washed dishes and everything, but at the moment when they were headed upstairs to the dormitory, right in the middle of the stairs where there is the curve (landing) he punched another deportee and sent him rolling down the stairs. The deportee fell unconscious at the bottom of the stairs." Tonatiuh rushed to check on the unconscious man, but the rest of the deportees grabbed the attacker and began beating him. The priest told them to take him outside. "They were still beating him and they had him facedown, pressing down on him. I called the army. I called the immigration authorities. I called the Red Cross. The Red Cross arrived and helped the unconscious man, but they said, 'The other one, he isn't breathing anymore. Not anymore, ya no. He is dead.' The army arrived, the state police and the ministerial police. They took me to make a declaration and I was there until three or four in the morning."

"I was scared that they wouldn't let me go," he explained. He and the migrants were released. The director skipped town and left the city, so Tonatiuh was subject to further questioning and interrogation, as the police asked for more witnesses. One of the bystanders volunteered to talk to the police. "This kid was watching from the window upstairs. He was not even down there. He just said, 'That was really ugly.' But they [the police] took him and blamed him for it. That innocent man, that innocent migrant who had nothing to do with it, they have him locked up there still." After going to speak with the police again and stressing that the accused was not one of the people fighting, Tonatiuh contacted a lawyer. Things escalated from there. The police stopped by the shelter on the following nights and made cryptic comments: "Are you saying that the police are lying?" and "You definitely need more protection here." These were threats. The lawyer called and told them that she would no longer help them, and told them it was too dangerous to proceed. "My whole declaration had been changed. All of the information that I gave them had been changed, even my signature. It was not my signature anymore." The director told him to let it go. "I didn't like that. It made me lose my philosophy of service and justice."

With so little confidence in the police and the possibility of justice, it makes clear just how much danger is present along the border, for everyone, not just those trying to migrate. This devastating event, tied directly to a migrant shelter, led to significant conflict and ultimately a reorganization of the personnel at the shelter, but it was kept out of the media and the shelter continues to operate. This vignette also serves as a reminder that deportees are not merely passive victims in the violence along the border. Being a migrant or a deportee in these spaces at times necessitates a ruthlessness, an ability to rise above the chaos and survive. The stresses of the journey and the pressures of increasing criminalization can lead to more violent outbursts like this one.

Migration is inherently about changing one's geography to change one's opportunities. However, very rarely do people go from a desperate set of options to a favorable one; rather, these are incremental changes often with a mixture of good and bad aspects.

Want better pay? Risk your life crossing the border, and live a precarious existence where you can be easily exploited. Fleeing violence? Claim fear and spend years seeking asylum, paying lawyers, wearing an ankle monitor, appearing before judges or detained in immigration detention. And finally, stuck at the border, deported, or unable to cross? Get kidnapped, extorted, tortured, and killed or join up, kidnap, torture, kill, and of course, die. These Faustian bargains have become part of the migration experience during the past decade of extreme cartel violence, reminding us once again that undocumented migration is not something people do without a great deal of pressure and desperation. These are not people crossing because they think there is an easy welfare state to exploit, but people who see few options forward. This interplay between hammer and nail, victim and victimizer, must be acknowledged because it is a major driver of violence and death on the border.

Certainly there are multiple ways that violence and death affect those attempting to cross into the United States. The dangers of the physical terrain of the desert, lack of food and water, checkpoints placed strategically to send people off into the most remote, dangerous areas possible, and of course the robberies and kidnappings discussed in this book, are all part of the hazards of migration. However, with recruitment, the sprawling havoc of a fruitless war on drugs makes it difficult to untangle which deaths are the result of migration and which deaths should be counted in the drug war's ever rising *executometro* (execution-meter). For those people who begin guarding the river, carrying a gun, and enforcing cartel order, their lives are worth little, but from a practical, empirical point of view, should they count as victims of the conflict, or victims of our ever-calcifying borders? In the next chapter we address death and disappearance, both as it relates to people because of their attempted migration and those who may engage in migration because of death.

CHAPTER SIX

The Disappeared, the Dead, and the Forgotten

They walk across the bridge, bleary eyed, dressed primarily in prison garb, baggy light-gray sweaters and blue slip-on shoes. Once on the other side of the river with its overgrown rushes poking up along the walkway, Ramon, a large, jovial agent from Grupos Beta, greets them in a group.[1] After giving them the standard introduction about the services they provide, such as a deportation slip that can serve as a temporary identification and ticket to social services around the city, he warns them ominously, "Do not go walking on your own." He later explains to me, "Every night a couple people decide they don't want to wait and they disappear. There is nothing I can do about it. But the number of people who disappear is piling up. Sometimes they use fake names and other times they just walk off into the night and we never see them again."[2]

Night after night, it is the same scene; people arriving by the dozens and then ... disappearing. Most make it to a destination, but the difficulty in keeping track of who does and who does not, especially since many deportees simply have nowhere to go in Mexico, is a pressing concern. The state government of Tamaulipas through the Instituto Tamaulipeco has taken a different approach than other border states. Rather than simply relying on federal aid programs for migrant support, their goal has been to get people out of the border region as soon as possible. They arrange travel and attempt to get everyone to a place where they can receive a money transfer to leave the state immediately. The fear of taking people to shelters, due to the frequent incursions and insecurity, has led to the military fortifying bus stations, and the government-depositing deportees there. All of these actions speak directly to the danger posed by being removed to the Northeast.

Oscar Misael Hernández asked in an op-ed, "When can we start to talk about *migranticidio* or migranticide?"[3] The killing of people for simply being migrants has reached an alarming level but has failed to galvanize the public, largely because the migrants come from all over, they are on their way somewhere else, and have for years suffered in silence as a complicated, large, and diverse group of people. This diversity of goals and destinations has made it hard to recognize the violence that has been engrained on human mobility, allowing us to neglect the systematic murder and disappearance of migrants and deportees.

This is the challenge behind the more than 30,000 disappearances that occurred between 2007 and 2016 in Mexico. Throughout the country, mass graves have been unearthed: 250 in Veracruz (2017), 193 in San Fernando, and 49 torsos were found in Cadereyta Jiménez, Nuevo Leon. Only 13 bodies were identified from the Cadereyta massacre, among them, migrants from Honduras, Mexico, and Costa Rica. In San Fernando, after the infamous massacre of 72 migrants, 11 of which have still not been identified, 47 mass graves were found the following year containing the 193 bodies and demonstrating that those 72 people were just the beginning of the violence, not the end. Three hundred bodies were found in Tijuana.[4] Over 850 clandestine graves have been found in Mexico by 2017.[5] The systematic kidnapping and assault of Central American migrants traveling on the train known as the *bestia* (beast) has been well documented.[6] While I was conducting fieldwork one migrant explained the recent changes to riding the train. "There are checkpoints and you have to pay them 150 dollars. If you don't have it, you can jump or they will throw you off, and not in a nice way. I jumped," he explained pointing to the scrapes and scratches still visible on his arms. While attempts to get migrants off the trains by allowing them free travel through Mexico were successful in reducing violence, these policies were quickly rescinded at the behest of the U. S. government as the number of Central Americans requesting asylum increased after 2013.

Less understood, but no less worrisome, is the predatory and violent ways that these same criminal organizations kidnap, extort, recruit, and even kill deportees and migrants along the U. S.-Mexico border. In chapter 4, Juanito described in detail the systematic disposal and obliteration of bodies, which has unfortunately become widespread. That white powder, reminiscent of salt, is a human life, and their family will wait years or decades to know, or may never know, what happened to their loved one. It also creates a problem for people attempting to recognize and make legible the costs of this war on drugs; namely, which of these deaths are products of our prohibitions on human mobility and which are the result of the conflicts within organized crime itself?

The asylum system is the most visible place where these two issues collide. The increase in people seeking asylum from Central America and Mexico shows the desperation and fear that is now a major driver of immigration. These requests have increased despite the fact that many people (especially Mexicans) do not know they have a right to request protection under the 1951 Convention Relating to the Status of Refugees. Moreover, other conventions such as the principle of *non-refoulement,* or the Convention Against Torture (CAT), protect people from being deported to a country where they are likely to be tortured. The courts have set the standard for protection as a 51 percent chance (more likely than not) that they will be tortured. While our figure of 7 percent being kidnapped does not get close to this number, it is important to recognize that this is a broad category (all deportees). As we explore the specific circumstances facing each individual—such as previous interactions with the cartels or pertaining to particular groups of people such as Americanized Mexican Americans—more and more people would easily meet this standard.

Laura was a victim of the general dismissal of due process and people's internationally protected rights at the border.[7] Police stopped her near McAllen, Texas, just across the border from Reynosa, Tamaulipas, and decided to call the border patrol when she could not produce identification. These informal relationships between police and border patrol terrify border residents, knowing that any interaction with the police can lead to a deportation. Because of this, border cities such as El Paso often take great pains to separate the two and discourage this process;[8] however, the state legislature in Texas passed SB-4, a variation on the "show me your papers" law from Arizona (SB-1070) mandating that police check immigration status.

For Laura, this would be a death sentence. "I can't be sent back to Mexico," Laura told Solis, beginning to cry. "I have a protection order against my ex—please, just let me call my mom and she'll bring you the paperwork."[9] Her ex-husband had threatened to kill her. This fear should immediately trigger the asylum process, whereupon she should be referred to an Asylum Officer (AO) for an interview to establish Credible Fear, a low bar, where the AO must decided if there is a 10 percent likelihood that she would face persecution. However, the agents refused to hear her pleas for help and she was forced to sign a removal. This is unfortunately not an uncommon occurrence. In the Migrant Border Crossing Study (MBCS), about one third of individuals indicate that they felt pressure or were forced to sign, and another third did not even know what type of form they signed (deportation, voluntary removal, expedited removal, etc.). Laura said to the agent, "You're sending me straight to the slaughterhouse," and she was right.[10]

Once removed, Laura's ex-husband found her and would drive by her home, shouting at her. Sergio, her ex-husband and now cartel member, had a history of domestic abuse and crime before being deported. One night she did not return and the next day they found her car incinerated and her body inside. As a victim of domestic abuse (VAWA), a victim of crime (U-Visa) and potential asylum case, there were multiple avenues for Laura to prevent her deportation, but none of them were honored or presented to her. She was killed about a week after being deported.[11]

This is part of a disturbing pattern. A man with head trauma was deported to Tamaulipas and kidnapped the same day where he was tortured and his family extorted for thousands of dollars. He was lucky to escape with his life.[12] On July 20, 2017, two bodies were found in the Josefa Ortiz de Domínguez neighborhood of Ciudad Juárez, Chihuahua. The bodies had been burned, and their severed heads were left in a red cooler in a different part of the city. They had been deported two months prior.[13] Nineteen-year-old DACA recipient Manuel Antonio Cano Pacheco was murdered in Zacatecas just three weeks after being removed.[14] He had lived in the United States since he was three years old but had been arrested twice for misdemeanor drug charges and then deported.

The previous chapters have outlined the ways people are controlled, recruited, and abducted. In this chapter we explore death, disappearance, the difficulty of searching for answers, and the dangers caused by mass deportation. With the magnitude of the conflict in Mexico, searching for the missing or identifying the dead has in and of itself been a slow, agonizing process. Add to this the complications of identifying migrants from Central America, as well as deportees who may have spent decades in the United States, and it is no wonder that this conversation is barely beginning. Unfortunately, we are nowhere near close to sorting out the true magnitude of violent deaths for migrants and deportees in Mexico. More research is needed to fully explore this situation and provide needed closure to the families and the loved ones they have lost. Not only does the search for loved ones who die during migration create new challenges inside Mexico, but the deaths of people through the routine violence of the "drug war" have also led thousands of people to leave their homes.[15] Understanding that death can be both the start and the end of migration shows how easy it is to fail to understand the complex relationships between violence, conflict, and human movement.

In December of 2017, the Caravan of Mothers of Disappeared Central American Migrants descended on Mexico City to demand answers. More than three dozen women embarked on a 22-state tour to demand help from the Mexican government to find their children who went missing during their attempts to migrate to the United States. Annually for the better part of a decade, the mothers have followed the train tracks through Mexico in protest for their missing loved ones. One mother, Clementina Murcia from Honduras, was quoted as demanding more attention from the Mexican government. "It is impossible that a movement by migrants and their mothers without money has found many children in Mexico and they (the state), with more resources than us, have not been able to find even one. We have spent many years demanding the same thing. We ask that the promises made before international organizations be worth more than wet paper."[16] This is the largest movement to date that connects the plight of migrants and the widespread violence in Mexico. Using a familiar Latin American tactic, the mothers have been able to successfully stand up to the state, whose silence, as noted by Murcia, is more than just a symptom of inability; it is deliberate.

Throughout the dirty wars of the 1970s and 1980s groups of mothers were able to protest against the violence of the state in ways that others were unable.[17] The most famous case is the Madres of the Plaza de Mayo in Argentina, who have spent decades and garnered international attention for their struggle. Gendered stereotypes of mothers as untouchable have been appropriated to demand accountability and transparency from the state within extremely repressive environments, breaking through the limits of state oppression. For example, in Argentina, while political dissidents were being imprisoned and disappeared, mothers were one of the only groups who were able to publicly criticize the dictatorship without being attacked or killed.[18] There are many other examples of mothers demanding political action throughout Latin America due to their success in combating oppressive policies in the region.[19] While it may still be acceptable to kill protestors and activists, groups of mothers continue to garner far more support. However, Mexico's conflict, in many ways a distorted copy of the state-sponsored violence and guerrilla conflict of decades past, requires even more ingenuity.

Leftist guerrilla movements attempting to change the political system in much of Central and South America typified the dirty wars of the 1970s and 1980s. These political struggles were born out of the conditions of exploitation, poverty, and abuse in the oligarchical Latin American societies where a small number of families and businesses controlled vast amounts of resources. In response to (or sometimes preceding) these uprisings, military dictatorships and extreme right-wing governments took power. Each of these conflicts had their own characteristics, with Central American countries such as Guatemala committing genocide against indigenous people,[20] while their neighbors, El Salvador and Honduras, attacked people for supposed politically dissident views, all with the aid and support of the United States.[21] In the Southern Cone, sophisticated military dictatorships in Chile, Argentina, and Brazil kept their violence silent for years, despite U.S. involvement in the coup d'etat in Chile and a firm presence throughout the process. Neoliberal policies and the so-called "Chicago school" of economics placed restrictions on social support programs while cutting taxes for the wealthy and businesses.[22] In the decades since, these conflicts have been reduced to a simmer but never fully ended. The economic situation has only been exacerbated by rising inequality throughout the region. Rather than open conflicts between the government and separatists or revolutionary groups, crime has become the new battlefront. Colombia in particular represents the murky lines being drawn between political dissidents and drug trafficking criminals.[23] As these groups have merged, the tone and framing of the conflict have taken new directions, but the form and intensity of the violence shows striking similarities, especially in Mexico.

With the figure of the drug trafficker as villain replacing the radical leftist guerrilla, it has been harder to galvanize a concerted reaction to the violence, which has in turn let the state off the hook for many human rights abuses.[24] There is a general acceptance that the drug trafficker is an illegitimate enemy, one who therefore can be killed and tortured and whose life is basically forfeit the moment he or she engages in this illegal world. In reality, it is much more complicated, especially in a country with so little economic mobility. Not only are drugs one of the few routes to economic stability, but the level of involvement and type of involvement vary dramatically. Despite this, the idea that it is completely natural for the government to kill drug traffickers has provided unique cover for the same type of atrocities committed during the dirty wars, with even less scrutiny. The military still runs rampant in Mexico, frequently using torture and even sexual violence as a method of interrogation.[25] Yet, internationally, there is no outcry. "This is not a 'dirty' war; it's a drug war" is a common refrain. What is wrong with combating drugs? While the critique of this conflict is growing, it is still not recognized as a war.

Sadly, the toll for family members of the dead and disappeared has been steep in this dirty drug war. Miriam Rodriguez was murdered in Tamaulipas in 2017 after finding her daughter's body and publicly accusing the killer by name. Marisela Escobedo Ortiz was gunned down in front of the Government Palace in Chihuahua, Chihuahua, where she was protesting the murder of her daughter.[26] Nepomuceno Moreno, a well-known activist, was killed in Hermosillo, Sonora. Sandra Luz Cuevas was killed in Sinaloa. Cornelia San Juan Guevara Guerrero was murdered in her home in the Estado de Mexico. The list goes on...[27]

However, as more and more people came forward over the past decade to demand answers for atrocities committed by the state, this narrative—"a drug war, not a dirty war"—has crumbled. The caravan of Central American mothers has been organizing this pilgrimage for the past 12 years, meeting with local groups and activists also searching for their loved ones. The Movement for Peace with Dignity and Justice popularized the caravan as a way to gather these local tragedies into a national narrative, delivering a blow to Felipe Calderón in 2009, who was not ready for the organized political backlash to the violence in Mexico. Javier Sicilia, an accomplished writer and poet, read a poem for his son who had recently been killed:

The world is not worthy of words
they have been suffocated from the inside
as they suffocated you, as they tore apart your lungs...

the pain does not leave me
all that remains is a world
through the silence of the righteous,
only through your silence and my silence, Juanelo.[28]

These emotional words resonated with thousands of families who had lost loved ones and helped turn the tide of the public by humanizing the violence and its real costs. It also directly challenged the government narrative. If the war were simply an attempt to weed out crime and stop drug trafficking, why would it cause such trauma and violence throughout society?

To begin, we must conceptualize death in these circumstances. Death can also be a social process, as some people are already marked as guilty or worthless through a system of racialized rightlessness.[29] Justice and rights have always been elusive or nonexistent for the poor and indigenous people of Mesoamerica. This complements the ways that these deaths and disappearances in Mexico have been written off, often by invoking the specter of "guilty victims." Their involvement in crime such as drug trafficking therefore makes their murder somehow not worth investigating.[30] This trope of the guilty victim has been a staple of the politics of death, with politicians immediately disavowing public outcry and fear over the deaths of women in places such as Ciudad Juárez by questioning why they were out at night, implying they were in fact asking to be killed by engaging in sex work.[31] This can be combined with the issue of "false positives" whereupon the dead are made to appear as enemy combatants or criminals.[32] The clearest examples of this are the perp-walks popularized in the early days of the drug war, when every person arrested was said to be a dangerous drug lord, and posed for the cameras in front of their cash, drugs, and weapons.[33] The dead were often given generic nicknames—*La Rata, El Gato, El Negro, El Quemado*—to further cement their status as bad people, who deserved, nay, needed to be killed. This fortified the idea that these are bad and scary people, and also guilty before an investigation or any semblance of a trial takes place.[34] This attitude was, unfortunately, widespread. When discussing a recent killing in Nogales, a young man exclaimed, "Good! I hope they kill each other!" Another local politician joked with me that we should put a 666 on the forehead of everyone from Sinaloa, since they were blamed for the violence in Nogales. Unfortunately, three quarters of the city would be marked since almost everyone living there was originally from Sinaloa.

This practice of locating, physically, the source of the threat was ubiquitous in Mexico. In Ciudad Juárez, the violence was caused by people from Veracruz.[35] In Tamaulipas it was because of the Potosinos and Duranguenses. In the mix with all of these enemies from other states was always the migrant and deportee as purveyor of insecurity, violence, and chaos. These processes of racializing and gendering death give us important clues as to why some deaths matter and others do not. In the case of migrants it is their dislocation and movement that allows us to comfortably disavow the tragic loss of life. For those who die in the desert, crossing through the treacherous terrain due to the explicit policies of the U.S. government that drive people into remote areas,[36] we wash our hands because they "chose" to take that risk. Inversely, authorities often blame deaths on "unscrupulous human smugglers" (often falsely calling them human traffickers) who abandon them to die. However, it is the height of hypocrisy to deliberately make it dangerous to cross and then blame smugglers for not doing a better job of mitigating these risks. These acts of law breaking, even laws that are purely administrative, have the rhetorical power to absolve the state, not only of direct blame but moral complicity as well. This extends to people kidnapped and forced to carry drugs, since when they were trying to cross the border they were in the process of committing a "crime," making later violence they suffer a violence they deserved. This has been one of the most common ways that courts in the United States disavow claims of coercion for drug trafficking. If you are intending to cross, it means that whatever happens is your fault.

Therefore, understanding how mobility acts as a catalyst or even an excuse for violence (and vice versa) can help us explain why it has been so difficult to even begin a conversation about missing and disappeared migrants. It is precisely this relationship to movement, to the border, and to the law that makes it so easy to kidnap, coerce, and kill migrants. For Central Americans traveling through Mexico, it is not necessarily nationalism or racism that drives mistreatment (although this certainly exists); rather it is their status as people engaged in illegal movement. This can be seen clearly as efforts to allow Central Americans free passage through Mexico had a notable impact, decreasing violence significantly. For Mexican migrants, generally, their journeys through Mexico are uneventful.[37] It is when they arrive at the border that their relationships to the border and their homeland change as they are suddenly labeled lawbreakers, and they become exponentially more vulnerable.[38] This is particularly true for deportees because they are now stranded in those border spaces, marked by their expulsion from the United States as someone who is related to that forbidden border mobility. They are visible in the plazas, government offices, and in the street. Residents of Nogales often referred to them as *"pollos asados,* roast chickens" because they would arrive in the city sunburnt from their treks through the desert. Also, human smugglers are often called *polleros,* or someone who raises (and slaughters) chickens.

Movement and place are therefore predicated on relationships: who is moving where and why. As an academic born in the United States, white, and male, my relationship to the border is different. I have SENTRI and GOES: fast passes through customs. After I turned 30, officials have rarely asked me a question beyond the first one—what I want to declare. Other people have decidedly different relationships to the border that attract a different type of attention. Moreover, this attention is not solely the domain of the state, as previous chapters have shown. A wide range of nonstate or parastate groups such as drug cartels and corrupt police are interested in who is being removed. Knowing when it is okay and when it is not okay to report crimes is an important part of this process, one that typically only residents of these border towns understand.

This adds another layer to the discourse of guilty victims that is constantly paraded forth by government officials in Mexico. More directly, searching for loved ones in Mexico is dangerous as it represents a direct challenge to the government and their ties to killers who are often operating with the direct or indirect protection of the state. The disappearance of loved ones has profound consequences for grief and mourning, since people must hide the emotional consequences of losing loved ones in order to avoid physical danger as well as the social stigma attached to violent death, especially disappearances, in Mexico.

Pauline Boss has dubbed this "ambiguous loss,"[39] and studied how the lack of finality, the questions about what happened and why, as well as the absence of a ritual for mourning, cause intense suffering for families. According to Boss "the greater the ambiguity surrounding one's loss, the more difficult it is to master it and the greater one's depression, anxiety and family conflict."[40] This can have a number of outcomes. Some people react with absolute certainty, denying death or trauma, pretending it never happened. For others, it leads to a failure to reorganize their lives to accommodate this loss, especially as it relates to changing economic realities. Moreover, by denying the symbolic ritual of death, such as funerals, it compounds the social isolation of death. Friends and extended family often disappear, or do not know how to support the loss of someone who may or may not be dead. This has devastating impacts on people's ability to return to a normal life, and can completely destroy social circles for the loved ones of the disappeared. It is therefore important that we try to understand death and disappearance, not only as a numerical calculation of bodies, but by the social and psychic holes left by these absences. One family that I was involved with for several years typified this phenomenon. The father Luis was kidnapped and disappeared, which led to them all leaving Mexico and relocating to the United States.[41]

> We walked into the Procuraduria General de Justicia del Estado in Hermosillo, Sonora (PGJE—state prosecutor's office). It was packed and sweaty with industrial fans churning away loudly, as people waited agonizingly in folding chairs packed into the lobby. We went straight to the front desk

where people were taking numbers. "I want to check on the status of a case," said Victoria Cuevas. When prompted by the clerk about the nature of the case, she stated emphatically, "*Desaparición de mi papá*—the disappearance of my father." The clerk tensed up and busied herself with the computer. Nothing. They sent us upstairs, and then to another police station.

She's nervous, picking at the peach-colored fingernail polish of her freshly painted nails. Little flecks of the paint fall to the floor in her car.

After hours of searching from office to office and station to station, we found the appropriate building, near Victoria's former home, only a few blocks from where he was abducted. It was a tiny station, with a waiting room and two adjacent offices, but no one to talk to. A man with slicked-back hair, an ostentatious silk shirt, and a Cartier watch came to the desk and asked if we had been helped. Victoria handed him a crumpled piece of paper where she had written her father's name and date of birth. "I want to check the status of my father, Luis Cuevas's disappearance."

The official looked at the paper intensely for a moment as if it contained some secret clues and then asked us to follow him back to his office. He asked a few more questions about who made the *denuncia* (police report) and her relationship to the victim and began to check their database. When he could not find anything, he invited a colleague to help him. After a futile search through the database on an outdated computer, they could not find anything that even remotely matched any combination of his name or circumstances. We left unceremoniously.

When we got into the car she began to cry through gritted teeth. "Ni siquiera existe un caso. (There isn't even a record of him.) It's as if he never existed."[42]

The Kafkaesque bureaucracy of Mexico's legal and policing institutions is further exacerbated by the physical danger of negotiating these spaces. Simply by making inquiries one is exposing oneself to retribution. Organized crime in the area actively seeks out people who go to the police and file reports known as *demandas,* largely due to Mexico's legal system where these statements are sufficient to send someone to jail.[43] It is well known that drug cartels have long infiltrated police departments in order to better receive information, intimidate those willing to make reports, keep tabs on rival criminals, and even hire police officers as part-time hit men and bodyguards.[44]

The invisibility of death occurs from the official state side, as well as through the murky, tangentially connected world of illicit organizations. Records, data, and information are inaccessible, and generally framed through the same accusations of guilty victims that reify the social stigma for anyone searching for answers. This same logic of silence, invisibility, and fear nurtures corruption and the criminal organizations. This system has created a deadly cycle, one that has made it harder and harder to find the truth.

OCTOBER 2008

"When I saw it, all I could hear was a ringing in my ears, everything went silent and I thought I would pass out. I didn't know I was screaming," said the oldest daughter, Maria. She was at home when it happened. Her father had run to his car and sped down the street. He was stopped a block away and young armed men had taken him out of his car and loaded him into the trunk. He struggled. The Nissan Maxima was covered in blood. The police took it and never returned the car. Later, they learned their father received a phone call instructing him that if he did not come out, they would come in and take him and his family.

"When Mom called us, she told us to sit down. She said he had been kidnapped and I just started crying. He is never coming back, I thought," explained Victoria. In the days that followed their mother told them not to talk to anyone, not to look, not to ask. "Pretend that he was never a part of our lives," she instructed. They received a ransom call, but heard nothing after the initial contact. This has become a common aspect of disappearances. The *levantón*, a kidnapping without the intent to return the person alive, has become part of the daily lexicon in Mexico.

The family fled Mexico and has been trying to adapt to a new life in the United States. The ruptures and conflicts that have followed show the importance of Boss's work on ambiguous loss. The lack of finitude, the inability to remove the last scintilla of hope that accompanies the lack of a body, has myriad effects on how people interpret and react to this tragedy. The Cuevas family was no different. For some, the response was absolute certainty, certainty to the point of denial. "I don't want to talk about it. I don't want people to know. They will look at us differently," said one sister. Others felt compelled to act, but balked at outright political or activist participation, partly because of the tension it caused within their family.

> I accompanied Victoria to meet with her paternal grandmother in Nogales, to conduct an interview and see if there was any new information. Victoria's grandmother, Imelda, had not been close with them growing up, and had a difficult relationship with Victoria's mother as well. Imelda discussed hearing the news, "When I got the call I was dropping off my great-grandson at kindergarten. I could barely hear the call because there was noise from the street. When I finally understood, my legs gave out and I fell on the street, breaking my nose." In the days following, men carrying automatic weapons, wearing masks, arrived at her house and made them wait in the living room while they searched the house. The fact that people were actively searching for her father excited Victoria. "If they are searching then they would know if he is alive or not," she exclaimed. Two of her cousins and an aunt joined the conversation. They brought out a bag of Luis's possessions. It was filled with receipts and scraps of paper for farming equipment and land in Chiapas. The aunt swore that he had run to Chiapas, Mexico's southernmost state, to live, but Imelda disagreed.
>
> This led to a number of uncomfortable conversations and intimate details of Luis's life that Victoria knew nothing about. Initially, she was excited about the Chiapas lead, but she grew increasingly skeptical and angry. "They were never there for us. They never knew my father," she said. Her sisters and mother grew irate that she had visited her father's family. "They are into the *Santa Muerte* and they work with drug traffickers. Who knows what could have happened to you!" exclaimed the oldest sister.[45]

This paralysis adds another layer of complexity to notions of grief within the context of Mexico's drug war. These divisions, motivated by self / social preservation in light of an overwhelmingly oppressive and dangerous regime, threatened to divide a family that was suffering from isolation, grief, and fear as they relocated to a new country. These differences in how people react to the physical absence of a person are the key to understanding Boss's concept of ambiguous loss.[46] The inability to locate the physical body necessitates an understanding of the psychic geography of loss, trauma, and suffering. The physical absence but psychological presence creates a rupture. The nature of violence erases, removes, or disposes of bodies in order to silence people and sew distrust among the population. This leads to greater power, control, and corruption within Mexico, especially as people struggle to conceptualize the violence, often unaware of the costs inflicted on their friends and neighbors due to this silence.

Judith Butler argues that we interpret mourning as a finite period, that loss somehow disappears after a time, negating the fact that loss fundamentally changes us.[47] We are no longer the same self. It is these relationships that constitute us, and the loss of these ties fundamentally alters us. In the case of loss that has no end, since there is no body to bury and no ritual to mourn, the lack of an official mourning period has an even more profound consequence. Ambiguous loss not only is a mourning that lacks finitude, but it lacks decisiveness. It lacks a name. We do not know or cannot define what is being mourned. Boss articulates that the lack of symbolic rituals regarding this loss further exacerbates the problem. For the Cuevas family, the lack of support was readily apparent. While they held a *misa* (mass), only a few of their friends came. "Some of my closest friends, people I had known since I was a child, did not say anything to me," explained Victoria. "I remember, later, after one of my friend's grandmother died, all my friends were worried about mentioning going out and partying in front of her as a show of respect. That same girl got mad at me for not showing up to her party the week my father was kidnapped!"

This lack of support caused ruptures in their social networks. "When your best friend just tells you to 'get over it already' you can't look at them the same way ever again," explained Victoria. This lack of formal recognition for loss, breaking away from the social facts that govern grief, necessitates a different space for mourning. This happens, in a way that is similar to all grief, through the unconscious, in dreams.

For the Cuevas family, dreaming became a principal site of resolution. There are dreams that answer the question of how their father died. Dreams he died in the ocean, or was burned to death. Dreams that he is at peace, or that he is suffering, would provoke reactions among the family members. Frequent dreams telling them to take care of each other, not to fight with one another and to make sure their mother is doing well. Sometimes he would appear in dreams with words of advice, warning or admonishing them for fighting among themselves. Victoria questioned why her father comes to her sisters in dreams but not to her. This is the manifestation of the subconscious challenge of grief and loss. Without knowing the fate of a loved one for certain, those lingering doubts and fears, the regret at family strife or the inability to search for justice, manifest physically. The mind therefore becomes the principal site of conflict for grief and resolution in Mexico.

The term *"amanecer muerto"*—literally, "to wake up dead"—has become common around Mexico. The mundane character of violence—omnipresent death, murder without murderers—points to the fact that homicide is not considered something that is actively done, but rather a passive event. It became increasingly common to ask "Cuántos amanecieron muerto hoy?" (How many people woke up dead today?). Santiago, a 15-year veteran of the municipal police, remembers when the police would get excited if there was a dead body: "People would say '*Un muerto?*—A body? What happened? Where? Let's go!' But now no one cares. It happens every day."[48] Another local business owner being extorted told me that he will not report the true identity of the people threatening him because, "If I say anything I will wake up dead *(amanezco muerto)*."

While Luis Cuevas is just one case, over 32,000 people have suffered similar fates in Mexico, leaving hundreds of thousands searching in silence.[49] We have to combine the number of disappeared with the bodies that have been found but not identified, their families located in Honduras, El Salvador, Guatemala, and, of course, in the United States, to know the true costs of this conflict. Are they counted in the missing people? Not likely. Efforts to locate loved ones have been largely futile, as is evidenced by the disappearance of 43 students in Iguala, Guerrero, in 2014.[50] Despite the high-profile nature of this case, none of the disappeared have been found. Efforts to locate them resulted in the discovery of multiple clandestine graves known as "narco" graves (*narcofosas*), but none of them matched the missing students.

GENDER AND DISAPPEARANCE

The messy, complicated consequences of death and disappearance are not borne uniformly by the whole population. As Muehlmann writes, "More than anything, [women's] experience with the drug trade is defined by the loss of sons and loved ones."[51] While men, particularly young men, have borne the brunt of the violence, so much so that it has caused the life expectancy for Mexican men to decrease,[52] it has left fractures among those left behind.

The Cuevas family represents just one configuration. Luis had been the only source of income, so relocating to a new country posed unique challenges and struggles as they were forced to adapt not only to the loss of a loved one but to a change in economic and social circumstances. These new stressors, heaped on top of the lack of closure, provide a potentially volatile cocktail as familial relationships must be renegotiated and adjusted to the new situation. Women are often overly tasked with the emotional burden of readjustment and change.

As many Latin American families still follow a patriarchal model of male income earners, this can be a shock to the family in myriad ways. Women's work has often focused on care, nurture, and negotiating the emotional world. The loss of economic stability can be devastating. While much has been discussed in terms of the increase in women migrants, undocumented Mexican migration is still overwhelmingly male. Ninety percent of Mexican deportees over the age of 18 were male in 2016.[53] Border patrol reports a similar percentage of apprehensions of male Mexican nationals. For those migrants with families, the cash flow of remittances may be the only contact they have with their families for years at a time. Scholars have also noted that for women who come to the United States it does not necessarily alter traditional gender roles, leaving many still dependent on a husband; only now, they are living in a foreign land away from family and friends.[54] Combine this with evidence that the conflict in Mexico targets young men, and the labor of negotiating death, loss, and grief also falls disproportionately on women. For children on both sides of the border, coping with the loss of a parent, either through the separation of migration, the violence of deportation, or the ambiguousness of disappearance, can have tremendous consequences.

However, this is not to say that women have not been the direct targets of brutal violence. Issues such as femicides, the killing of women for being women, have garnered international attention, not without some controversy. Some people have claimed that femicides are a myth, that this is simply part of the larger patterns of crime along the border.[55] Critiquing scholars who have made sloppy interpretations of data and lumped every woman killed into the category of gender crime (a difficult assertion to prove), the anti-femicide group has claimed that since not all of these murders have a direct gender motive, then the phenomenon as a whole is fake.[56] On the other end of the spectrum scholars have claimed that these murders are the direct result of NAFTA, global capitalism, and machismo, often with little evidence.[57] However, as Heather Agnew points out, this often overlooks the important changes, the corruption, and the violence that arrived at the border in the 1980s and 1990s as sophisticated and wealthy criminal organizations took over the region.[58] Clearly, many of the women killed along the border were abducted, raped, and disappeared because of their gender, but not every one.[59] More careful, empirical work is needed to fully understand this phenomenon, especially with regard to how drug trafficking, crime, and gender intersect.

DISAPPEARANCE AND MIGRATION

While the challenges faced by the Cuevas family are immense, this is only one example that demonstrates but a few aspects of this enormous problem. The different situations of the thousands of families dealing with an unnamable, often unspeakable loss create unique problems. For the deaths of migrants, this loss manifests in unique and conflicting notions about crossing the border.[60] The extreme difficulties of locating people who are on the move, and almost impossible to keep track of, even if they are alive, means that the possibility of finding some form of closure is even more difficult.

Death connects to migration in a variety of ways. For the Cuevas family, death sparked their migration to the United States as they fled not only the potential danger in Mexico, but also the social stigma of death. Others may be returning to Mexico due to the death of a loved one, as the years living in the United States without papers ticked by but they never returned and the reunions never materialized. Others come to the border in search of missing loved ones only to find their family member perished during the treacherous journey through the desert. Thousands have died along the U.S.-Mexico border, particularly in the harsh desert in southern Arizona where migrants were pushed after additional patrols in urban areas made it more difficult to cross.[61] Understanding exactly how many people have died and identifying the bodies is a herculean task. Bodies decompose quickly and can be buried or scattered by animals in the desert, or simply washed away in the arroyos (seasonal riverbeds). While the United States has often been described as purposefully negligent, in Mexico it is worse. It is dangerous. State actors are actively complicit, not just in strategic plans that have led to people's deaths, but in actually murdering, kidnapping, and extorting people. While I do not want to downplay the violence of enforcement policies that funnel desperate people into dangerous regions of the border, the resistance to searching, studying, and naming the dead is far greater in the context of Mexico's period of hyperviolence. This leads us to ask, How long can this conflict last? How many people will be silenced? When will it be too much to bear? These remain open questions as violence and insecurity continues to disrupt life throughout Mexico. However, this is not to say that people do not resist and push back. One of the most important ways people do this is through their relationships to each other, and the strength of love and friendship to protect themselves against the desperation and violence they face.

CHAPTER SEVEN

Resistance, Resilience, and Love

The Limits of Violence and Fear

Today Zacatecas was very agitated. He paced around the room at La Choza, exaggerating his usual hunched-over, lanky gait, and ran his hands through his short black hair. I asked what was wrong and he told me that he was going to start "cuidando el rio." He said: "Look, Antonia (a Honduran migrant he had been dating) is gone. I don't have anything. The last 13 years of my life don't exist here (in Mexico). What else am I going to do? If they catch me crossing again they are going to lock me up." Later that day he got a phone call that Antonia had been caught by the border patrol. A big smile lit up his face and all his friends started making fun of him. He immediately began going to work every day, doing whatever he could to save up some money. Zacatecas, a veteran border crosser, did the calculations. "If they just caught her and this is the second time she got caught then it will be ten days." He had taught her how to pretend to be Mexican so they would not send her back to Honduras.[1] "I don't love her and she doesn't love me," he said. "But at least we have each other." His work, even though it was low paying and inconsistent, meant that he would not hang out in the plaza with us. He saved his money, not eating out. He was simultaneously excited and stressed. "How can I provide something for her?"[2]

Despite the horrific violence, it is this desire for connection and humanity that persist within the chaotic and dangerous atmosphere of the border; people look to each other for protection, warmth, and humanity. For even the most skilled migrants— people with numerous contacts, access to capital, and knowledge of the border's unwritten rules—getting through this situation requires help. Without the deep friendships and emotional ties built through shared hardship and the suffering involved in migration, it would be impossible.

The most tender, heartwarming moments come when people are reunited. A young man from El Salvador named Antonio, whose brother had just been murdered by the Mara Salvatrucha because the family had failed to pay their extortion tax, explained tearfully that he had lost contact with his wife. He rode the train and she took a bus for more protection, but she had not arrived at the border. That night, she arrived at the shelter in Nuevo Laredo and the two embraced for what seemed like an hour, the tears of happiness and relief overcoming them.

These ties are emblematic of the strength and tenacity that drive migration. That struggle to survive and to create a better life for oneself and one's family is the reason, the only reason, people are willing to sacrifice so much. The connections between friends and lovers become one of the principal safeguards for protection throughout the migratory journey. True, these relationships often collapse under the strain of desperation, the scarcity of resources, and the pressures of life-and-death situations. Therefore these ties are often viewed as both temporary and resilient, capable of dissolving at any moment, but easily re-formed in the future when circumstances permit. Because graft and deceit have become extremely common throughout the border, the ability to identify people who you can trust, and avoid those who you cannot, is invaluable. This chapter explores these relationships, their importance, and how aspects of immigration enforcement actively rupture the bonds between people, making it increasingly difficult to trust and care for one another. The understandings of relationships among migrants and service providers (locals, shelter workers, and coyotes) are still very limited;[3] however, their importance cannot be denied. A trustworthy friend can be the difference between being kidnapped and finding a safe place to sleep, of getting work or being forced to cross a backpack of drugs. A better understanding of how certain policies and practices create wedges between people, shattering these relationships and increasing the incentives to be cutthroat and adversarial, can help us understand some of the hidden costs of our current approach to immigration enforcement. This helps us explore the ways through which enforcement practices directly exacerbate the vulnerability of deportees. By eroding important aspects of care, love, and friendship that have been one of the most important, albeit frequently ignored, forms of support for migrants, enforcement measures have the power to drastically improve or hurt people, even after they are deported.

There are three main types of enforcement-related issues that have an impact on the relationships between migrants: lost possessions, anti-smuggling initiatives, and anti-human trafficking measures. First and foremost among the enforcement practices that have an enormous impact on deportees is the loss of possessions while in U.S. custody. The lack of possessions makes navigating the border even more difficult and dangerous. In addition to the loss of possessions, the Operation Against Smuggling Immigrant Security and Safety (OASISS) puts coyotes and migrants at odds with one another, leading to increased violence between the two in the form of abandonment, extortion, and safe houses. Anti-smuggling initiatives have also blurred with anti-human trafficking programs, creating a more punitive atmosphere surrounding a variety of activities along the border. In addition to adding fuel to the anti-coyote narrative, anti-trafficking initiatives have impacted a variety of survival strategies. This has blurred the distinctions between sex work, human trafficking, and intimate relationships in the context of deportation and migration.

"HOW DO I GET THE MONEY TO GET OUT OF HERE?" MIGRANT POSSESSIONS ON THE BORDER

Upon repatriation, 34 percent of deportees report having possessions taken and not returned. This includes money, cell phones, and perhaps most importantly, identifying documents.[4] All of these belongings provide essential protection for people once they are deported. In fact, when asked in the MBCS survey as to what they were most afraid of or worried about upon deportation, not having their possessions was the most common answer; 22 percent of deportees who were afraid cited this as the main cause of their fear. Twenty-one percent who lost possessions report losing their cell phones. In today's digital era this can mean losing contact information and the ability to get in touch with people in both Mexico and the United States, stranding them at the border. Another 20 percent report losing money, with a median of $55 reported lost. While this may not seem like a lot of money, it is the difference between being stuck on the streets at the border or in a safe hotel room, with a bus ticket back home as soon as possible. Additionally, of the 70 percent of respondents who were carrying Mexican identifying documents when they were apprehended, 26 percent lost them while in custody.[5] This is the most devastating possession to lose, simply because without these documents, it is extremely difficult to receive a money transfer and replacing them is almost impossible without returning to the interior of Mexico, usually to one's birthplace.[6]

For Ramiro, an army veteran, he was at a particular disadvantage because he was deported during an election season. "They wouldn't give me a new ID (Credencial Electoral) because an election was coming. I had to wait six months and all that time the cops would stop me and harass or arrest me for not carrying an ID." Mexico's anti-voter fraud laws limit the government from issuing new voter IDs before an election. This extends the time that deportees have to wait for some sort of identification that would allow them multiple benefits such as protection from extortion by authorities, but also in the form of being able to access money.

The frequency with which deportees arrive at the border without identification has led to one of the most tangible circumstances where trust becomes a tradable commodity: money transfers. Some deportees will specialize in receiving money sent by family members for a small fee; however, since the money must be sent directly to a third party, it is easy for people to abscond with the cash. In an effort to combat this problem, local governments have made arrangements with specific businesses (Soriana, Moneygram, Western Union) to accept deportation slips as proof of identity, but in my experience these agreements are inconsistent at best and have also led to the proliferation of fake deportation documents in an effort to launder money (i.e., cash sent to Mexico under a fake name).[7] One cannot expect to be able to use the slip of paper and grainy webcam photo to receive money everywhere along the border. Even when these arrangements work, it can be risky, since gangs monitor the areas where deportees are known to pick up money, waiting for them to collect their cash before assaulting them. This happened frequently outside of the bus station in Matamoros. People would monitor who came and went from the bus station and deportees had to walk to the nearby supermarket to collect money.

Because of these risks, deportees with their identifying documents often offer to have cash sent in their names and then hand it over to their (literally) undocumented acquaintances, for a fee. Monterrey offered this service to others at the shelter, a practice that was frowned upon, but not forbidden, given the reality of the situation. Some shelters started allowing money transfers to be made inside, but this quickly became dangerous with the large amount of cash on the premises and the propensity of these arrangements to attract drug traffickers trying to launder funds. Monterrey would give people his full name and have the money sent to the nearby Santander Bank. They would pick up the money together and he would give them the cash, minus a few bucks or the promise of a burrito and a soda (depending on some complicated haggling by the fast-talking Monterrey). Often these schemes are the result of a whole group of people collaborating, and the money is treated communally. However, it does not always work out so well, and the fear of being robbed is real and everpresent.

Eusebio, a middle-aged Guatemalan migrant, had been living at the shelter for over a month in exchange for his help around the place. Normally, in Nuevo Laredo, people had to leave after a week (still longer than most shelters), but trusted people often were allowed to stay on in exchange for helping out. He was also known to use his identification to receive money transfers.[8] One day Eusebio did not show up and a deportee began asking the shelter staff for him. "He was supposed to bring me 500 dollars that my family sent me. Have you seen him?" Eusebio never returned, causing an embarrassment for the shelter who had vouched for him by allowing him a privileged position working in the kitchen and being able to come and go as he pleased.

Add to this how closely guarded personal information has become because extortion is so common. For instance, giving the names and contact information of family members to pick up a wire transfer can lead to someone calling back and requesting more money, claiming it was lost or stolen or simply pretending to have kidnapped their loved ones. About 17 percent of respondents reported that they or their family had been targeted by extorting phone calls either claiming to have kidnapped a loved one or claiming that they had successfully crossed the desert. The calls, rampant in the borderlands, both in the United States and Mexico, are known as "cyber kidnapping" or "virtual kidnapping."[9] Extortion through trickery has become so common because the violence is terrifying, which makes it easy to convince people that bad things will happen if they do not comply. Any personal information can be used to extort money from concerned relatives.

Extortion is a familiar story, ubiquitous in border towns. This is but one simple example of how limited resources, handed to someone deemed trustworthy, can have devastating impacts. The loss of people's possessions increases their vulnerability. True advocates may be hard to find, but one often overlooked form of advocacy comes from human smugglers, hired to escort people through the desert. While we typically think of human smugglers as parasites on the suffering that is migration, they are often offering a much-needed service. Finding a competent and honest guide can be the difference between life and death.

WHO TO TRUST? GUIDING
THROUGH THE DESERT

One of the most difficult and complicated tasks for migrants is meeting, assessing, and finding a trustworthy guide to take them across the river and through the vast expanses of wilderness along the border. While we have discussed some of the contention over the role, motives, and nature of coyotes in chapter 2, the process of choosing a guide and essentially entrusting one's safety to them contains an important message about the potential support offered through this arrangement. The coyote-migrant relationship is a unique one because people must trust their well-being to their guide on the dangerous journey through the desert. The coyotes know where to go when they run out of water, how to flag down authorities when they need medical attention, and the fastest, safest ways through the desolate terrain of the border. A mistake can cost migrants their lives. Despite the illegal nature of human smuggling, the choice about which guide to select is dictated not only by the likelihood that they will successfully arrive at their destination but by the likelihood that they will survive.

The same issues of trust involved with money transfers impact the migrant-coyote relationship. First, migrants must find someone who they believe will take them safely to their desired destination. It is not uncommon for people to be led around the desert in circles and brought to a house they believe is in the United States, when in fact they are actually still in Mexico. Other times, people can be kidnapped, extorted, and abandoned. Kidnapping and extortion often involve increases in the price to cross once people arrive at a safe house. All of this is in addition to the life-and-death nature of migration, whereupon the U.S. government has deliberately made it more dangerous and deadly to cross through the harsh desert.[10] Guides must be competent, know the terrain, and be able to find more food or water or, in an emergency, look for help.

A recommendation from a friend or family member is extremely valuable. While scholars have suggested that these recommendations are common, MBCS data found that while fully 75 percent of migrants were satisfied by the services provided by their guides, only 45 percent say that they would put a friend or family member in contact with the coyote.[11] "If I recommend him to someone and then something happens to that person—they'll blame me! No, it's not good to recommend."[12] There are costs to recommendation because of the potential dangers of crossing. While most people seem to expect a level of hardship for themselves, the prospect of putting other people in that situation, especially the life-or-death reality of the desert is more difficult.

Part of this unwillingness to recommend stems from the increased professionalization of human smuggling on the border, and the other major factor is the increased prosecution of human smugglers. This leads to increasingly less personal, or direct, contact with coyotes. Already, fewer people rely on coyotes who are from their hometowns, most now meeting guides at the border who live and work there.[13] These increasingly professionalized guides have additional concerns. For starters, local guides were generally experienced migrants, who would also cross and work for periods of time, especially during seasonal migration, charging small amounts to a group of people, mostly friends, to guide them through the desert together. This meant crossing once or twice a year and being apprehended a handful of times. Now, for people whose primary source of income is smuggling migrants, they have to cross more, which alerts the border patrol to their work as a guide because they have multiple apprehensions and, likely, multiple criminal charges for illegal entry and reentry.

The latest iteration of the desire to arrest and prosecute smugglers is the Operation Against Smugglers, Initiative on Safety and Security (OASISS). It relies on the disjointed legal geography of the border whereupon laws on one side of the border are exploited in conjunction with supposed protections on the other. However, for migrants, it makes it more likely for people to be abandoned in the desert, or threatened with violence if they are suspected of having cooperated with authorities. According to a press release by CBP, "The program enables the prosecution of Mexican human smugglers, through Mexican courts, using information obtained via interviews conducted by Border Patrol agents while in U.S. custody."[14] Border patrol or ICE agents in the United States will take a statement about who the guides are from migrants in U.S. custody and then deport both the witness and the guides back to Mexican authorities (usually with a clearly marked OASISS tag on their deportation form). They are relying on the fact that a statement is sufficient to convict someone and incarcerate them in Mexico, but requires more evidence in a U.S. court of law. This practice falls somewhere between extradition and extraordinary rendition. They are sent back with an accusation of criminal activity, to be prosecuted in another country based on evidence gathered in the United States. The difficulty in prosecuting individuals for smuggling in the United States has been circumvented by this binational program that began in 2005. Little data is available outside of sporadic press releases, and certainly more research is necessary to determine its long-term impacts on relationships between migrants and their guides.

It is often hard to find and interview people with knowledge of this program, since few migrants know what it is called or how it works. All enforcement programs are complex and the details are not shared with those people being processed through them. However, I have interviewed many people who reported being interrogated about who their guide was (most refused to cooperate, although those with particular grievances such as car accidents cooperated actively),[15] but only a few who had been part of the program. One man named Rogelio explained that he was separated from the rest of the migrants and deported directly to the Procurador General de Justicia de la Republica (PGJR— similar to our federal prosecutor). A young man named Luis who was in the same group of migrants as Rogelio had OASISS written on his paperwork when they were deported. Luis had crossed the border many times and admitted to the agents that he used not one but two fake names on previous apprehensions. He told the border patrol, "Así no me llamo en México" (That's not my name in Mexico). They were all put in handcuffs and separated from the other migrants. Rogelio did not know what had happened exactly, and did not know or did not divulge who had fingered the young man, who according to him was not the coyote.[16]

This is the problem with efforts to arrest and stop human smuggling; it erodes the relationships and trust that are essential for people's safety. These arguments are largely ignored, as protecting and increasing the safety of deportees and migrants is anathema to the Consequence Delivery System (CDS). However, as the pressure to report who the guide is increases, it becomes more and more dangerous for both migrants and coyotes to trust one another. Aside from simply taking extra precautions such as preemptively abandoning the group if it is likely that the authorities are approaching, a potentially deadly option, there are other pitfalls. If I am the coyote, should I risk having someone report my identity to an agent and subsequently spend years in jail? Rather, as the guide, with more knowledge about enforcement practices, should I preemptively report that another member of the group is the guide to divert suspicion? I do not know if this is what happened to Luis in the story above, but the possibility remains.

Moreover, the use of this program has coincided with the rise of so-called "cyber coyotes" who simply direct the migrants through the desert over a cell phone. Migrants expressed feelings of being abandoned, tricked, and alone in the dangerous desert and uniformly hate this practice. Especially since this research has shown us that not only do coyotes guide people through the desert to their destinations, but they often know how to find food such as edible cacti (nopales, tunas, etc.). They also can find water by locating arroyos where subsurface water is easily accessible or even cattle troughs that, although dirty, can provide life-saving sustenance. In addition to stories of people being abused by coyotes, there are tales of intense loyalty and help. Amado, 18, from Veracruz who paid a $2,700 fee, described his experience: "Really, it's luck—it's a game if you make it [across the border] or not. But my guy crossed my father before. He's not like these other guys who will

Figure 7. Tijuana, Baja California. A couple walks up the bank of the canal known as "el Bordo." Photo by Murphy Woodhouse.

leave you. I was vomiting blood [while crossing] and he stayed with me." Another migrant asserted: "He's a good person. There were women in our group and he treated them all well. We made it safe and sound."[17] These connections can be the difference between life and death.

Policies that drive wedges between guides and migrants, particularly those designed to obtain confessions from migrants about the identity of their guide, do the opposite of the stated intentions of the enforcement program. Simply creating new and creative ways to incarcerate people does nothing to increase the safety of migrants. For all of the criticisms about evil smugglers that we hear from law enforcement, at what point do we take a step back and realize that increased criminalization always makes things more dangerous, not less. Nowhere is this more visible than in the interpersonal relationships between migrants. These are important sources of support, comfort, and care that are often overlooked by focusing on the big-picture geopolitical issues of migration.

LOVE, SEX, AND RELATIONSHIPS
ON THE BORDER

Zacatecas and Antonia had a relationship that was far from perfect. Jealousy and distrust shaped much of their interactions. The intense danger, scarcity, and violence of migration added a cynical layer to many of the romantic relationships, and yet a tenderness and support did exist underneath the tendency to seek material comfort, support, or protection.

Juan Manuel, a deportee who had been injured and was living at the shelter as a worker, cleaning, cooking, and making sure people followed the rules, asked me to sit down with him. He was thin and in his early forties with a salt-and-pepper ponytail that hung down between his shoulder blades as it peeked through the opening of a baseball cap he usually wore. I thought he might have been annoyed with me, disrupting dinner and sitting down with the migrants to talk over food as had become my custom. "I am starting to have feelings for Helga," he explained.

Helga was from Guatemala and had been staying at the shelter for a few weeks at that point. Although not quite five feet in height, she had a commanding presence and had already asserted herself at the shelter, helping herself to food in the pantry and giving orders to the other guests. Some of the paid employees had begun to grumble about her being too bossy, which caused Juan Manuel, who usually kept to himself listening to rock and roll in his spare time, to get in some heated arguments with the others, including the head priest. Helga's story was a mix of tragedy, perseverance, and strength, with the later figuring prominently.

She had been sold as an infant and sexually abused by her adopted father, until the civil wars in Guatemala destroyed her community. "I watched the Kabiles[18] kill babies. They led me into a trench (*trinchera*) and they were going to execute me. A priest came and stopped the military from killing us," she recounted.[19] She fled to southern Mexico as a child and was given refugee status, but the camps were hard to live in, so she eventually left for Cancun. However, through the promise of employment in the cantinas as a waitress she was sucked into the world of sex traffickers and was forced to work as a prostitute. She was finally able to escape and was now headed to the United States. Juan Manuel was in awe of her toughness and the amount of suffering she had endured. "I've never met anyone like her!" he said.

My impression of Helga was that she was a survivor, tough as nails and willing and able to do anything to get ahead. She would admonish other migrants at the shelter and make up new rules that suited her, and sometimes her stories were inconsistent. I have no doubt that the level of trauma she had endured makes recounting her life difficult, but it gave some people around the shelter pause, doubting her story. Eventually, the conflict boiled to a head and Helga and Juan Manuel were asked to leave. They traveled together to neighboring Piedras Negras, Coahuila, to cross, but got stuck there. Helga left Juan Manuel and crossed with another man. He showed up again at the shelter heartbroken and with a bruised ego.[20]

This story illustrates the challenges and potential comfort offered by relationships. For Juan Manuel, this was a ray of hope in an otherwise difficult existence. His injury meant that he walked with a limp and was for all intents and purposes stuck in a border town, deported after years of living in the United States. He had often confided in me that he did not know what or when his next steps in life would be. For Helga, a consummate survivor, it is important not to judge the hustle needed in these situations. Prostitution is often cynically referred to as the *cuerpomático*, a play on the word for an ATM—*cajero automático,* and body, *cuerpo.* Many relationships along the migrant trail become transactional in a way that is hard to judge from the outside. Yes, there is an exchange that happens, but that does not mean that it is wholly without love. When I see the harsh realities people face, I conclude that the dissolution of Juan Manuel and Helga's relationship, as well as countless others, is a product of the hardship they live. That is why it is important to understand and value these moments of tenderness as evidence of solidarity, support, and care, even in the direst of moments. Zacatecas's own cynicism was precisely what made his relationship with Antonia so profound.

"Yeah, I broke my own rules but it was just for *calentura* (lasciviousness*)*. It wasn't real," he had explained to me a few days earlier.[21] He laid out his rules that you can't be interested in women if you can't even take care of yourself. This was evidenced by how he had learned to navigate the border and the traps laid out for migrants. Later that day, as we were walking back toward the shelter, a woman approached him, asking if he was looking to cross. She claimed that her family had already arranged for her to cross but that she needed a man to go with her. She was scared of going alone and needed someone to stand in as her husband to protect her from unscrupulous coyotes or others. "It's all paid for. You don't need to pay anything. Just come with me," she said, sweetening the deal. He laughed and walked away. "What was that about?" I asked. "She is a kidnapper," he explained in a matter-of-fact tone. "They try and play on your manhood, make you think that you can protect someone, when in reality you can't even take care of yourself. It is a trap, especially when it sounds too good to be true." Zacatecas went on to explain how being a deportee stuck here is an extremely emasculating experience. With little to no work, and a lack of money or even sufficient food, deportees are set to wander the streets and *"charrolear"* (beg).[22] "When someone says they need your help, your protection, it is easy to fall for that," said Zacatecas.

This phenomenon is not isolated to migrants and plays a prominent role for service providers and aid organizations.[23] Lázaro, the Oaxacan caretaker for the shelter who walked with a limp, was chatting with me one evening after the chores had slowed down. He told me a story of a woman from Honduras who claimed she was kidnapped and raped and did an interview, crying and everything. Then a week later he heard her talking on the phone in the plaza saying that she had a group ready to cross, but they are hers and she needs to get paid. She had already done it once and was doing a second group. Lázaro was angry and crushed that someone would lie about such an experience to gain access to a shelter and migrants to cross them as a coyote.[24]

Flat stereotypes of victims and victimizers plague research on migration, but the reality is much more complex. For the young woman who approached Zacatecas, it is hard to understand her situation because we simply do not have enough information. Was she being forced to recruit kidnapping victims? It would most likely depend on very subjective perspectives about the ability of people to freely make choices in times of desperation. Once people begin down the road of participation in organized crime, it becomes more and more difficult to stop, to resist, and to extricate oneself.[25] This became apparent with a group of young women who were staying at the shelter. A rumor began to circulate that Josefina, a young woman from Oaxaca, had been *"jalando tacón,"* a euphemism for prostitution that roughly translates to "pulling on heels." The assumption that her new clothes and a purse meant she had been engaging in prostitution led to a devastatingly vicious cycle of rumors. Officially she had been working at the *Tianguis* (flea market), selling used clothes, but no one believed her. She began to face harassment as the men at the shelter began speculating that she charged 1,000 pesos (less than 100 USD) for sex, gossiping endlessly about her in obscene and often vicious ways. She quickly left the shelter with a man she claimed was her husband. I say "claimed" simply because the paternalistic atmosphere and intense scrutiny of female migrants in shelters necessitates these relationships, making female economic activity suspicious unless it is carried out under the obvious auspices of a man.

Regardless of whether or not the rumors about Josefina were true, the narratives around migration, the often patronizing religious organizations that are omnipresent in migrant aid efforts, as well as a highly masculine atmosphere, make engaging in other activities such as prostitution socially unacceptable and often lead to people being ostracized. Since the aid economy, generally controlled by religious organizations, has overtly

moralistic and paternalistic regulations, people are frequently kicked out
for breaking, or even for the suspicion of having broken, these moral
taboos. Assertions about misbehavior are often wrapped in assumptions
about masculinity and infidelity. After chatting with an ex-gang member
from Honduras, whose wife was in the United States, Zacatecas noted
viciously, "His wife is fucking other guys."[26] The cynical attitude that
women were not to be trusted, and doing so was a slight to one's own masculinity, was toxically pervasive in the highly gendered spaces of migration.[27] The overarching narrative, packaged and presented to the outside
world of the suffering, deserved migrant, working to support *HIS* family, is
replicated internally through checks and balances on relationships and
behavior. This often includes completely innocuous romantic relationships, but also mutually exploitative relationships and prostitution. Prostitution is not, in fact, uncommon among migrants.

> I met Zacatecas and Monterrey at their new place to make some lunch. We
> had bought a couple pounds of thin sliced beef milanesa and were prepar-
> ing the grill, which consisted of a couple cinderblocks and an old oven
> grate. Their next-door neighbors, Wilbur and Denia, came by and chatted
> with us for a minute. They were both from Honduras, but had been here for
> a few months living as a couple. He was skinny with light skin and a scrag-
> gly black goatee and baggy clothes. Wilbur lit up a joint as he chatted about
> struggling to find work, but preferring Nuevo Laredo to San Pedro Sula.
> His girlfriend, Denia, looked a few years older with bleached blond hair.
> Zacatecas came up to me and whispered not so subtly, "The *guera* likes you.
> *Te la rifan*—they will sell her," I nodded and pretended not to understand.
> He reiterated bluntly that she would sleep with me for some money, but I
> continued to ignore him and feign ignorance with my typical gringo grin.[28]

Was Wilbur a boyfriend or a trafficker? I suppose it depends on how
we understand relationships, survival, and agency within the intensely
violent landscape of migration.[29] In the recent rush to prosecute human
trafficking, little of the debate has truly explored the complex relationships that abound in situations where scarcity and survival are daily
concerns. In the sense of forcing someone to engage in sex work we can

see a sliding scale. In this case, as well as the hypothetical case of Josefina, it is doubtful that someone put a gun to their heads, threatened
them, or abducted them, but neither can we say that this is a decision
that was entered into without considerable outside pressure and stress.
One could assert that no migration, or at least very little undocumented
migration, ever occurs without limited options, crushing poverty, and
very real structural constraints. If the option to lead a healthy, happy
life and provide a future for their children in their native country was
possible, fewer people would attempt the dangerous journey across the
border, not to mention engage in sex work, or other dangerous activities such as drug trafficking. These are fundamentally the acts of people who are not free to pursue their lives, and if that is not coercion, I
do not know what is.

Unfortunately, in the legal realm it most definitely does not count as
coercion. For Wilbur, the Honduran boyfriend, it certainly could get
him arrested as a human trafficker. The punitive side of anti-trafficking
measures is fully developed and in overdrive, broadly incarcerating
individuals as traffickers, when in reality they are smugglers paid by
migrants to take them across borders (generally, a mutually agreed-
upon arrangement rather than some sort of coercive situation) or even
boyfriends. And yet, when it comes to the victims, the protections of
the state are extremely limited. All suspected victims of human trafficking are supposed to be screened for T-visa eligibility, which was
created in 2000 as part of an initiative to encourage people to testify
against human traffickers. However, since their creation, T-visas have
been vastly underutilized. For instance, U.S. Citizenship and Immigration Services received a total of 1,848 T-visa applications in fiscal year
2016, 1,737 of which were approved, well under the cap of 5,000.[30] And
yet a total of 6,228 T-visa applications were still awaiting a decision as
of that year.[31] In comparison, Immigration and Customs Enforcement
arrested 1,952 people for human trafficking as part of the Homeland
Security Investigations (HSI) program in 2016 alone, with over 7,000
arrests since 2010.[32] Since multiple agencies arrest people for human

trafficking, it is particularly shocking that one agency arrests more people for trafficking than the total number of people granted relief in that same period. It is easy to conclude that alleged victims of trafficking clearly face a much higher degree of scrutiny than those arrested.

Worldwide, the anti-trafficking phenomenon has had a number of unwanted side effects. An example is punishing people and countries for the prevalence of irregular migration, which has led to crackdowns like the anti-Rohingya campaigns by the Thai government. In 2015 the Thai government refuse to allow Rohingya refugees from Myanmar to land their boats in Thailand because the U.S. State Department classifies them as victims of trafficking and not refugees. In their effort to join the failed Trans Pacific Partnership (TPP), the Thai government was trying to improve their classification in the annual Trafficking In Persons report (TIP). This led to dozens, perhaps hundreds of deaths as boats with an estimated 6,000 occupants were left marooned at sea.[33] Moreover, scholars have critiqued the lack of methodologically sound statistics about the size of trafficking as an industry, often classifying all sex work as trafficking due to the strong anti-prostitution lobby from the Christian right that has worked closely with anti-trafficking feminist groups.[34] Moreover, wage exploitation is far more prevalent than sexual slavery, and yet sexual exploitation receives the vast majority of the media coverage.[35]

As with many debates, the conversation about human trafficking has become polarized to the extent that both sides deny the complete validity of the other. In my research I have documented numerous stories such as Juanito's, the kidnapping victim from chapter 4, where women are kidnapped, raped, and used in the sex industry. I have also seen more complicated aspects of sex work used as a tool for desperate people trying to escape a dire situation. However, some of these relationships, such as a woman traveling alone who begins a romantic relationship with a guide, seem, at least in many of the cases I have witnessed, to be genuinely tender. I have no easy answers about how to judge these entanglements. How can you judge someone else's relationship, their motives, or their reasons at all? One thing I do know is that many times, efforts to prosecute human traffickers have had the unfortunate side effect of putting people at odds with one another, afraid of accusations and distrustful of being close to anyone.

These complicated questions lead us to doubt whether or not human trafficking is a valid framework for understanding forced mobility, exploitation, and slavery. Perhaps the degree to which the trafficking framework has been hijacked by law enforcement means that instead of discussing victims of trafficking we should specifically address abuses such as labor or sexual exploitation, labor violations, or kidnapping and extortion. These are specific actions that can be proven or disproven, and documented. Increasing protections against labor exploitation is paramount to address the linkages between debt, labor, and the financing that has driven prices for coyotes to such exorbitant sums.[36] Moreover, the trafficking framework creates an extra layer of complication that can separate people and drive wedges between them, which in turn creates more violence and danger on the border. During fieldwork I began to hear rumors that women will accuse the men in their groups of being human traffickers as a way to legally go to the United States. One migrant told me that his girlfriend accused him of violence in order to get papers. "She lied to them to get papers and here I am deported!" While it is impossible to verify this statement, the implications are troubling.

These rumors may have been hyperbole, but the fear is real enough that people begin to act differently, distancing themselves and being fearful of caring for one another. This erodes the closeness and humanity that has become the lifeline for so many people. Similar to the ways that the removal of people's possessions leads to greater exploitation when receiving money transfers, anti-trafficking laws have the potential to insert themselves within people's relationships and remove the care and love that still exists among migrants and deportees. Acknowledging that solidarity, care, and love are among the strongest forms of social capital when trying to successfully navigate the border, helps us understand how people survive and even thrive after such devastating violence and trauma.[37]

REUNITED

Zacatecas set out to work, finding jobs to do during the day, a construction gig here, landscaping there. He struggled, but got enough money saved up to get his own room at La Choza and buy food for when Antonia came home. He calculated perfectly how long it would take for her to be deported: "One previous apprehension, so two weeks for reentry ... Hopefully, they believe that she is Mexican and she remembers everything I taught her." Sure enough, Antonia arrived in the predicted ten days to a warm reception. Zacatecas showed up at the shelter to greet her and they headed off to his newly rented (and decorated) room at La Choza.

Personal relationships have the power to pull people back from the danger and violence of the drug war. The emotional ties created through shared experiences of migration and removal create important bonds, bonds useful for allowing people's humanity to show through in even the darkest times. The relationships people build during their experiences at the border are important tools for resisting recruitment and not participating in criminal activities. This care and love is a bulwark against the darkness and violence, and yet, it is not without its pitfalls. This chapter explored the complicated interplay of people's relationships and how policies and practices often have unintended consequences that drive wedges between people. Despite this, people persevere. Zacatecas and Antonia are but one example of this strength through companionship. Their relationship had its ups and downs. Zacatecas was caught crossing and detained. Antonia crossed the border again with another man but somehow both found their way back to each other and at the time of this writing they are living together in Nuevo Laredo, Tamaulipas.

For Antonia and Zacatecas, to have someone to look forward to made all the difference in the world. For many fleeing violence, the only thing they have waiting for them upon removal is danger and fear. The next chapter gives a brief overview of the asylum system in the United States and ways to protect those who are fleeing the very violence discussed in this book.

CHAPTER EIGHT

"Who Can I Deport?"

*Asylum and the Limits of Protection
against Persecution*

"WHO CAN I DEPORT?" the judge barked at me. I was testifying on behalf of a man who had been in the United States for over twenty years. His entire family were U.S. citizens. He had been arrested for using a fake identity to cross the border. He had witnessed his friend murdered in front of him and had left Mexico in fear. After arguing that this man would face danger in Mexico because he would be perceived to be wealthy and essentially a foreigner in what is no longer his home country, I struggled to respond to the judge's blunt question, knowing full well that I had to placate the judge because he, and he alone, would determine the fate of this individual. What I wanted to say was we should recognize that the harm and danger people are being placed in, due to removal, is far more serious than the law assumes; that people are being systematically targeted after deportation; and that people who have spent a lifetime in the United States have a right to be here with their families. I didn't say this though. I tried to explain to the judge that, yes, there are many people who come, work, and want to go back to Mexico, but others are tied to the United States after their years living and working here which makes return difficult, often dangerous.[1] The judge's palpable frustration at my argument displayed a truth of the immigration courts: they are designed and incentivized to remove people, en masse and as fast as possible.

The asylum system includes a very precise set of guidelines outlining which types of violence can be considered *valid* fears of persecution.

Judges attempt to determine which forms of violence classify individuals for protection. Achilles Mbembe writes of necropolitics, defined as the way that our politics shape which types of deaths and violence are presented as acceptable or legal. They ask: "Under what practical conditions is the right to kill, to allow to live, or to expose to death exercised? Who is the subject of this right? What does the implementation of such a right tell us about the person who is thus put to death and about the relation of enmity that sets that person against his or her murderer?"[2] The racial and colonial hierarchies that designate these rights are never more apparent than at the border and among those asking for protection. In the asylum courts, however, it fits the mold of *necroliberalism*,[3] whereupon we see the supposed gifts of our liberal democracies being bestowed or withheld, on the basis of a set of standards few would recognize as our legal system. Rather than simply a politics that decides whose deaths matter, necroliberalism points out which potential murders should be prevented by granting clemency.

This is precisely the role of the immigration judge: deciding whose deaths, or rather, which types of deaths should matter and thus should be spared. Is there state involvement or is it "just" crime? Can they relocate internally in their home country? Did someone actually harm them or was it simply a threat (meaning one should stay long enough to be harmed, but not quite long enough to be killed before leaving, a tricky endeavor)? These types of questions seek to exclude, or validate, certain types of violence as being worthy or unworthy of protection.

To this point I have focused on the ways that the conflict over drugs has reshaped migration, precisely because people in motion are extremely vulnerable and exposed. However, for this last chapter I would like to explore one of the unintended side effects of my research on violence facing deportees: my role as an expert witness in asylum hearings. I had never intended to take this role, and barely knew of its existence until I finished my PhD, but as an academic who is constantly attempting to maximize the public impact of my scholarship, it has been an intriguing and edifying consequence of my research. In fact, I wrote this book the way that I did in order to publicly spell out the arguments that are relevant to a great many individuals fearing deportation. Therefore this chapter should serve as a catalyst for more academics to use their knowledge in the courts and contribute to the legal struggles of thousands from across the globe.

Often scholarship and research connect back to the people we study in interesting or strange ways. Generally, applied or public intellectuals tend to think in terms of shaping public opinion, working with the media, or drafting policy proposals. Rarely does legal consulting factor into this conversation. Under the Obama administration, many held out hope that cleverly crafted research could provide the necessary information to prod lawmakers to reform immigration. This was largely a failure. As this book is being written, it is even less likely that such an effort will have success under the Trump administration, with its overtly nativist, anti-immigrant stance. In this sense, the legal protections that already exist for people with precarious legal status become all the more important, and the appropriate aid of academic experts provides much-needed evidence to buttress asylum claims.

Often, a statement or testimony by an expert is the only major piece of evidence offered in their defense.[4] In immigration court people are not guaranteed the right to counsel, there is no jury, and the burden of proof is on the individual, not the state.[5] The decision to rip apart a family, often with U.S. citizen children left to pick up the pieces of a broken home, is done in mere minutes. It bears repeating the oft-quoted phrase that immigration court is "death penalty cases in a traffic court setting."[6]

However, even within this limited timeline, and the few possible options available for people trying to stay in the United States, the courts are overwhelmed. The average length of time of a Mexican immigration case is 923 days, with the longest wait in Colorado where the average is 1,259 days until completion.[7] This is both a challenge and a possibility for immigrants and advocates. For those waiting in immigration detention, the years incarcerated are torture. This has been called the long hallway approach to asylum deterrence that simply places people in never-ending detention in the hopes that they simply give up and sign a deportation form.[8] However, additional cases, with competent lawyers presenting evidence and testimony, will drag out even longer, and for the people who are out on bond, this provides other opportunities for them to regularize (marriage, children reaching 21 years of age, etc.). If each case is met with full resistance, with lawyers fighting each motion, adding new possible defenses, presenting evidence from (multiple) experts, and appealing decisions, it will have huge consequences for the underfunded immigration court system.

ASYLUM AND THE CONVENTION
AGAINST TORTURE

While I will not provide an exhaustive overview of the asylum system, knowledge of its basic structure is important for understanding the precise ways that judges decide which types of fear are valid, and therefore whose life is valid. That being said, there are several conundrums for which I do not have the answer; above all, the seemingly random nature of immigrant detention. A recent ruling in the U.S. Supreme Court found that immigrants can be detained indefinitely, meaning that judges are not required to offer them periodic bond hearings.[9] Again, this hinges on the definition of immigration rulings as administrative and not criminal proceedings, despite the fact that deportation can have extreme consequences. However, every day, upon turning themselves into authorities to ask for asylum, some people are sent to "processing" centers while others are released with a "Notice to Appear." There are two thoughts on this. First, that it is based on who failed the initial review for asylum, known as credible fear or reasonable fear depending the individual's criminal and immigration history.[10] However, a closer look reveals that many people who pass this initial interview and are allowed to apply for asylum remain in detention. More likely—and this is the suspicion of activist organizations—it is simply a logistical issue, based on whether or not there is bed space available in detention. This has been one of the major shifts with the Trump administration, as more and more people are required to fight their cases from a detention center with limited access to information, legal aid, and help from relatives who often cannot visit because they themselves are undocumented.

If there is no space in detention, some asylum seekers are released with the opportunity to pursue their cases outside of detention; nevertheless, many of these individuals are given GPS-ankle monitors and subjected to other "alternatives to detention" such as home visits and randomized phone call check-ins. Moreover, these ankle monitors, known as *"grilletes"* in Spanish, have become so ubiquitous that individuals are often required to wear them even while they are in detention.

This is just one of the many random elements that appear in the course of any given asylum application. Scholars have referred to this system as refugee roulette because a favorable outcome has far less to do with individual circumstances than it has to do with luck or, perhaps more accurately, geopolitical factors far beyond one's control.[11] For instance, the country of origin is probably the strongest predictor of success. Chinese asylum seekers have a 21% denial rate, while refugees from Central America and Mexico face much more difficult odds. Seventy-seven percent of Guatemalans are denied, as are 80% of Hondurans, 83% of El Salvadorans, and 90% of Mexicans, the highest denial rate of any country in the world.[12] This is largely due to the relationship between the United States and an asylum seeker's home country. In the case of China, our at times tense relationship regarding trade issues and human rights violations leads to more favorable views toward Chinese nationals seeking protections, whereas there is a persistent fear of opening the opportunity for millions of Mexicans or destabilizing the favorable relationship between the United States and Mexico. This is especially true as the Obama administration began (and the Trump administration continues) to convince Mexico to prevent Central American asylum seekers from easily reaching the United States through enforcement measures along Mexico's southern border.

The odds of a favorable outcome are even worse for people who do not have an attorney. Since this is not a criminal proceeding, lawyers are not provided by the state and must be hired, which has led to a shortage of competent immigration attorneys as well as to predatory practices. Notary publics often claim to be able to resolve an immigration case, but simply take people's money. In Latin America *notarios* have a significantly different role and often are able to practice law in many legal situations, whereas a notary public does not denote the same amount of skill and power in the United States. The difference in terms has become an extremely persistent point of exploitation.

The shortage in competent legal representation is further exacerbated for people in detention, who might be moved frequently and to remote areas. This makes it more expensive to meet with a lawyer face to face and get documents or conversations translated. These factors, as well as the general attitude of some judges that no one (at least from Latin America) is eligible for asylum, all cause many people who otherwise are afraid for their lives to never file for asylum in the first place. There are multiple barriers meant to drive people away from applying for asylum even before the opportunity to be heard in court. Substandard conditions in detention; officers at the ports of entry turning people back to Mexico or making people wait on the bridges; a general climate that labels refugees as "illegals" and lawbreakers—all contribute to this attrition. The system is designed not only to make it difficult for people to win, but to keep people out of the process in the first place. A single day's Master Calendar hearings demonstrate the multiple ways that people are systematically discouraged and weeded out of the asylum process.[13]

Today was strange—just women were in the courtroom.[14] At first there were 18 women, five wearing orange, one in red, and the rest in dark blue or gray jumpsuits. The room was full, and instead of women on the left and men on the right as customary, both sides of the room were filled with women. The courtroom itself is rather small, making it feel tight and overly intrusive with so many people there. Hanging on the wall was a print by Diego Rivera of a woman kneeling before calla lilies, and another picture I did not recognize of a woman brushing her hair. These images stood out in the drab, cramped prefab room with no windows, striking an odd tone. I was seated behind the only woman in red in the courtroom. She was shaking nervously, bouncing her feet up and down, clutching onto some papers, fidgeting. There was a tattoo of a sword on her forearm and the name of a loved one next to it. The judges went through some of the cases and dismissed a handful of people who did not speak English or Spanish, including several indigenous women from Guatemala and one Brazilian.

The ICE attorney, a young woman with glasses, sat at her table to the left of the judge, the translator sat at his left hand and one table remained open for the respondent or lawyer. There were only two lawyers that day and their clients were addressed first: one was attempting to get Cancellation of Removal and the other was a victim of Female Genital Mutilation in Guinea. The judge scolded both lawyers for not filling out the appropriate paperwork and one did not even know her client's preferred language.

The lawyers stepped out after their clients had been processed. Then the judge turned to the unrepresented "pro se" group, calling them up by their names and Alien numbers. Six requested more time to find a lawyer or for their absent attorneys to file paperwork. The judge called Armenia. She stood up to address him. She had no previous crossings, and a U.S. citizen sister. The judge asked, "Do you fear harm in your country of origin?" The translator repeated it. "Sí, Yes," she responded. "Will you pursue protection through the asylum system?" "No," said Armenia meekly. The judge ordered her deported to Honduras. This process repeats four more times. "Yes, I am afraid." "No, I will not seek protection." Only three decided they will claim asylum, and the judge ordered them to wait until the end.

He turned to the 23-year-old woman in red in front of me. Her name was Helena. She grew up in El Paso, and had gone to high school here, spoke fluent English, and had just given birth to twins six months ago. She looked tiny in the cramped courtroom, barely five feet tall and thin. She came to the United States at the age of one. The judge asked if she feared harm in Mexico. "I have never been to Mexico, so I don't know," mumbled Helena. He went over her criminal record, "It is not that bad. I won't go into it since there are people present, but it has something to do with the world's oldest profession," he said with a chuckle.

The judge looked at Helena's documents and saw that her father was a U.S. citizen and began questioning her about the specifics. "Was he a naturalized U.S. citizen? Was he naturalized before or after you were born?" These distinctions mattered because she could become a citizen and not have to deal with the entire, complex asylum system, something that the judge was very keen on. Helena did not know the answers. "He wasn't around," said Helena. The judge asked if her mother could send an affidavit. "My mom won't answer me. She is undocumented and too afraid to help me." The judge looked upset, "I can't give you Cancellation of Removal because it is not considered a hardship to separate you from your children, even though they are six months old. The asylum process will take months or possibly a year too." Helena asked again if she could be released on bond, stressing that her babies were born premature. He responded, "Now, that makes me think you are not serious about the process if you only want to be released." Helena asked if she could just sign the deportation but the judge convinced her not to, stressing that she should get a lawyer, because she had a claim under violence against women (VAWA). She slunk back to her cell, demoralized and wiping away tears.

The last three, the only ones who asserted their rights to asylum, remained sitting in front. The judge turned to them and explained the four elements needed for asylum, giving an extremely pessimistic vision of asylum. "Nothing I see here would qualify you for asylum," he said, despite having spent less than a minute with each one. "You will need a lawyer. If you do not have one, I will treat you exactly how I would treat a lawyer. You need to have all of the documents presented in English and no one here could translate for you. It has to be done by a certified translator.[15] If you even meet the requirements it will take six to eight months." One woman asked about the possibility of being released. "It's possible, but again if your life were really in danger that would not be a concern," he replied. The women took the pamphlets offered them and filed out with tears streaming down their cheeks.

WHO IS PROTECTED? THE NEXUS

While this particular judge holds an extreme view of asylum, there is a wide range in opinions about how this system should be interpreted. However, some general background is needed to give this courtroom observation context. "A refugee is a person with a well-founded fear of persecution *on account of* race, political opinion, religion, nationality or membership in a particular social group."[16] While the first categories are easier to define, a protected social group (PSG) is far more complex. It must be immutable, meaning that you cannot change it. It has to represent a social distinction inasmuch as the rest of society will recognize you as pertaining to that group. It also must be particular, narrow, and homogenous, meaning that broadly defined groups of people are excluded. Some common PSGs include LGBT persons from countries that routinely persecute them, such as Uganda, Russia, and some Middle Eastern nations among others. Victims of domestic violence were also considered a PSG, until then-attorney general Jeff Sessions ruled that neither victims of domestic violence nor those targeted by gang and other "non-state" actors should receive protection.[17] It is too early to tell the overall impacts of this ruling. Another potent group are families who have been systematically targeted, meaning that if one or several family members have been targeted, then you can be protected because of your immutable association with them. Some other PSGs have met with limited success, including landowners, witnesses of crimes (whistleblowing as a political activity), small business owners being extorted, former police and bus drivers from Central America.

The important thing to remember is that violence cannot be specific to the individual. This is the most challenging aspect for refugees when giving an interview with the asylum officer. When asked why they are afraid, most people will name a specific person or group after them, never identifying this persecution as stemming from their membership in a particular group. There often is an underlying reason that can be reduced to a particular social group, but this is not always readily apparent, especially for people who have a limited understanding of how the asylum system works. Therefore violence specifically against you personally is not valid, as judges are quick to point out; only violence directed at a group is considered valid.

Moreover, the issue of internal relocation is frequently an issue. For example, for Mexican nationals, ICE attorneys always ask me if the respondent would be able to relocate to Mexico City or Cancun. Mexico is a large country and it is difficult to assert in all cases that someone could not safely relocate to another region of the country. However, certain issues such as long-standing regional animosities, and even the propensity to view deportees with years of experience in the United States as having an imputed "American" nationality, create complex layers of vulnerability for deportees attempting to relocate within Mexico as the previous chapters have clearly demonstrated.

Another form of protection, one that is, unlike asylum, available to everyone regardless of immigration or criminal history, is the Convention Against Torture (CAT). It states that "No State Party shall expel, return (*"refouler"*) or extradite a person to another state where there are substantial grounds for believing that he would be in danger of being subjected to torture."[18] This does not require a nexus, as with asylum; however, it requires much more explicit involvement of the state or, at the very least, extreme acquiescence from the state, who will not intervene to prevent torture from occurring. Another major difference is the protections people receive when they win. Those who win asylum are entitled to many benefits while people who win CAT will remain in a legal limbo, generally undeportable, but not eligible for citizenship or permanent residency.[19]

CONNECTING IMMIGRATION AND BORDER ENFORCEMENT TO ASYLUM

Most of the discussion of enforcement that has filled the pages of this book relates to the criminalizing apparatus of involving police and sheriffs departments in immigration enforcement activities, as well as prosecuting people for illegal entry and reentry through Operation Streamline. Recently, these processes have collided with asylum seekers in a particularly heinous way. The Trump administration's "zero tolerance" policy has led to criminal prosecutions of all undocumented immigrants before they are allowed to proceed to the asylum system. Once arrested, charged, and convicted, even for the first offense, a misdemeanor, they are incarcerated for as little as a week to several months, during which time they have been separated from their children. This happens because most asylum seekers prefer to cross into the United States and flag down a border patrol agent to whom they will claim fear of persecution to initiate asylum proceedings, rather than crossing the bridge and claiming fear at the point of entry.

There are a complicated set of reasons why crossing through the desert is so prevalent: general fear of the ports of entry, a suspicion that they will simply be sent back to Mexico, or perhaps it is at the behest of coyotes who charge to guide them only a few hundred yards into the United States. However, there are some legitimate reasons to cross through the desert or the river instead of through the ports of entry. At the time of this writing, there are several ongoing lawsuits that seek to determine whether or not the Trump administration can bar people who cross illegally from applying for asylum. Traditionally, however, there are more options for people who are "Entry Without Inspection" (EWI—crossed between ports of entry) than for those who are "Arriving Aliens" (AA—crossed at the port of entry). This includes the ability to request a voluntary departure, rather than a formal deportation, which will carry a ban on applying for a visa or other form of immigration relief.[20] Moreover, generally, Arriving Aliens have had a harder time getting out of detention since they may only be released at the discretion of ICE, whereas people who cross the border "illegally" may be granted a bond by an immigration judge.

This has been one of the principal issues that has confused the American public, journalists, and lawmakers alike. People simply do not realize that crossing the border and claiming fear to an authority is a legitimate way to initiate the asylum process. This lack of awareness is prevalent in the media—calling people "illegals" who, despite the technical inaccuracy of the term in a broad way, are in fact not engaged in anything even remotely illegal. They are pursuing their legal right to asylum. Necroliberalism demonstrates the process whereupon certain individuals and the classification of actions play a role in determining whether a life deserves to be saved, or whether it should be locked up, punished, and sent to a potential death.

In addition to these issues, there are the other insidious ways that the Trump administration has been limiting access to asylum. In coordination with new policies charging asylum seekers with misdemeanor illegal entry charges, Customs and Border Protections officials (Office of Field Operations [OFO]) have been stationed at the physical boundary of the United States to check people's papers before they are physically present on U.S. soil. Since the ports of entry are actually set back into the United States, once someone arrives at the port to claim fear they are already present in the United States (making them asylum seekers rather than refugees). There have been several attempts since Donald Trump was elected to discourage, turn back, or stop people from being physically present in the United States as a way to further decrease their access to asylum. Most notably were the mechanisms that returned people back to Mexico to wait for an appointment to process an asylum claim.[21] Claims are being made that "there is no room" and people must wait for an appointment, but this is likely false, especially since more room could be made by releasing people to pursue their cases. By making asylum seekers wait in border cities, it subjects them to the violence that I have discussed at length in this book and encourages them to cross between ports of entry out of desperation. This is a concerted strategy to prosecute and separate families, one that puts all of the abuses committed against immigrants from previous administrations to shame.

Oddly enough, despite the strange and convoluted interactions of various policies, practices, and two distinct legal systems, the Trump administration has (at times) blamed their systematic separation of children from their parents on coyotes. Officials have been claiming that coyotes are systematically placing unaccompanied minors with adults who are strangers in order to pretend to be a family unit and cheat the asylum system. "They are like slaves, they keep these kids and make them cross again and again," said an ICE agent, giving a tour of the processing facility in El Paso.[22] While any assertions of widespread asylum fraud should be taken with a great deal of skepticism considering how few people are actually granted asylum,[23] this claim has several layers of confusing misinformation. First, in all of my years working with migrants and smugglers I have never heard of coyotes forcing people together to make a joint asylum claim. People are generally aware that once you are in custody the relationships end, as you do not want to tie your future to anyone else. While it is not uncommon for people to fake familial relationships because those interpersonal relationships hold so much power and provide protection during the journey (see the previous chapter), this is generally not true once people cross.[24] Moreover, if, as this ICE agent says, children are being forced to cross multiple times pretending to be part of multiple fraudulent family units, it would be extremely easy to identify them, since processing includes fingerprinting and photography. In addition, one would expect a systematic process like this would significantly decrease the number of unaccompanied minors crossing the border. It has not.

No matter what the rationale, the separation of children fleeing violence from their parents is a horrific development in the ever-expanding Consequence Delivery System (CDS) approach. The idea of creating consequences for people for the sin of attempting to reunite with family members, earn a decent living, or even escape violence or death has sunk to a new depth, one that includes brutalizing children. While families have been separated by our immigration system for years, actively separating a family unit that has braved the dangerous journey and arrived at the border is a new development. There are reports of children as young as one-year-old being separated from their mothers, who are processed, charged, and incarcerated with no knowledge of where their children are located.[25]

At the heart of this practice is once again the CDS, which has been a central issue throughout this book. This approach to enforcement has created different levels of harsher and harsher punishments in order to make the process of immigrating so horrific that no one will attempt it. While many advocates and scholars have critiqued the "prevention through deterrence" narrative that began with Operation Gatekeeper, it has now morphed into something far more technocratic and individualistic that merits further examination. A better understanding of how necroliberalism constructs good and bad migrants, the deserving and the undeserving, and those deaths that will matter versus those that are forfeit will help our understanding of these processes. By sending asylum seekers who enter between ports of entry into Operation Streamline, the so-called "zero tolerance" court program designed to charge people en masse for entering the United States without inspection, it effectively veers refugees into the criminal system. Not only does this result in the separation of families, but it criminalizes them, making their asylum claims even more difficult.[26] The process of criminalizing migrants has reached new heights, effectively moving the bar yet again about what it means to be a criminal. This shifting legal terrain has caught many unawares concerning how their actions, once accepted as commonplace, can now result in months or even years of jail time and separation from their families.

A CALL TO SCHOLARS

I present this discussion, especially the overview of the legal landscape, not to suggest that this is how it should be, nor to assert that this is the only way to interpret asylum. It is not. There are many countries who draw from the same framework and have completely different interpretations of what constitutes violence and a nexus. However, plenty of organizations and scholars have challenged specific readings of asylum law and have attempted to shift the way the law is understood or interpreted.[27] That is not the goal of this final chapter. Rather, I present this discussion to help people understand the realities of a system that asylum seekers, lawyers, and "experts" must contend with. Further, despite the uphill battle, the asylum system and the immigration courts are one of the strongest options available to immigrants who fear persecution and deportation. This is a call for more academics and scholars to get involved and directly advocate for people in courts, providing much-needed documentation of the violence facing deportees in their home countries. For many scholars, our principal "public" activity is to critique policies and laws. While acting as an expert does not preclude this activity, it takes a wildly different shape, one where we are simply asked to provide our extensive empirical knowledge of situations facing deportees in other countries.

While this book has been directed at a wider audience concerned with the violence facing deportees, this chapter is also dedicated to my colleagues who have the tools and background knowledge to contribute in the courts. As academics, it is our job to step back and craft research that answers questions held by the broader community. In my case, this broader community also involves lawyers, both those challenging the practices and policies of immigration enforcement, but also those fighting individual cases and struggling to provide convincing evidence for a judicial system stacked against people seeking relief from removal. I want to present some of the challenges and pitfalls of doing this work, as well as the simple ways that academics are sometimes ill equipped to provide the types of answers necessary for a court setting.[28]

Academics have a role to play, one that requires a good deal of maneuvering to make it fit with our training and theoretical sensibilities, but could easily be included in our academic preparation.[29] First, as social scientists we attempt to generalize to a wider population, whereas courts are only concerned with the individual case at hand. I have had prosecutors attempt to pin down exactly how many people I have interviewed who were kidnapped in a precise way, within a one-year time period, coming from an exact shelter and crossing the border through one particular small town. Or going through a list of the thousands of municipalities in Mexico to ask if I had conducted research in each of them to be able to assert that that municipality would be a dangerous place to relocate an asylum seeker. However, perhaps more important than the awkward methodology of an expert social scientist in a court of law, are the complicated epistemological and ontological questions that we must face. The role of expert requires us to embrace a unique form of post-positivism.[30] Gone are the endless asterisks and nuances fundamental to contemporary scholarship, replaced by a necessity to seize and embody power in ways that we understand to be highly problematic. This means that empirical knowledge of the history, culture, and legal systems of the countries where we work takes on new significance. Moreover, as an expert, we are asked to present ourselves in a different way than as academics.

When I walk into a courtroom, my suit is pressed and my shoes shine. My watch matches my belt and I look like an expert. I revel in my status of the moment, soaking it up and overtly trying to convince the courtroom of it as I speak. I embrace and exploit my whiteness, my masculinity, my physically imposing stature, heightening everything for the theatre of power. This space of the law, the courtroom, is a place of domination, of control, of power in action, the state reshaping its repressive apparatus. On the stand I embrace all the stereotypes, from dangerous foreign lands to the romantic ethnographer who risks life and limb to return with a profound truth that can be used to save the "natives." These words would cause a revolt in anthropology, but they can save lives.

This book sprang from the dilemma of scholarship in service of the people we study. How can we, as scholars who research vulnerable populations subject to violence and death, reconcile the standards and needs of our disciplines and simultaneously make our research matter for the people who share their stories with us? How can we explore the academic nuances of violence while aiding in the legal battles of those trapped in this milieu? How can we increase the utility of ethnographic research without compromising its depth, richness, and complexity? Many have wholeheartedly rejected the trope of the expert, asserting that this mantle denigrates local knowledge and reifies the hierarchy of formal education and the vanguardist tendencies of academia. However, we do not live in a vacuum, and this rejection can have the pernicious effect of forcing the valuable and powerful insights of ethnographers to disappear from many public debates. When facts and even reality are so frequently disregarded, we cannot afford to shed the trappings of power, expertise, and privilege that come with our profession and our credentials, knowing full well the problematic nature of embodying that power without reflection and praxis. We know to critique these constructs, but by removing ourselves from spheres where the power of expertise can lead to tangible change, we are doing a disservice to the people we work with and care about. This can include participation in the media, writing or speaking for nonacademic audiences, teaching outside of our universities, or, frequently, testifying. This is not to say that we should not be wary of the individual rewards and spotlights that develop around romantic stories of researchers that devolve into some sort of (generally) white savior. However, one can easily make the critique that a unique brand of celebrity culture within academia creates exactly these pitfalls, even for those who critique the colonial process of academics offering their "expert" views. Therefore, the balancing act between centering ourselves as researchers and experts versus highlighting the voices and opinions of those who participate in our work is a constant tension of contemporary ethnographies.

These are only a few of the potential pitfalls. With such high stakes, however, we must fully engage in the messy world of action, reflection, critique, and analysis simultaneously. The victory of Trump and his xenophobic platform has created a clamor for more applied or activist engagement by academics. Critical, long-term engagement is of the utmost importance as we must avoid the desire to jump from one "hot" topic to another. This will require both shifting the prestige hierarchy of working outside of academia and addressing the slow, laborious, and frustrating process of making our academic labor compatible with the needs of more dynamic perspectives of advocates, who also arrive with epistemic baggage and constraints of their own.

The future is bleak as I write these words. I do not know what is in store, but one thing is for sure: if the planned mass removals and eliminations of protections proceed, the violence toward those deportees will only escalate. If we lose protections such as the Convention Against Torture (CAT) or asylum in general, then we will have to find new avenues to resist, create, and maintain public outcry or simply mitigate the disaster at hand. For now, the likelihood of any sensible immigration reform is extremely low; therefore these legal avenues remain one of the most important venues of resistance. Before, many people were content to accept deportation and attempt to cross back. Now, they are fighting, investing in their futures and facing the daunting legal system. As individuals there is not much hope for success, but as the numbers of cases pile up and the appeals drag each case on for several years, nothing will alleviate that pressure but meaningful reform. Hopefully, this book can help expand people's understandings of the violence of deportation and the impacts of the current approach to deportation in the United States, providing important points for arguing that people legitimately face harm and torture if deported. It will be a long road, but one of the major paths toward reform will be the court system collapsing under the weight of millions of immigration cases.

SEEKING ASYLUM AND SEPARATING FAMILIES: A NOTE FROM A NEW FATHER

I spent my first Father's Day with over a thousand people who were marching on the detention center being constructed in Tornillo, Texas. This tent city, a makeshift camp to house children, is yet another example of the approach of the Trump administration: equal parts cruel and incompetent, taking action with little or no understanding or knowledge of logistics, consequences, or even, ironically, the law. It is hot outside; at barely 9:00 a.m., the temperature already hovers near 100 degrees. My nine-month-old son Oliver keeps throwing off the hat we borrowed from a friend. He starts to cry and squirm. My wife begins to nurse him, leaning against the chain-link fence that separates us from the tent city. It is a painful reminder of the sustenance and love only a mother can give, and that which is being withheld. At the time, we were deep in the family separation crisis that the Trump administration began in El Paso, Texas. As I write this, there are almost 15,000 children still in Tornillo and hundreds of children who have yet to be reunited with their parents.

I have not known how to respond to this intolerably cruel practice of separating families, and it is clear that my usual analytical framework is not sufficient. I became a father during the course of writing this book, and despite many years of researching violence in Mexico, of interviewing and witnessing the often gruesome stories depicted in this book, there is something uniquely painful about this tragedy. While other administrations have caused the separation of families, none have done so in such an explicitly inhumane way.

Therefore, I write this section as a father and not as an academic. I look at my beautiful child and his amazing mother who provides him with so much love and care that I cannot help but feel a deep despair at the fact that there are children in this world whom our government would deliberately deprive of such love and care. Oliver was lucky enough to be born on this side of the border, as was I. His mother, Carla, was also born in the United States, but was raised entirely in Mexico. Like many children, he will grow up in a bilingual, bicultural household and it is my hope that he knows both the United States and Mexico as his home. I fear, however, that this will make him feel split in two by one country that hates and fears the other. The roll of the dice that decided to whom and where he was born has entitled him to the basic human dignity and protection of his parents. How can we deprive other children of that dignity simply because their parents dared to seek help or were born on the wrong side of a line? When people come to the United States looking for help, how can we justify punishing them for it? If ever there was a time to reflect on the moral heart of our nation, this is it.

Conclusions

Requiem for the Removed

"His name was Ezikiel Hernandez, I think. He was one of the first to build his house, his *nongo* here," said Ramon. "He loved his dog." A large brindle mutt that looked as much Saint Bernard as Pit Bull greeted us. We stood on the sand banks that washed up near the border in the concrete canal known to Tijuanenses as "el Bordo." A group of deportees was trying to figure out who their late friend and companion really was.

Hugo, a local activist, had been trying to find next of kin since they found him dead in his makeshift tent last week. Unfortunately there were a lot of people with the same name, and without his birthdate or the specific hometown it would be hard to find out who he really was before.[1]

Who was he before he was deported, before he came to live here in an urban river of sewage? This zone of human suffering, where people come to escape the pain of banishment, is located right in the shadow of the country many still call home. About a thousand homeless people, more than 90 percent of whom were deported from the United States,[2] lived directly under the American flag flying at the border wall. These are the socially dead, neither Mexican nor American. They have essentially become nothing in the months and years since removal. This open-air drug market, where people shoot heroin and smoke meth to even out the high, is a refuge of exclusion that leaves us wondering about the potentially worldwide impacts of mass deportation.

The Bordo is a unique, if complex example with which to open the concluding remarks of this book. Studies from Laura Velasco and Sandra Albicker at the Colegio de la Frontera (COLEF) in Tijuana show that this population, aside from being largely made up of deportees, is filled with people who have long histories in the United States, with higher-than-average levels of education, bilingualism, and of course, felony convictions.[3] They are mostly older, and many were regularized under the Immigration Reform and Control Act (IRCA), only to be removed at a subsequent date as a result of criminal convictions. Although many started using drugs before deportation, removal resulted in what is known as "switching," whereupon deportees began using different types of drugs, often more serious forms.[4] One deportee explained to me, "I had done cocaine in the U.S. but it wasn't until I was deported that I met crystal (methamphetamine)."[5] While being careful to acknowledge the complex factors that lead to addiction and drug abuse, I want us to question how the trauma of removal and banishment contributes to these tendencies. Could the Dreamers become the rejects and drug addicts of the Bordo de Tijuana? The disruption from place, the violence and the rejection of forced movement, sending people back to the country where they were born but no longer know, has an extremely harmful effect on people.[6] Many arrive at the border knowing nothing about Mexico and often without any form of identification. For longtime U.S. residents like the Dreamers they are essentially stateless people with no record of their existence in their former home and banned from the place they know. Like Ezekiel Hernandez, how many will be lost in those currents with no one to identify them and tell their stories?

This is not to say that people do not or cannot return to Mexico—many do, particularly those who did not put down strong roots in the United States. For people who successfully partitioned their social lives from the economic tasks and labor of migration, it becomes easier to leave and return to family and friends back home. However, for those who distance themselves from the strict purpose of economic migration—working to improve their lives in an often-distant country—

the return becomes more problematic. In this book we have followed a number of people throughout their deportation journeys, but what happens next? Why is it that some can return to Mexico and reintegrate into the population while others, such as those that live in the Bordo, are unable to adapt? To fully answer this question will require years of additional research, as well as greater attention to the impacts of deportation as it relates to conversations about stigma,[7] mental health,[8] and addiction.[9]

This book has chronicled the ways deportation has become intertwined with Mexico's violent conflict. The twin processes of mass removal and the turmoil created by a militarized crackdown on drug traffickers have produced a toxic cocktail of violence that has placed migrants and deportees in a particularly precarious situation. This highlights how a nonstate form of structural power controls much of the border, with unwritten rules for the illegal world that one must learn in order to understand and navigate the region. The disturbing result of this unstable environment is the unique way in which people in movement are exposed to violence in extreme forms. To be identified as a migrant is essentially to be a dislocated human being. Migrants are always defined as from or belonging to somewhere else. This dislocated geography is at the heart of why violence against migrants persists. Deportees are particularly vulnerable as they are often classified as failed migrants, where the rhetoric of the romanticized migrant evaporates and their own government treats them as a problem, or even something to be feared.[10]

This link between movement and violence leaves us in a challenging position. We have a vocabulary for the casualties of the drug war in Mexico. Researchers have discussed *jovenicidio* and *feminicidio* as the targeted killing of youths and women respectively[11], even showing that the high mortality rate among young men has decreased the life expectancy on a national scale in Mexico.[12] We discuss the disappeared people, exploring the impacts of ambiguous loss on the families of drug war victims, but we have a problem when it comes to identifying those who disappear while migrating. This classification problem means that we can often lump victims of diverse geopolitical phenomena together, blurring the lines between conflict and forced movement. However, as Oscar Misael Hernández asks, when should we start talking about *migranticidio?* Being killed because one is a migrant may be a new phenomenon, but it is also an extension of decades of mistreatment and abuse. Moreover, this trend seems to be exploding worldwide.

Recent videos of migrants being tortured by whipping and being burned in Libya echo the horrors of migration in Mexico.[13] Moreover, as increased enforcement in the Mediterranean has halted migrant journeys in Africa, evidence from Libya shows that migrants have been sold as slaves. The violence associated with the mass movement of people, both those fleeing conflict and poverty, has been climbing steadily. Around the world, the massacres of the Rohingya[14] and the refusal to aid Syrian refugees are further examples of the ease with which extreme violence and lack of compassion surround migrants. Reece Jones has discussed the inherent violence in borders, where intensely militarized controls have become the norm.[15] He outlines not only the historical precedents for partitioning space and the violence of designating who is inside and who is outside the body politic, but also the ways in which those permissions and prohibitions have evolved over time. For refugees, their movement, itself the very thing that can save their lives, has been consistently hampered or halted by authorities without reflection on the damage this causes. Alison Mountz has discussed the ways asylum seekers are pushed back, offshore, as states designate certain islands as "extraterritorial," which prevents people from arriving there and being able to claim asylum.[16] To those who cite security concerns regarding refugees and immigrants, there is little to no evidence of dangerous individuals infiltrating Western countries through the long, arduous, expensive, and nearly impenetrable asylum system. There are far easier avenues for migration for anyone of means.

With wait times in the years, and the potential to spend months or even years in immigration detention awaiting trial, declaring asylum is the least attractive avenue to migrate. This has been dubbed the "long hallway" approach.[17] By creating a long and uncertain process, akin to walking down a long tunnel that you cannot see the end of, it encourages people to give up. For those who arrive at a port of entry at our southern border, one must first convince an agent that this is a viable plea for help and get them to initiate asylum proceedings, something that has become increasingly challenging. Agents frequently deny asylum seekers, telling them that we are no longer accepting people or they must make an appointment months in advance.[18] If people are able to initiate an asylum claim, they are generally sent to one of the immigration detention centers for months or years awaiting trial. Those with resources or contacts can hire a lawyer, and those who cannot have almost zero chance of getting bonded out, much less winning an asylum claim. The legal process itself is long, costly, and difficult. As with undocumented migration, asylum is simply not a process that anyone who is not absolutely desperate will attempt. The dangers outlined in this book make a clear case for a reexamination of the reality faced by deportees upon return to Mexico, one that lawmakers and judges should take into account.

POLICY IMPLICATIONS

This book places a dilemma before lawmakers, judges, and prosecutors. I have argued that the processes of removal are inherently violent and place people in an inordinate amount of danger. There are many things that could be done from a policy perspective to either expand our definitions of danger, torture, and violence to include more people who are facing removal, or to simply provide additional legal avenues to migrate. It always bears repeating that for everyone who would push people to "come legally" or "get in line," for poor people throughout Latin America, there is no line. The most common form of migration is through family petitions, but contrary to claims made by the Trump administration, these visas are limited to immediate family and will generally take decades to be processed, especially if the applicant is from Mexico.[19] The attack on so-called "chain migration" is really an attack on the fundamental idea of immigration law in the United States: all families deserve the right to be together. This was in fact the unifying principle of our original immigration laws,[20] but has been slowly eroded due to the increased criminalization of migration.

Getting officials and lawmakers to recognize these concerns will be a long battle. On one level, this will require constant political and social pressure to recognize people's families as being important units, to create more favorable conditions for refugees, and to halt or reduce the criminalization of migration. However, this places a dilemma in front of policy makers and advocates: Do we work to try and improve the conditions of deportation, making it safer and easier to return to one's country of birth, or do we concentrate our efforts in using this danger as an argument to slow or stop removals of people afraid to return? Is it defeatist to ameliorate conditions in Mexico for deportees? In an important way, protecting Mexican nationals upon repatriation to Mexico should be the purview of the Mexican government, and yet, why is it so haphazard, varied, and often managed by NGOs, churches, or by the state government instead of the national government? This inertia hinges on the lack of connection of deportees, especially as people are arriving who have spent more and more time in the United States and have fewer and fewer ties to Mexico.[21] Scholars, advocates, and activists must be engaged on multiple fronts, not just through the provision of services but challenging these larger narratives of "unbelonging" that surround migrants. While making it safer for returnees could hurt asylum claims, the fact of the matter is that very few of the hundreds of thousands of people being removed annually want to pursue such an option. Moreover, the high burden for asylum makes it unlikely that these conditions alone would be sufficient grounds for relief.

It is important, therefore, to recognize the conflicting motivations, desires, and goals of migrants. Most people would never entertain applying for asylum, due to the weeks if not years in detention, or at the least showing up to court and paying thousands of dollars for legal counsel. Challenging the myth that asylum itself is easily abused and that it is full of frivolous appeals is important, not only for those seeking to exclude immigrants, but also for advocates whose interactions consist almost entirely of people already part of that system.

This research, combining random sample surveys with ethnography, helps grapple with the distinct populations among deportees, each with diverse motives and circumstances. Those with strong ties who consider the United States and not Mexico as their home will fight to stay, or will cross back at all costs.[22] Others see migration in economic terms: being detained for long periods or fighting charges in immigration court is an economically unproductive activity when families in Mexico will be forced to provide for themselves. Many migrants I interviewed stated they would prefer temporary work visas above everything else. They hate their life in the United States, and describe it as a process of suffering. Every pitiful taco and chewy, store-bought tortilla only solidifies their desire to return home. This is not to suggest that temporary work visas are the solution, far from it. The reliance on work visas opens people up to exploitation by employers and does not let people change their minds about the length of stay or their place in the world. However, we need to be cognizant of the multitude of desires and goals that shape human mobility. One way to shed light on these issues is to follow people after they are returned to Mexico in the weeks, months, and years after removal. What happens? How are they treated and how do they handle the challenges of migration and deportation over the years? The various trajectories of the people in this book can shed a light on some of the long-term issues facing deportees.

ZACATECAS AND MONTERREY

These two friends and roommates spent a few months in Nuevo Laredo, until jealousy about Antonia, the woman who diverted Zacatecas away from joining the Zetas, led to them parting ways. Monterrey successfully crossed the river and spent a few more months living and working in Laredo, Texas, before braving the walk around the checkpoint on

I-35. He bounced around for about a year, not spending more than a few months anywhere: San Antonio, Houston, North Carolina, Illinois, North Dakota, Tennessee. He met a woman named Heide who had grown up in Mexico but was a U.S. citizen. She wanted to go back to Brownsville, Texas, where she was from to finish school but Monterrey had a difficult time finding work in the depressed border economy. He was caught driving his truck through a checkpoint and deported again. The pair returned to Monterrey, Nuevo Leon, to visit his family, but tensions were increasing as they had almost no income and were unable to find a stable place to live and work. They split up and she returned to the United States, but he was unsuccessful in his attempts to cross and is currently living in Nuevo Laredo again.

Zacatecas, on the other hand, stayed with Antonia in Nuevo Laredo until she left to cross with another man.[23] He crossed again but was apprehended and incarcerated due to his prior DUIs. He was deported and found himself in Nuevo Laredo once again with his old friend Monterrey. They met up to share resources and live the border deportee life once again. Antonia and Zacatecas again reunited, but only time will tell if they can remain together.

LÁZARO

Most of the people at the shelter in Nuevo Laredo moved on quickly after my fieldwork. On each return visit, there were fewer and fewer familiar faces. There have been a total of six different directors over the course of this research. In 2017, Lázaro left and began working at another shelter in central Mexico that caters only to special cases, helping people transition back to life in Mexico. After six years on the border during some of the most intense violence, it had an impact on him. The trauma of seeing the young man from Sinaloa beaten, bloodied, and naked sticks with him. "I had those images in my mind, of what happened in front of me," he said, still angry about the many times he witnessed police and military collaborating with organized crime. "[People know] how dan-

Figure 8. Tijuana, Baja California, Mexico. A man sleeps in an alley next to a busy street in the Zona Norte of Tijuana. Photo by Jeremy Slack.

gerous and risky it is to be deported now, without money, without identification, practically completely vulnerable! They can't get money or anything. If they ask for a favor from someone they are exposed to get robbed. But no, for me, I would panic to be in their place."

When asked what the government could do, he explained, "People come back here without knowing their country anymore. They have roots here, but living in the U.S. they already took all the culture, the way to live. By right, they are gringos now. How can you take everything from them?"[24] The U.S. government must understand that despite the labyrinthine immigration laws, the simple truth is that after decades of life in the United States, people now belong there.

For Mexico, "the security ... is horrible, man. It is difficult and insecurity is advancing all the time and more and more during the elections. Organized crime is dominating again. There are no options. One, you go to the United States, or second, you get into organized crime. It won't end."

WHERE DO WE GO FROM HERE?

In an age of vehement anti-immigrant scapegoating and paranoia about foreign criminals, it might seem a mistake to focus so much of this book on individuals who have criminal records rather than on the thousands of deportees with no criminal history. We know that noncitizens are less likely to break the law,[25] and yet that discourse has fallen flat. Many people will simply shrug and say, "What's the problem then? If they don't commit crimes then they will be fine." This does not acknowledge the myriad ways that people are labeled as criminals, often for benign or administrative violations.

There are already tomes about migration, written exclusively about that immigrant subject, the one lauded by the Left as the perfect *homo economicus,* family "man", valedictorian, entrepreneur, and so on. Unfortunately, these stories do not simply make immigrants more sympathetic; they also create an impossibly high standard. For people like Zacatecas and Monterrey with DUI charges and illegal entry charges, they will never be considered a national treasure as far as the discourse around the Dreamers is concerned; however, they are also not a significant threat. They are human beings like all others and deserve the right to work and get ahead in life.

We need to develop an alternative script to criminalization, one based on the connected nature of deportees to their communities in the United States. Simple mea culpas about the lack of crime among immigrants allows for the creep of criminalization to take hold. More and more people are successfully labeled criminals without attention to the nuances of changing understandings of what constitutes a crime. Most of the individuals whose stories you have just read have deep connections to the country that just expelled them, resulting in painful ruptures in families and lives. As scholars, we need to embrace an alternative approach—one that recognizes the failings of some immigrants, and also recognizes the basic fact that immigrants belong here: they have ties and families, and deportation causes immense emotional and physical harm. This raises the question of belonging to a place. Giving the state absolute authority to decide who is and who is not allowed in a particular place as part of group of citizens is fraught with complications and will undoubtedly stoke racial tensions for decades to come.[26] However, it is extremely common for courts to decide in favor of the status quo, meaning that if you have been living in a house for decades, farming or ranching on land, or have been in possession of something, even something as abstract as information, then generally the case can be made that you are the rightful owner. Why is it different for people who have lived in the United States for decades? At what point can we simply accept that someone belongs? Ten years? Twenty years? Thirty years?

The arcane, confusing, and highly subjective rules of immigration law relied upon to decide who does and who does not belong are remnants of older times. We were once interested both in selectively allowing quotas of people from specific nations (for explicitly racist purposes), but also, we placed a premium on keeping families together. Neither of these constructs should escape interrogation. When does the regulation of immigration become a mask for far-reaching policies of racial exclusion and disenfranchisement, as was evidenced with the quota system? Who has the right to decide who truly belongs and who should be expelled? What constitutes a legitimate family and how can we reinforce the basic right to be with loved ones? By questioning the very notion of the state as the sole grantor of legal status, it forces us to abandon stereotypical notions of the "deserving" immigrant that leave behind the complicated, human, and flawed individuals.

Let me leave with a last story that helps us to question notions of where people belong even after breaking the law:

> Ramiro grew up in Compton in the '80s and '90s and joined the Compton 155 street gang while in high school. "We did not do much, other than drink and tag stuff, but we felt like we were hard," he explained. However, Ramiro decided he needed a change and joined the army, serving in the 82nd Airborne. He had been in the United States since he was seven and had been naturalized as a Lawful Permanent Resident when he was a teenager.

After serving in the military he was arrested and charged with illegal discharge of a firearm. He served three years in prison and upon release he was deported to Mexico. While his army service could have allowed him to naturalize and become a citizen, he had not felt it necessary and was shocked to find out that he was to be removed to Mexico with a lifetime ban. His young daughter and wife still in Los Angeles, Ramiro struggled to make a life in Tijuana. He worked in an old folks home for a while in Rosarito, but ended up struggling with substance abuse, getting addicted to crystal meth. Ramiro speaks English better than Spanish, has his entire family in the United States, and spent his entire adult life there. He has an infectious smile and laugh, with his grin lighting up his round face from underneath a small mustache. "I know I screwed up, but I paid my dues and did my time, three years in prison. I was in detention for a year fighting my case. The judge said that if I had served in combat he would allow me to stay in the United States ... At the end of the day, I am an honorably discharged veteran and when I die, I will die as an American."

I present this story to close the book as a reminder of the profound challenge of immigration. On the Right and the Left, few people would struggle to argue that a man with a felony conviction and substance abuse should not be deported; however, his profound connection to the United States, exemplified by his service in the military, makes us question the linkage between crime and deportation. The pro-immigrant Left has turned a blind eye to the complicated cases of drug addicts and criminals who, while a minority, do exist among undocumented immigrants. To discuss such cases is considered heresy, giving fodder to the anti-immigrant Right. And yet, this book is full of these complex and difficult stories, such as Don Gerardo, with a history of breaking and entering and 25 years in jails and then being deported to a country he no longer knows. I hope this book will push us to have a deeper conversation about what it means to remove people from the country, regardless of their criminal history.

Scholars have focused on the exponential growth of removable offenses,[27] or even how removal leads to greater contact with crime and criminality.[28] However, very rarely do we discuss what should be done with the thousands of people with serious convictions. Where do they belong? Should we continue policies of removal that often simply out-source the problems of crime created by our racial and class systems, pushing the problem to Mexico, which exacerbates the already tenuous security situation? The types of upbringings that lead people like Ram-iro to join a gang are uniquely American. At what point do we take responsibility for those immigrants who grew up in the United States, with its inadequate schools, segregated neighborhoods, and racially charged atmospheres? Deportation, in many ways, represents the ulti-mate dream of turbocharged law enforcement in the United States—lock them up and then remove them from society forever. The ability to drop people off on the other side of the line, the place where the map is blank, is the dream of the law and order contingent. If only we could excise all lawbreakers from the body politic (provided they are the right color)! This already mimics many of our other treatments of criminals, as we have removed their right to vote for long periods, curtailed their move-ment under parole, limited employment options, reduced school options or removed student aid, or even restricted their ability to rent a home.

We can add deportation to this laundry list of consequences related to criminal convictions and incarceration. However, as the brilliant work of Daniel Kanstroom shows, deportation and immigration law more broadly is able to operate in such a distinct legal milieu because removal is not viewed as a punishment, but as an administrative action.[29] At its core, the principal argument of this book is that removal is a harmful, dangerous, and inhumane process, one made worse by our converging drug and labor prohibitions. Yes, both Mexico and the United States should work to decrease the danger created by the actual process of removal, but there is a deeper challenge here; namely, deportation should not be a first resort. Currently the burden of proof is on the indi-vidual, and not the state as it is in criminal court; therefore individuals must prove they should not be removed, rather than the state proving that they deserve to be removed. It is no surprise that people rarely actually win an asylum claim in the courts.

CONCLUSIONS

The overlapping categories of refugee, displaced person, victim of civil conflict, and migrant must be parsed out, often alongside painstaking work to identify, investigate, and interrogate how people died and why.[30] And yet, this becomes even more complicated in situations of active conflict, where journalism is hampered and access to information is limited. The danger present for activists and advocates working to provide answers or even direct aid in these situations is often intense. In the research presented here about Mexico, the risks of aiding migrants have significantly limited the scope and effectiveness of possible actions. In order to stay afloat, many organizations completely remove themselves from politics and human rights conversations, focusing instead on providing immediate services such as food, shelter, and clothing. At one shelter in the Northeast, a member of the Zetas put a gun to the priest's head and told him that under no circumstances should anyone enter or exit the shelter after 8:30 p.m. The priest complied. These curfews and controls of the migrant population have become emblematic of the dangers of migration and the intense controls of mobility that exist along Mexico's northern border. And yet, the United States continues its march toward increased criminalization and deportation, removing people for simple infractions such as driving without a license or other traffic-related offenses.

The dream of fascism is to locate and eradicate the possibility of danger by excising a particular group of individuals. This implies that only specific types of victims and criminals matter, which is evidenced by the Trump administration's efforts to highlight victims of crimes committed by immigrants, and set up hotlines to report immigrant crime. As Lisa Marie Cacho illustrates, however, these attempts to crack down on specific groups of people inevitably cross into the rest of the population. It is only when the white, wealthy, and suburban individuals become the victims and not the perpetrators that the injustice of this draconian project is visible.[31] It will take decades to sort through the violence that has been done, both in terms of the death, disappearance, and destruction in Mexico and the millions of people whose lives have been upended by immigration policies. Children growing up without their parents will not forget this injustice. The relatives of the dead will eventually search for answers and, with any hope, hold people accountable and demand real and lasting change in both the United States and Mexico. If not, then the slums of el Bordo, where broken people are left to die with no way of knowing who they really were, may become the norm for expelled people all around the world. As the mass movement of people across borders becomes increasingly violent and dangerous we must stop to consider the true consequences of militarized borders and deportation of people with legitimate fear of persecution. Not only does the violence of forced removal place people in extreme danger, separating families and banishing people from the place they call home, it exacerbates a complex and volatile conflict in Mexico.

However, not all is hopeless: after fourteen years of fighting to return to the country he calls home, to the country he served, Ramiro was given his citizenship. This required a pardon by the governor of California followed by two more years of court battles, assistance by the ACLU and numerous expert witnesses. His high-profile activism made this victory possible, as members of the Senate and Congress had come to visit the organization he ran, a support house for other deported veterans. He bore the brunt of years of accusations, insults, and threats but he persevered. Not everyone will have the profile or the unique circumstances, but his story is a reminder that despite the daunting nature of the problem, the only way to change it is by not giving up.

A NOTE ON RESEARCHING IN
VIOLENT ENVIRONMENTS

I wanted to add a note in this book for current and future scholars who may follow some of the same paths that I have, negotiating challenging environments and attempting to understand, shed light on, and hopefully stop some of the darker practices in the world. It is tempting as scholars for us to idealize these research experiences, portraying ourselves as social justice crusaders cloaked in a bravado that obscures the challenges, stress, and emotional toll that is exacted upon our loved ones and ourselves. There is rarely a space for us to discuss these challenges, and it does a disservice to the next generation of researchers who are thrown into the deep end in accordance with the sink-or-swim mentality that permeates ethnographic training. The idea that some people can cut it and others cannot is ludicrous, dangerous, and hubristic. No one successfully navigates a project on the extreme forms of violence such as are documented in this book without a well-developed cultural understanding of the region, excellent language skills, and most importantly, support both locally and at one's home institution. I learned this as I bounced around during graduate school, spending a summer researching in the City of God in Rio de Janeiro. I already spoke Portuguese well, but lacked the understanding of civil society, government, and history that I had developed in the years I spent in northern Mexico. This dissuaded me from jumping into a complicated morass of researchers (foreign and domestic), journalists, NGOs, and government officials who were all carving out their own niches while trying to come to terms with crime, violence, and drugs in Brazil. I returned to Mexico just before the violence began to erupt in previously unheard-of ways. Already situated as a researcher along the Arizona / Sonora border I was in a unique position to develop a research project that was able to wrestle with the chaotic world that was being reshaped around us daily.

After about five years of working in Nogales, Sonora, my colleagues Daniel Martínez, Scott Whiteford, and I decided to expand our work to include many areas that had been hit even harder by violence such as Tamaulipas and Ciudad Juárez. It was both an opportune time and an extremely difficult one. Having lost ties with most universities on the U.S. side of the border due to travel bans, many Mexican academics and NGOs were eager for collaboration (even when financial support was limited). On the flip side, navigating the dangerous atmosphere was a constant concern.

I, as well as every other researcher and journalist at the time, spent hours watching gruesome videos of narco-killings posted on *Blog del Narco* and other blogs (I am particularly indebted to Michael Marizco's *Border Reporter* and the *Borderland Beat*, which were the best resources for information about Sonora), news sites, and government statistics. This served multiple purposes. First, it kept me up to date on what was happening (at least as much as was possible in the turbulence of those years), but perhaps most importantly it reminded me that what I was doing, and what I was studying, is not some abstract idea. It is not a curiosity or a fabrication of sensationalist media. This was and is a very real and dangerous place and time to be asking questions. Throughout the years doing this work I would constantly run into journalists and other academics who would explain to me why *they* were safe. Explanations ranged from practices in how they would report the news such as omitting names or details, to giving money and sodas to the kids acting as lookouts on the street corners who would warn them about impending danger. Each conversation had a hollow ring to it, and I left with more doubt than ever about safely being able to work in this atmosphere. Many of the people I spoke with quickly quit, moving to another state in Mexico or to the United States; others have been killed. This knowledge, the videos, and the personal stories I collected served as a constant reminder that one can minimize risk, but this is inherently a dangerous activity.

It reminded me of Werner Herzog's excellent film *Grizzly Man* about Timothy Treadwell's death, when he and his girlfriend were mauled to death by a grizzly bear. Much of Treadwell's work with the grizzlies reminded me of a certain kind of journalist, who would explain how other people were in danger but he was smarter, more skilled, and therefore immune to the danger around him (yes, usually but not always a him). Similarly, the people who have spoken out against Treadwell for "staying too late in the season," "interacting with an unknown bear rather than the ones who had grown accustomed to his presence," remind me of how people dissected the attacks and deaths of their comrades. Many have gone so far as to accuse murdered journalists of collaborating with drug cartels or simply of foolishly reporting things they should not have, raising questions about whether continuing as a journalist but not reporting on the violence and corruption is worth it. The simple fact of the matter is: It is a bear. It cannot be controlled or tamed and it will eat you if it feels like it. The same is true of drug trafficking in Mexico.

Of course, I too played the game of making sure my trips were planned, slowly introducing myself into dangerous contexts, talking with local key informants and following the general trends in violence and conflict. I used tracking apps to share my location, although they often drained my cellphone battery and thus I had to be mindful. I had race, gender, and nationality on my side and exploited it to full effect. My fear, at least my most pressing fear, was that people would associate me with law enforcement. As a tall white man I fit the stereotype. I was told a number of times I looked like a cop. I probably should have ditched the leather bomber jacket, but it was often freezing and I didn't have the time to replace it. The best I could do was be sympathetic, open, and transparent. I would never lie, but also sometimes put away my notepads and packed up my recorder, simply because the situation did not allow for it. I presented myself as a good-natured oddity, the gringo with good Spanish who could joke around and hang out in places others avoided.

I never forgot, though, that all of this was simply working around the edges of a fundamentally violent and chaotic world where life has little value. I never fooled myself that my actions created a legitimate form of protection; rather I was simply lowering the danger by a few percentage points, nothing more. I tried to write a letter in case something happened to me. I say "tried" because it was extremely difficult to finish. Thinking about leaving behind a posthumous statement became a terrifying proposition, which persisted in the back of my mind but also remained at the bottom of my to-do list. I never finished it.

The constant pressure of working in these environs also took its toll on me personally and professionally. On one particularly difficult research trip to Tamaulipas in 2012, the team of researchers had found that one of the agents from civil protection (the local organization that was giving rides to deportees) had kidnapped an elderly woman who was waiting for her son to be deported and forced her to perform oral sex on him. We discussed what to do. They had tried to get a recording of the woman's story but his threats to kill her, and his claim that he was a member of the Zetas, caused her to flee the city. The man was there every day around our team of researchers talking and laughing, continuing to kidnap women. He put his arm on my shoulder when I first met him. With the researchers in Tamaulipas so exposed because they lived there, we discussed whether or not I should go to the police station and report the abuse. Ultimately we decided that the danger was too great and the likelihood of actual action was too scarce to warrant action. I left crushed and sickened. When I got back to the University of Arizona in a few days, I simply could not stomach reading *Anti-Oedipus* and engaging in the typical pedantic grad school performance.

Throughout this research, which was often conducted a few nights a week in Mexico (about an hour away from school and home), I struggled with the push and pull of responsibilities in graduate school versus the deeply violent, personal, and destructive nature of this research. At first, it was the simple fact that our team of researchers, after spending hours interviewing people about their often near-death experiences attempting to cross the border, would simply pack up our folders, get in a car, and drive across it. The guilt associated with spending mere hours (and frequently complaining about the two-hour border line) for what takes days, thousands of dollars, and costs people's lives, was palpable at first. It did not last. After months and years of repeating this, it gets hard to sustain empathy. Faces and stories tend to blur together, the questions on the page become a wrote script—a phonetic compilation of sounds coming out of my mouth that people may struggle to understand while I struggle to recreate the same earnest conversations with feeling and empathy. The first two years were easier because we were a team, we would talk about the stories we heard on the long drive home, although at least a few people would always fall asleep before we arrived in Tucson at 12:00 or 1:00 a.m. This camaraderie was invaluable, and I can honestly say that I would not have been able to complete this project without the team members who showed up to do surveys over the years. Being alone in the field was a struggle, and bouncing between cities, each with its unique constraints and context, took its toll on me. I say this not to elicit sympathy, nor do I want to absolve myself of any bad behavior on my part, but rather as an acknowledgment to scholars engaging in or considering engaging in this type of work. It becomes too easy to return triumphant, crafting concise, clean articles, books, and presentations that wash out the human costs of studying violence.

This combination of, on the one hand, tragic, deeply personal, and violent experiences during fieldwork and, on the other, a university system that is simply not set up to accommodate or even value this type of work has become a constant theme in my life. I feel extremely fortunate to have been part of the Drugs, Security and Democracy (DSD) fellowship, because it provided access to a group of like-minded colleagues, almost all of whom were deeply engaged on the ground in similar situations. We have attempted to address these concerns about how to handle the emotional stress associated with this type of research. I have witnessed considerable attrition from my colleagues who find it too painful to write about and subsequently receive the cold, distanced anonymous critiques of peer review about these deeply personal subjects. Being connected to a network of scholars who experience similar types of trauma, violence, and loss while in the field was an invaluable part of my education. While I had close colleagues in my graduate cohort, many did not have a clear picture of what the work I do entails and it is hard to communicate such field experiences to some peers. I also quickly got tired of explaining it to people, as typical reactions made me feel like a crazy person or someone attempting to create a kind of masculine heroic image.

This discussion is not meant to prioritize the violence we are exposed to over the reality of death and violence that we document. However, immersing oneself in the suffering of others has a cost, often called secondary trauma.[1] Academia lacks a support structure to help the people who are doing this important work to cope with the process of conducting research and then, most importantly, how to write it up, publish it, and handle the critiques of our peers. This shortfall has caused so much important work to go unpublished and unreported. I hope there are more resources and networks for scholars who struggle through the messy, violent, and impotent feelings of conducting research. I wanted to write this note for everyone who comes back from research under the impression that it is easy for people to coherently analyze traumatic experiences, crafting succinct and elegant narratives out of tragedy. This process is always fraught, and it is a skill that needs development, and often, teaching and learning. Abandoning the idea that there are those who can and those who cannot, and instead returning to one of the fundamental roles of a scholar—to honestly engage in the challenges and costs of one's work, with an aim to write and teach honestly about it—is necessary for producing better research in violent contexts.

NOTES

CHAPTER ONE. THE VIOLENCE OF MOBILITY

1. Personal communication, January 15, 2015, and January 15, 2018.

2. Ureste 2015.

3. Kanstroom 2007.

4. Extortion, especially by authorities, has been a common problem for decades, but rarely if ever did it result in the level of violence such as torture or murder that has now become commonplace.

5. Gibler 2011.

6. Grayson 2010.

7. This and all other names are pseudonyms.

8. Personal communication, October 14, 2011.

9. Prior to 2006 it was uncommon for people to be charged with illegal entry and illegal reentry; instead, most people would sign a voluntary removal and be sent back to Mexico. Now people with illegal-entry charges are considered criminals and can be sent to prison, whereas people with voluntary removals only have administrative violations on their records.

10. Campbell 2011.

11. See O'Neill (2015) for an in-depth discussion of the intermingling of religion, security, and reform. There are some individuals such as Alejandro Solalinde who have become effective advocates for migrants, but most shelters are too afraid to engage in these activities, particularly those in regions with more organized crime.

12. Alexander 2012.

13. Lowen and Isaacs 2012; Gilmore 2006.

14. Alarcón and Becerra 2012.

15. Removals are always events, not people, so individuals may be counted multiple times in these figures. www.politicamigratoria.gob.mx/es_mx/SEGOB /Repatriacion_de_mexicanos_2007.

16. Alarcón and Becerra 2012.

17. Gutierrez 2012.

18. De León 2013; Slack et al. 2015; K. L. Hernandez 2010.

19. Hiemstra 2012.

20. Slack et al. 2015.

21. K. L. Hernandez 2010.

22. Jones 2016; Raeymaekers 2013.

23. Kanstroom 2007.

24. Ramji-Nogales, Schoenholtz, and Schrag 2007, 2011.

25. Marks 2014.

26. Marcus 1995; Gupta and Ferguson 1992.

27. These collaborators were important for developing the survey and / or conducting interviews in the different sites. However, the majority of this book stems from my ethnographic research that was during the same period, as well as for several years afterward. See the Acknowledgments and the appendix for a full description of this collaboration.

28. These surveys built on a smaller researcher project from 2007–09 that was run by Daniel Martínez and consisted of surveys in Nogales, Sonora (see Martínez et al. 2017). We received funding from the Ford Foundation to expand border-wide.

29. Slack et al. 2015; Slack et al. 2013; Martínez et al. 2017.

30. Field notes, November 5, 2013.

31. Nail 2015.

32. Nail 2015: 3.

33. See Brotherton and Barrios's (2011) discussion of social bulimia by Jock Young (1999).

34. Thompson 2017.

35. Tyner and Inwood 2014: 771.

36. Bustamante 2002, 2011.

37. De Genova 2002.

38. Cresswell 2006, 2010.

39. Spener 2009.

40. Andreas 2000.

41. The rapid process was initially thought to be mutually beneficial as most economic migrants from Mexico wanted to be released quickly to either return to Mexico or cross again. This has changed with the advent of harsh criminal charges.

42. Heyman 2001.

43. Andreas 2000.

44. Testimony of Michael J. Fisher, Chief, U.S. Border Patrol, U.S. Customs and Border Protection, before the House Committee on Homeland Security, Subcommittee on Border and Maritime Security: "Does Administrative Amnesty Harm Our Efforts to Gain and Maintain Operational Control of the Border?" *House Committee on Border and Martime Security*, Washington, DC, DHS, October 4, 2011.

45. Frankly, there are not many valid defenses to this charge, so it makes sense that there is very limited representation. Moreover, due to the cookie-cutter nature of the charges (as well as the expense) several public defender's offices have refused to take the misdemeanor illegal-entry charges, meaning that private lawyers are contracted to fulfill these duties.

46. Lydgate 2010.

47. Lydgate 2010; Kanstroom 2007, 2012.

48. Kanstroom 2007.

49. Martínez, Slack, and Martínez-Schuldt 2018.

50. Ibid.

51. See Hiemstra 2012.

52. Grillo 2011.

53. Nevins 2002.

54. Martínez et al. 2014.

55. Slack et al. 2016; Nevins and Aizeki 2008; Nevins 2002; Dunn 1996.

56. Espenshade 1995; Eschbach, Hagan, and Rodriguez 2003; Eschbach et al. 1999.

57. Hughes et al. 2017.

58. De León 2012, 2015.

59. Ibid.

60. Martínez et al. 2014.

61. Reineke and Anderson 2016; Martínez et al. 2014.

62. See Boss 2006.

63. Throughout this book I have tried my best to separate these stories. I never include secondhand stories or rumors unless I identify them as such,

relying only on things that happened directly to the people I was interviewing and doing my best to verify the facts whenever possible.

64. He may have been younger. Migrants often lie that they are older so they are able to travel more freely in Mexico, but once they arrive in the United States, they will admit they are minors, something more difficult to lie about.

65. Field notes, April 23, 2014.

66. Veterans were typically Lawful Permanent Residents (LPRs) who were eligible to naturalize, but never did. After a criminal conviction they were typically subject to removal due to the 1996 IIRAIRA laws.

67. Cacho 2012: 7.

68. Abrego et al. 2017.

69. Personal communication, May 8, 2014, Tijuana, Baja California.

70. There were several attempts to evict people, such as the 2013 eviction that led to a large encampment being set up nearby. However, in 2016 it seems to have been cleared out for good, with people dispersing into the rough, *Zona Norte* area of Tijuana.

CHAPTER TWO. I WANT TO CROSS
WITH A BACKPACK

1. Martínez et al. 2017.
2. Arreola 1993.
3. Chesnut 2012.
4. Price 2005.
5. Field notes, July 5, 2006.
6. Robles 2008.
7. Notimex 2008.
8. McCombs 2008.
9. Field notes, September 19, 2008.
10. Kristeva 1982.
11. As a researcher who had never considered studying drug cartels, these events created an ethically complicated space for research. Should one pursue predetermined research questions, ignoring the growing maelstrom that has radically changed the place where research is conducted? This would be a disservice to place and to the people we interact with every day, whose lives are impacted by this complex geopolitical struggle (see Starn 1991). However, directly engaging in research on such a violent and terrible conflict is simply beyond the scope

or ethical and individual boundaries for most researchers. Care must be taken not to simply parrot the meta-analysis and disjointed research of many typical armchair academics. How should we combine ethnographic research on an intense topic that, by definition, rejects observation and categorization?

12. A. Hernandez 2010.

13. Staff 2015.

14. Lopez 2009.

15. Castillo, Aranda, and Urrutia 2010.

16. Osorno 2012.

17. Staff 2017a; Maldonado Aranda 2012; Grayson and U.S. Army War College, Strategic Studies Institute 2010.

18. Martínez 2015.

19. See the interactive map at http://static.apps.cironline.org/border-seizures/.

20. Personal communication, Nogales, Sonora, February 4, 2010.

21. This and all other names are pseudonyms. Interview conducted with a deportees staying at a migrant shelter in Nogales, Sonora.

22. Personal communication, July 19, 2011.

23. Adapted from field notes, September 4, 2009. See also Slack and Whiteford 2011.

24. This has been confirmed from multiple sources, but I was not able to locate anyone who actually participated in the strike or negotiations.

25. Source MBCS Wave II.

26. Personal communication, May 27, 2014.

27. Izcara Palacios 2012a / b, 2014.

28. Spener 2009.

29. Slack et al. 2013.

30. Weber 1965.

31. Staff 2016a, b.

32. Named "porque te bajan todo" (because they take everything off of you).

33. Personal communication, April 8, 2010.

34. Personal communication, May 13, 2010.

35. Due to the sensitivity of this line of questioning, for the purposes of our surveys, we only asked about witnessing sexual violence against women. In one-on-one interviews, when appropriate, we did ask about personal experiences.

36. Personal communication, May 13, 2010.

37. El Diario, April 24, 2009.

38. Martínez 2013.

39. Worried about being identified as someone from enemy territory, he hid the fact that he was actually born in Michoacán.

40. All burreros I have met and interviewed are male and none of them had heard of a female burrero.

41. Other areas along the border such as the Valle de Juarez do rely on forced labor or individuals not well known locally to cross drugs more frequently because the trip is considerably shorter.

42. CBP 2015.

43. Personal communication, Nogales, Sonora, April 29, 2011.

CHAPTER THREE. *TE VAN A LEVANTAR*—
THEY WILL KIDNAP YOU

1. Chapter opener adapted from field notes, November 12, 2013.

2. Staff 2012b.

3. Izcara Palacios 2014.

4. Izcara Palacios 2014: 9.

5. See Spener 2009.

6. Field notes, December 7, 2013.

7. Personal communication, Nogales, Sonora, April 9, 2009.

8. Field notes, Nuevo Laredo, Tamaulipas, October 12, 2013.

9. Field notes, Tijuana, Baja California, July 2, 2012.

10. Personal communication, January 15, 2018.

11. Field notes, Nuevo Laredo, Tamaulipas, October 23, 2013.

12. Slack and Martínez n.d.

13. I met a few people who deliberately went on a bus to Reynosa on what is called a "viaje de primera" (a first-class trip), where they are registered with the drug cartels and are required to sit in a specific seat wearing specific clothes and this will ensure them safe passage. Other scholars such as Simon Izcara (2012) have raised questions about this practice but little is known about it.

14. This is not meant as a criticism. The aid is much needed and extremely important, especially in light of the thousands of deportees who arrive in Tijuana. However, the combination of social factors, especially for deportees who no longer have any roots in Mexico, makes it easy to get stuck living in this situation for months, even years.

15. Heyman, Núñez, and Talavera 2009; Núñez and Heyman 2007; De Genova 2002.

16. Personal communication, January 15, 2018.

17. Staff 2017c.

18. Personal communication, Tijuana, BC, May 8, 2014.

19. Personal communication, February 12, 2016.

20. It occurred to me later that he could have robbed the other migrants and I became worried, but no one reported any theft.

21. Personal communication, January 15, 2018.

22. Lowen and Isaacs 2012.

23. Adapted from field notes, November–December 2013.

CHAPTER FOUR. THEY TORTURE YOU
TO MAKE YOU LOSE FEELING

1. Juanito's life is still very much in the balance. To protect him, identifiable information has been removed from the chapter. It is important to note that he has been involved with the writing of his story. The decision to include graphic details of his experience is his. While there is a danger of falling into the trap of highly pornographic violence, the danger of sanitizing his story and eliminating the pain poses a greater threat. This chapter centers on Juanito's story to make it a personal form of violence, rather than a nameless, impersonal, and disembodied critique of horrors.

2. Staff 2017a.

3. Turati 2015.

4. Based on three years of ethnographic work with deportees in five Mexican cities, with a total of 27 kidnapping victims interviewed and 83 more surveyed.

5. While it is impossible to verify every aspect of Juanito's story, there was significant documentation including a chronology of his arrests and removal, a psychological evaluation that listed him as suffering from a "Major Depressive Episode" and PTSD (DSM—IV), and a medical examination that included documentation of scarring compatible with his descriptions of torture.

6. This is based on 1,010 post-deportation surveys in six Mexican cities with people who had crossed the border without papers and been apprehended and deported to Mexico. I will have a full methods section that explains this in the introduction to this book. For more detail see Slack et al. 2015.

7. Rose 2011.

8. CNDH 2011; Staff 2012.

9. INEGI 2017.

10. Ibid., www.beta.inegi.org.mx/contenidos/proyectos/enchogares/regulares /envipe/2017/doc/envipe2017_presentacion_nacional.pdf.

11. Isacson and Meyer 2013.

12. Comparison of CBP data, www.cbp.gov/sites/default/files/documents /USBP%20Stats%20FY2015%20sector%20profile.pdf; Instituto Nacional de Migración statistics, www.politicamigratoria.gob.mx/es_mx/SEGOB /Repatriacion_de_mexicanos_2015.

13. I want to thank Murphy Woodhouse for his work on this chapter, both in recording our interview with Juanito and in crafting a narrative out of this horrific story.

14. Budget cuts led to unexpected releases and removals.

15. Grupos Beta is the humanitarian arm of Mexico's National Immigration Institute.

16. Bowden and Cardona 2010; Gibler 2011; Magaloni 2003; Sicario, Molloy, and Bowden 2011.

17. Ureste 2015.

18. Wright 2005, 2006.

19. Juanito assured me that the young man from Ecuador who survived and told police about the massacre was not let go. The Zetas had not meant for him to survive.

20. Grayson 2010; Longmire 2011.

21. CNDH 2011.

22. Balderas 2016.

23. This is outlined in greater detail in the previous chapter.

24. Interview conducted by Murphy Woodhouse.

25. While little of this can be substantiated, there have been numerous reports of similar practices spreading throughout Mexico (see Aristegui 2014).

26. Shay 2003, 2010, 2014.

27. Gibler 2011.

28. Bourgois 2003; Muehlmann 2013.

29. Campbell 2009.

30. Muehlmann 2013.

31. I reviewed his medical documents that were the result of the broken leg. These records also contained documentation of his torture.

32. Slack and Martínez n.d.

33. Coronado and Orrenius 2003; Dingeman and Rumbaut 2010; Orrenius and Coronado 2005.

34. Cantor, Noferi, and Martínez 2015.

35. La Ley General de las Victimas (General Law of Victims) is intended to guarantee the human rights, protections, and access to justice for victims of violence in Mexico.

36. J. Martinez 2017.

CHAPTER FIVE. GUARDING THE RIVER

1. Field notes, Nuevo Laredo, Tamaulipas, December 10, 2013.

2. Meaning he was from Guadalajara, Jalisco, Mexico.

3. Massey, Durand, and Malone 2002.

4. This approach draws on feminist geopolitical frameworks from human geography (see Massaro and Williams 2013).

5. Osorno 2010, 2012.

6. Grillo 2011.

7. In my research it was largely state police in the Northeast who were engaged in this type of activity. However, that is based on information from only a handful of individuals who escaped or were let go, often leaving someone else behind.

8. Staff 2017d.

9. Vigil 2010.

10. Zilberg 2004.

11. Personal communication, August 1, 2012.

12. I did not quite know what to do so I gave him twenty dollars and offered him a ride to the bus station.

13. Hartsfield 2011.

14. Muehlmann 2013.

15. See Sicario and Bowden 2011.

16. Field notes, November 5, 2013.

17. It should be noted that I thought of just trying to pay for their tickets, but I did not have nearly enough money to pay for their travel, and did not want to send them across the country without any way to support themselves, knowing that it would be even more difficult for them to receive a money transfer later on than it was for me.

18. Meyers 2003.

19. I should note that the only person who could speak to his involvement was Vanda.

20. Personal communication, January 15, 2018.

21. Zaitch 2002, 2005.

22. This made it extremely hard to get firsthand accounts of people who joined the Zetas, at least in the context of my fieldwork. Once people joined, even those I knew fairly well would disappear.

23. Reineke 2016.

24. For some reason, Joaquin "El Chapo" Guzmán's fame made many people directly attribute their work to him. No one else got this recognition; most people were even afraid to mention the Zetas by name, let alone Miguel Trevino or Heriberto Lazcano. Chapo's fame and strategy of being the named boss and employer, branding him as a Mexican Pablo Escobar, undoubtedly increased his reputation but also scrutiny from the government.

25. It should be noted that it is not always completely a result of the structural difficulties of migration. Both Zacatecas and Monterrey's stories show how a lot of these problems can be self-imposed, due to chaotic lifestyles, alcoholism, or law-breaking behavior.

26. Abrego et al. 2017.

27. Slack et al. 2013.

28. For a discussion of debt and repeat migration, see Johnson and Woodhouse 2018.

29. Abrego et al. 2017; Coleman and Kocher 2011; Coleman 2008.

CHAPTER SIX. THE DISAPPEARED, THE DEAD, AND THE FORGOTTEN

1. Grupos Beta is a Mexican government organization tasked with providing aid to migrants. They often patrol the desert to rescue migrants lost on the Mexican side of the border, or attempt to locate dead bodies, as well as providing some assistance for deportees. However, they are not in every border city, and have different levels of funding and staffing in each location.

2. Field notes, Matamoros, Tamaulipas, September 30, 2013.

3. Hernández 2018.

4. Nieto 2017.

5. Agren 2017.

6. Martínez 2010.

7. Stillman 2018.

8. It still frequently happens anyway, as it did in Laura's case; however, it is highly informal and often based on the fact that police officers and border patrol officers know each other and are friends, likely to call each other in these types of situations. This makes it hard to track interagency collaboration since it is unofficial.

9. Stillman 2018.

10. Ibid.

11. Ibid.

12. Daly 2017.

13. Staff 2017b.

14. Schmidt 2018.

15. Ríos 2014a, b.

16. Movimiento Migrante Mesoamericano 2017.

17. Robben 2005.

18. Ibid.

19. Tully 1995; Catela 2000.

20. Oglesby and Ross 2009.

21. Binford 2016; Danner 1994; Bourgois 2001; Miranda and Ratliff 1992.

22. Peck 2004; Tilly 1998.

23. Tate 2015; Braun 1994.

24. Gibler 2011; Wright 2011.

25. Amnesty International 2016.

26. Staff 2010.

27. P. Martinez 2017.

28. Archibold 2011.

29. Cacho 2012.

30. Gibler 2011.

31. Wright 2005, 2006.

32. Mastrogiovanni 2014.

33. Muehlmann 2013.

34. Due to the popularity of a documentary called *Presumed Guilty*, which highlighted the problems of having a guilty-until-proven-innocent legal system, judicial reforms have been enacted but it is too early to know exactly how this will change Mexico.

35. Alarcón and Becerra 2012.

36. Rubio-Goldsmith et al. 2006.

37. It is generally considered a bad sign by shelter workers if a Mexican migrant was traveling on the train or hitching rides. Sometimes they will

not let them stay in the shelter since most migrants will simply take a bus, whereas bandits and gang members take the trains to rob and kidnap others.

38. Many scholars have written about the lack of rights for migrants using Giorgio Agamben's (1998) theories of the state of exception, the sacred man and the camp. I do not want to discuss it here simply because these concepts have been used quite extensively, often without adding a significant depth to the discussion other than pointing out the limited rights of noncitizens, something that is readily apparent.

39. Boss 2006, 2009, 2010.

40. Boss 2009: 7.

41. The father was kidnapped and disappeared in their hometown, not as a migrant, but the experience of loss led to their migration out of Mexico. This experience also demonstrates the complex stresses placed on a family.

42. Field notes, July 30, 2012.

43. See Magaloni 2003. However, Mexico is currently undergoing a massive judicial reform and, at the time of this writing, it is unclear what final form it will take.

44. Sicario, Molloy, and Bowden 2011; Bowden 2002; Blancornelas 2004.

45. Field notes, Nogales, Sonora, July 8, 2012.

46. Boss 2006.

47. Butler 2006.

48. Field notes, March 2, 2010.

49. Staff 2017b.

50. GIEI 2015.

51. Muehlmann 2013: 59.

52. Aburto et al. 2016.

53. According to Mexico's National Migration Institute, www
.politicamigratoria.gob.mx/es_mx/SEGOB/Repatriacion_de_mexicanos_2016.

54. Sandoval-Cervantes 2017.

55. Powell 2012.

56. Hooks 2014.

57. Wright 2005, 2006.

58. Agnew 2015.

59. As with many polemical debates, there are valid critiques as well as overstatements. The contentious nature of this debate has become counterproductive. We should not be in the business of determining the importance

of an issue simply by its overall size and quantity. Clearly, the death of women is important and should be studied.

60. Reineke 2016.

61. Nevins and Aizeki 2008; Nevins 2002; Eschbach et al. 1999; Cornelius 2001, 2005.

CHAPTER SEVEN. RESISTANCE, RESILIENCE, AND LOVE

1. This was before many Central Americans began claiming fear and seeking asylum. During fall 2013, few people knew they had this option, although the vast majority were eligible according to my research. I encountered a handful of people who sought asylum, but most were more interested in evading the authorities and passing for Mexican. It was not until 2014 that it became common practice to claim fear.

2. Field notes, Nuevo Laredo, Tamaulipas, December 10, 2013.

3. See Vogt 2016.

4. Martínez, Slack, and Heyman 2013.

5. Ibid.

6. Several state governments have opened facilities along the border to help people recover identifying documents. Most notably Oaxaca state has a facility in Tijuana, but for residents of other regions, it is still incredibly difficult or impossible. Even for those shelters that have attempted to facilitate this process, the results have been mixed.

7. Similar to my experiences trying to get the El Salvadoran couple out of Tamaulipas, these anticorruption measures often have unintended consequences.

8. He had residency in Mexico through asylum.

9. "Secuestro ciber" or "secuestro virtual."

10. Martínez et al. 2014; Rubio-Goldsmith et al. 2006.

11. See Slack and Martínez 2018.

12. MBCS Survey: He was 50 years old and from Oaxaca. He paid a $600 fee and had no tie to his guide.

13. Martínez 2015.

14. USBP 2017.

15. Most people cross on foot until they are past border patrol checkpoints, at which point they are picked up by vans and driven to a safe house. Often

road accidents occur when the vans are attempting to escape from the border patrol.

16. Personal communication, Nogales, Sonora, July 19, 2011.

17. MBCS Survey: He was 32 years old and from Jalisco. He paid a $1,300 fee and had no tie to his smuggler.

18. Soldiers.

19. Field notes, Nuevo Laredo, Tamaulipas, December 8, 2013.

20. This is of course on Juan Manuel's side of the story.

21. Field notes, Nuevo Laredo, Tamaulipas, December 6, 2013.

22. Upon learning of ethnography and participant observation Monterrey urged me to go *charrolear* (beg for change) one day. Considering the experiences I had had being threatened, I decided against it. I also suspected that Monterrey thought it would be funny more than anything else.

23. Of course, this was also a methodological concern, usually circumvented by follow-up interviews and making it clear that there was really nothing that I could provide to help anyone. However, it should also be noted that having been kidnapped and raped and working as a coyote are not mutually exclusive experiences.

24. Personal communication, November 26, 2013.

25. Izcara Palacios 2016.

26. Field notes, Nuevo Laredo, Tamaulipas, November 11, 2013.

27. It is worth noting that most of my interactions were with men at the shelters. Shelters typically have some religious affiliation, which often leads to policies strictly separating men and women. While I did interview many women, the interactions were far more limited because men were forbidden in certain parts of the shelters (and vice versa).

28. Adapted from field notes, December 16, 2013.

29. For a full discussion see Marcus and Snajdr 2013.

30. USCIS 2017.

31. USCIS 2017.

32. ICE 2017.

33. Associated Press 2015.

34. Weitzer 2011.

35. Sanford, Martínez, and Weitzer 2016.

36. Izcara Palacios and Yamamoto 2017; Johnson and Woodhouse 2018.

37. See also work on the funds of knowledge that highlight the strategies and methods people use to survive and flourish despite scarcity and hardship (Vélez-Ibáñez and Greenberg 2005).

CHAPTER EIGHT. "WHO CAN I DEPORT?"

1. Personal communication, April 23, 2018.

2. Mbembe and Meintjes 2003.

3. I would like to thank the anonymous reviewer for this term and its additional insight to my argument.

4. For people who are high profile enough to achieve media coverage of their story, this can serve as corroboration, but usually evidence is relegated to an individual telling his or her story with the possible aid of a police report or death certificate if appropriate.

5. Kanstroom 2007.

6. Marks 2014.

7. See Transactional Records Access Clearinghouse (TRAC) Immigration (Syracuse University), "Immigration Court Backlog Tool: Pending Cases and Length of Wait by Nationality, State, Court, and Hearing Locations," http://trac.syr.edu/phptools/immigration/court_backlog/.

8. Mountz 2010.

9. See *Jennings v. Rodriguez*.

10. These are the initial interviews generally conducted by an asylum officer after an individual claims fear. The credible fear standard, reserved for people with no previous deportations or criminal history, is based on a 10 percent likelihood that the person will meet the asylum standard, whereas reasonable fear requires a 51 percent likelihood.

11. Ramji-Nogales, Schoenholtz, and Schrag 2011.

12. TRAC Immigration, "Continued Rise in Asylum Denial Rates: Impact of Representation and Nationality," http://trac.syr.edu/immigration/reports/448/.

13. HBI 2018.

14. Field notes, October 25, 2017.

15. This seems to be an outlier and is not considered standard practice.

16. INA § 101(a)(42)(A).

17. 27 I&N Dec. 316 (A.G. 2018).

18. Convention against Torture and Other Cruel, Inhuman or Degrading Treatment or Punishment, www.ohchr.org/EN/ProfessionalInterest/Pages/CAT.aspx.

19. Ramji-Nogales, Schoenholtz, and Schrag 2011.

20. AIC 2015.

21. Morrissey 2017.

22. Field notes, March 28, 2018.

23. It should be noted, however, that many people decide to skip their court dates and simply live in the United States with a removal order. If they are caught for anything they will be deported. However, noting the difficulty, cost, and general fear and distrust people have of the courts and authorities in the United States, it is not surprising that many people would rather just risk it and live on the run.

24. This is not to say that it has never happened, but that it is extremely rare.

25. Nathan 2018.

26. However, it is not yet known if judges will treat these as a prior criminal offense or not, especially if it is the person's first time in the United States.

27. Bien 2003; Schenk 1994; Aleinikoff 1991; Sinha 2001; Landau 2004.

28. At times, academics will suggest policy changes, and make arguments for ways to right injustices or alleviate suffering. I would argue that our role in the courts is more mundane, but still important. Rather than critiquing a system, this is a realm where empirical background knowledge, typically referred to as "country conditions," becomes invaluable. Often we forget the value of descriptive knowledge in our academic pursuits and yet, in the broader world, specific knowledge about a place is often the most sought after.

29. Campbell, Slack, and Diedrich 2017.

30. Ibid.

CONCLUSIONS. REQUIEM FOR THE REMOVED

1. Field notes, Tijuana, Baja California, June 5, 2014.

2. Albicker and Velasco 2016.

3. Ibid.

4. Robertson et al. 2012.

5. Field notes, Tijuana, Baja California, March 21, 2014.

6. See Duncan 2014.

7. Albicker and Velasco 2016; Schuster and Majidi 2015; Brotherton and Barrios 2009; Golash-Boza 2014.

8. Duncan 2014.

9. Robertson et al. 2012.

10. Alarcón and Becerra 2012.

11. Wright 2011.

12. Aburto et al. 2016.

13. Elbagir et al. 2018.

14. Kiragu, Rosi, and Morris 2011.

15. Jones 2016.

16. Mountz 2010.

17. Ibid.

18. Borderland Immigration Council 2017.

19. U.S. Department of State, Bureau of Consular Affairs, "U.S. Visa Law and Policy: The Visa Bulletin," https://travel.state.gov/content/travel/en /legal/visa-lawo/visa-bulletin.html.

20. Kanstroom 2007.

21. See Martínez et al. 2017.

22. Martínez, Slack, and Martínez-Schuldt 2018.

23. It should be noted that both these stories are told from the perspective of Monterrey and Zacatecas, and therefore any relationship complications should be viewed as one-sided interpretations.

24. Personal communication, January 15, 2018.

25. Cantor, Noferi, and Martínez 2015; Orrenius and Coronado 2005; Coronado and Orrenius 2003; Martínez, Martínez-Schuldt, and Cantor 2017.

26. Kanstroom 2007.

27. Golash-Boza 2009, 2015; Coleman and Kocher 2011; Coleman 2007, 2008.

28. Martinez and Slack 2013.

29. Kanstroom 2007, 2011, 2012.

30. See the Fatal Journeys Report compiled by the International Organization on Migration for the premier source on quantifying and identifying migration-related deaths worldwide.

31. Cacho 2014.

APPENDIX

1. Stamm 1995.

REFERENCES

Abrego, Leisy, Mat Coleman, Daniel E. Martínez, Cecilia Menjívar, and Jeremy Slack. 2017. "Making Immigrants into Criminals: Legal Processes of Criminalization in the Post-IIRIRA Era." *Journal on Migration and Human Security* 5(3).

Aburto, José Manuel, Hiram Beltrán-Sánchez, Victor Manuel García-Guerrero, and Vladimir Canudas-Romo. 2016. "Homicides in Mexico Reversed Life Expectancy Gains for Men and Slowed Them for Women, 2000–10." *Health Affairs* 35(1): 88–95.

Agamben, Giorgio. 1998. *Homo Sacer: Sovereign Power and Bare Life.* Stanford, CA: Stanford University Press.

Agnew, Heather Robin. 2015. "Reframing 'Femicide': Making Room for the Balloon Effect of Drug War Violence in Studying Female Homicides in Mexico and Central America." *Territory, Politics, Governance* 3(4): 428–45.

Agren, David. 2017. "Mexico Maelstrom: How the Drug Violence Got So Bad." *The Guardian*, December 26. Accessed December 12, 2018. www.theguardian .comworld/2017/dec/26/mexico-maelstrom-how-the-drug-violence-got-so-bad?CMP%20=%20share_btn_fb.

AIC. 2015. "'Arriving Aliens' and Adjustment of Status: Practice Advisory." Edited by American Immigration Lawyers Association (AILA). Washington, DC: American Immigration Council.

Alarcón, Rafael, and William Becerra. 2012. "¿Criminales o víctimas? La deportación de migrantes mexicanos de Estados Unidos a Tijuana, Baja California." *Norteamérica* 7(1): 125–48.

Albicker, Sandra Luz, and Laura Velasco. 2016. "Deportation and Stigma on the Mexico-US Border: Trapped in Tijuana." *Norteamérica, Revista Académica del CISAN-UNAM* 11(1): 99–129.

Aleinikoff, T. Alexander. 1991. "The Meaning of 'Persecution' in United States Asylum Law." *International Journal of Refugee Law* 3(1): 5–29.

Alexander, Michelle. 2012. *The New Jim Crow: Mass Incarceration in the Age of Colorblindness.* New York: New Press.

Amnesty International. 2016. *Mexico: Sexual Violence Routinely Used as Torture to Secure "Confessions" from Women.* Mexico City: Amnesty International.

Andreas, Peter. 2000. *Border Games: Policing the U.S.-Mexico Divide.* Ithaca, NY: Cornell University Press.

Archibold, Randal. 2011. "Violence Suffocated a Father's Poetry, but Not His Voice." *New York Times,* May 13. Accessed December 12, 2018. www.nytimes .com/2011/05/14/world/americas/14sicilia.html?pagewanted = all.

Aristegui, Carmen. 2014. "'Templarios' extraían órganos a ninos; hay versiones de que comían el corazón: Castillo." *Aristegui Noticias.* http:// aristeguinoticias.com/1803/mexico/templarios-extraian-organos-a-ninos-hay-versiones-de-que-se-comian-el-corazon-castillo/.

Arreola, Daniel David. 1993. *The Mexican Border Cities: Landscape Anatomy and Place Personality.* Tucson: University of Arizona Press.

Associated Press. 2015. "Malaysia and Thailand Turn Away Hundreds on Migrant Boats." *The Guardian,* May 14. Accessed January 12, 2018. www .theguardian.com/world/2015/may/14/malaysia-turns-back-migrant-boat-with-more-than-500-aboard.

Balderas, Oscar. 2016. "Sobrevivr a lo imposible: Mis 7 anos como esclava sexual de Los Zetas y Cártel del Golfo." *Vice News,* August 10, 2016. Accessed September 8, 2016. https://news.vice.com/es/article/sobrevivir-imposible-mis-7-anos-esclava-sexual-zetas-cartel-golfo.

Bien, Rachel. 2003. "Nothing to Declare but Their Childhood: Reforming US Asylum Law to Protect the Rights of Children." *Journal of Law and Policy* 12: 797.

Binford, Leigh. 2016. *The El Mozote Massacre: Human Rights and Global Implications.* Revised and expanded edition. Tucson: University of Arizona Press.

Blancornelas, Jesus. 2004. *El cartel: Los Arellano Felix, la mafia mas poderosa en la historia de America Latina.* México, D.F.: Debolsillo.

Borderland Immigration Council. 2017. *Discretion to Deny: Family Separation, Prolonged Detention and Deterrence of Asylum Seekers at the Hands of Immigration*

Authorities along the U. S.-Mexico Border. Edited by BIC. El Paso: Hope Border Institute.

Boss, Pauline. 2006. *Loss, Trauma, and Resilience: Therapeutic Work with Ambiguous Loss.* New York: W. W. Norton.

——. 2009. *Ambiguous Loss: Learning to Live with Unresolved Grief.* Cambridge, MA: Harvard University Press.

——. 2010. "The Trauma and Complicated Grief of Ambiguous Loss." *Pastoral Psychology* 59(2): 137–45.

Bourgois, Philippe. 2001. "The Power of Violence in War and Peace: Post–Cold War Lessons from El Salvador." *Ethnography* 2(1): 5–34.

——. 2003. *In Search of Respect: Selling Crack in El Barrio,* vol. 10. Cambridge: Cambridge University Press.

Bowden, Charles. 2002. *Down by the River : Drugs, Money, Murder, and Family.* New York: Simon & Schuster.

—— and Julian Cardona. 2010. *Murder City: Ciudad Juarez and the Global Economy's New Killing Fields.* New York: Nation Books.

Braun, Herbert. 1994. *Our Guerrillas, Our Sidewalks: A Journey into the Violence of Colombia.* Niwot: University Press of Colorado.

Brotherton, David, and Luis Barrios. 2009. "Displacement and Stigma: The Social-Psychological Crisis of the Deportee." *Crime, Media, Culture* 5(1): 29–55.

——. 2011. *Banished to the Homeland: Dominican Deportees and Their Stories of Exile.* New York: Columbia University Press.

Bustamante, Jorge A. 2002. "Immigrants' Vulnerability as Subjects of Human Rights." *International Migration Review* 36(2): 333–54.

——. 2011. "Extreme Vulnerability of Migrants: The Cases of the United States and Mexico." *Migraciones internacionales* 6(1).

Butler, Judith. 2006. *Precarious Life: The Powers of Mourning and Violence.* New York: Verso.

Cacho, Lisa Marie. 2012. *Social Death: Racialized Rightlessness and the Criminalization of the Unprotected.* New York: NYU Press.

Campbell, Howard. 2009. *Drug War Zone: Frontline Dispatches from the Streets of El Paso and Juárez.* Austin: University of Texas Press.

——. 2011. "No End in Sight: Violence in Ciudad Juárez." *NACLA Report on the Americas* 44(3): 19–22.

——, Jeremy Slack, and Brian Diedrich. 2017. "Mexican Immigrants, Anthropology and U. S. Law: The Pragmatics and Ethics of Expert Witness Testimony." *Human Organization* 76(4).

Cantor, Guillermo, Mark Noferi, and Daniel E. Martínez. 2015. *Enforcement Overdrive: A Comprehensive Assessment of ICE's Criminal Alien Program*. Edited by American Immigration Council. Washington, DC: AIC.

Castillo, Gustavo, Jesus Aranda, and Alonso Urrutia. 2010. "Muere Tony Tormenta luedo de ocho horas de tiroteos con efectivs federales en Matamoros." *La Jornada*, November 6, 2010. Accessed December 12, 2017. www.jornada.unam.mx/2010/11/06/politica/007n1pol.

Catela, Ludmila da Silva. 2000. "De eso no se habla: Cuestiones metodológicas sobre los límites y el silencio en entrevistas a familiares de desaparecidos políticos." *Historia, antropología y fuentes orales*: 69–75.

CBP. 2015. *United States Border Patrol: Southwest Border Patrol—Total Illegal Alien Apprehensions by Fiscal Year*. Edited by Customs and Border Protection. Washington, DC: CBP.

Chesnut, R. Andrew. 2012. *Devoted to Death : Santa Muerte, the Skeleton Saint*. New York: Oxford University Press.

CNDH. 2011. *Informe Especial Sobre el Secuestro de Migrantes en Mexico*. Edited by Comision Nacional de los Derechos Humanos. Mexico, DF: CNDH.

Coleman, Mathew. 2007. "Immigration Geopolitics beyond the Mexico-US Border." *Antipode* 39(1): 54–76.

———. 2008. "U.S. Immigration Law and Its Geographies of Social Control: Lessons from Homosexual Exclusion during the Cold War." *Environment and Planning D* 26: 1096–114.

——— and Austin Kocher. 2011. "Detention, Deportation, Devolution and Immigrant Incapacitation in the US, Post 9 / 11." *Geographical Journal* 177(3).

Cornelius, Wayne A. 2001. "Death at the Border: Efficacy and Unintended Consequences of US Immigration Control Policy." *Population and Development Review* 27(4): 661.

———. 2005. "Controlling 'Unwanted' Immigration: Lessons from the United States, 1993–2004." *Journal of Ethnic and Migration Studies* 31(4): 775–94.

Coronado, Roberto, and Pia M. Orrenius. 2003. *The Impact of Illegal Immigration and Enforcement on Border Crime Rates*. Dallas: Federal Reserve Bank of Dallas.

Cresswell, Tim. 2006. "The Right to Mobility: The Production of Mobility in the Courtroom." *Antipode* 38(4): 735–54.

———. 2010. "Towards a Politics of Mobility." *Environment and Planning D: Society and Space* 28(1): 17–31.

Daly, Michael. 2017. "Mom Deported Because She Didn't Change Lanes." *Daily Beast*, August 8. Accessed December 12, 2018. www.thedailybeast.com/deported-by-the-us-kidnapped-by-the-cartels.

Danner, Mark. 1994. *The Massacre at El Mozote: A Parable of the Cold War.* New York: Vintage Books.

De Genova, Nicholas. 2002. "Migrant 'Illegality' and Deportability in Everyday Life." *Annual Review of Anthropology* 31: 419–47.

De León, Jason. 2012. "'Better to Be Hot Than Caught': Excavating the Conflicting Roles of Migrant Material Culture." *American Anthropologist* 114(3): 477–95.

———. 2013. "The Efficacy and Impact of the Alien Transfer Exit Programme: Migrant Perspectives from Nogales, Sonora, Mexico." *International Migration* 51(2): 10–23.

———. 2015. *The Land of Open Graves: Living and Dying on the Migrant Trail.* Berkeley: University of California Press.

Dingeman, M. Kathleen, and Rubén G. Rumbaut. 2010. "The Immigration-Crime Nexus and Post-Deportation Experiences: En / countering Stereotypes in Southern California and El Salvador." *University of La Verne Law Review* 31(2): 363–402.

Duncan, Whitney L. 2014. "Transnational Disorders: Returned Migrants at Oaxaca's Psychiatric Hospital." *Medical Anthropology Quarterly* 29(1): 24–41.

Dunn, Timothy J. 1996. *The Militarization of the U.S.-Mexico Border, 1978–1992: Low-Intensity Conflict Doctrine Comes Home.* Austin: CMAS Books, University of Texas.

Elbagir, Nima, Raja Razek, Sarah Sirgany, and Mohammed Tawfeeq. 2018. "First They Were Burned, Then They Were Whipped, Then Their Families Were Sent Videos." *CNN,* March 21. Accessed December 18, 2018. www.cnn.com /2018/01/25/africa/libya-sudanese-migrants-torture-intl/index.html.

Eschbach, Karl, Jacqueline Hagan, and Nestor Rodriguez. 2003. "Deaths during Undocumented Migration: Trends and Policy Implications in the New Era of Homeland Security." *In Defense of the Alien* 26: 37.

Eschbach, Karl, Jacqueline Hagan, Nestor Rodriguez, Ruben Hernandez-Leon, and Stanley Bailey. 1999. "Death at the Border." *International Migration Review* 33(2): 430–54.

Espenshade, Thomas J. 1995. "Unauthorized Immigration to the United States." *Annual Review of Sociology* 21(1): 195–216.

Gibler, John. 2011. *To Die in Mexico: Dispatches from Inside the Drug War.* San Francisco: City Lights Books.

GIEI. 2015. *Informe Ayotzinapa: Investigación y primeras conclusiones de las desapariciones y homicidios de los normalistas de Ayotzinapa.* Edited by Grupo Interdiscipinario de Expertos Independientes. Mexico D. F.: GIEI.

Gilmore, Ruth Wilson. 2006. *Golden Gulag: Prisons, Surplus, Crisis, and Opposition in Globalizing California*. Berkeley: University of California Press.

Golash-Boza, Tanya. 2009. "The Immigration Industrial Complex: Why We Enforce Immigration Policies Destined to Fail." *Sociology Compass* 3(2): 295–309.

———. 2014. "Forced Transnationalism: Transnational Coping Strategies and Gendered Stigma among Jamaican Deportees." *Global Networks* 14(1): 63–79.

———. 2015. *Immigration Nation: Raids, Detentions, and Deportations in Post–9 / 11 America*. New York: Routledge.

Grayson, George W. 2010. *Mexico: Narco-Violence and a Failed State?* New Brunswick, NJ: Transaction.

——— and U.S. Army War College, Strategic Studies Institute. 2010. "La Familia Drug Cartel Implications for U.S.-Mexican Security." http://purl.fdlp.gov/GPO/gpo3105.

Grillo, Ioan. 2011. *El Narco: Inside Mexico's Criminal Insurgency*. New York: Bloomsbury Press.

Gupta, Akhil, and James Ferguson. 1992. "Beyond 'Culture': Space, Identity, and the Politics of Difference." *Cultural Anthropology* 7(1): 6–23.

Gutierrez, Thelma. 2012. "Detainees Fear Deportation to Mexico." *CNN*. Accessed December 18, 2018. www.cnn.com/videos/us/2012/03/30/deportations-after-dark.cnn.

Hartsfield, Cathy Ho. 2011. "Deportation of Veterans: The Silent Battle for Naturalization." *Rutgers Law Review* 64: 835.

HBI. 2018. *Sealing the Border: The Criminalization of Asylum Seekers in the Trump Era*. Edited by Hope Border Institute. El Paso, TX: Hope Border Institute.

Hernandez, Anabel. 2010. *Los senores del narco*. Mexico, D.F.: Grijalbo.

Hernandez, Kelly Lytle. 2010. *Migra! A History of the U.S. Border Patrol*. Berkeley: University of California Press.

Hernández, Oscar. 2018. *Podemos hablar de migranticidio?* Edited by Colegio de la Frontera. Matamoros: COLEF.

Heyman, Josiah McC. 2001. "Class and Classification at the US-Mexico Border." *Human Organization* 60(2): 128–40.

———, Guillermina Gina Núñez, and Victor Talavera. 2009. "Healthcare Access and Barriers for Unauthorized Immigrants in El Paso County, Texas." *Family and Community Health* 32(1): 4–21.

Hiemstra, Nancy. 2012. "Geopolitical Reverberations of US Migrant Detention and Deportation: The View from Ecuador." *Geopolitics* 17(2): 293–311.

Hooks, Christopher. 2014. "Q&A with Molly Molloy: The Story of the Juarez Femicides Is a 'Myth.'" *Texas Observer,* January 9.

Hughes, Cris E., Bridget F. B. Algee-Hewitt, Robin Reineke, Elizabeth Clausing, and Bruce E. Anderson. 2017. "Temporal Patterns of Mexican Migrant Genetic Ancestry: Implications for Identification." *American Anthropologist* 119 (2): 193–208.

ICE. 2017. *ICE Arrests Nearly 2,000 Human Traffickers in 2016, Identifies over 400 Victims across the US.* Washington, DC: Department of Homeland Security.

INEGI. 2017. *Encuesta Nacional de Victimización y Percepción sobre Seguridad Publica (ENVIPE).* In ENVIPE, edited by Instituto Nacional de Estadisticas y Geografia. Mexico, D. F.: INEGI.

Isacson, Adam, and Maureen Meyer. 2013. "Border Security and Migration: A Report from South Texas." Washington, DC: Washington Office of Latin America.

Izcara Palacios, Simón Pedro. 2012a. "Coyotaje y grupos delictivos en Tamaulipas." *Latin American Research Review* 47(3): 41–61.

———. 2012b. "El declive del contrabando de indocumentados en México." *Mexican Studies / Estudios Mexicanos* 28(2): 351–76.

———. 2014. "Coyotaje and Drugs: Two Different Businesses." *Bulletin of Latin American Research* 34(3): 324–39.

———. 2016. "Post-Structural Violence: Central American Migrants and Drug Cartels in Mexico." *Revista de Estudios Sociales* 56: 12–25.

——— and Yasutaka Yamamoto. 2017. "Trafficking in US Agriculture." *Antipode* 49(5): 1306–28.

Johnson, Richard L., and Murphy Woodhouse. 2018. "Securing the Return: How Enhanced US Border Enforcement Fuels Cycles of Debt Migration." *Antipode* 50(4): 976–96.

Jones, Reece. 2016. *Violent Borders: Refugees and the Right to Move.* New York: Verso Books.

Kanstroom, Dan. 2007. *Deportation Nation: Outsiders in American History.* Cambridge, MA: Harvard University Press.

———. 2011. "The Right to Deportation Counsel in *Padilla v. Kentucky*: The Challenging Construction of the Fifth-and-a-Half Amendment." *UCLA Law Review* 58: 1461.

———. 2012. *Aftermath: Deportation Law and the New American Diaspora.* New York: Oxford University Press.

Kiragu, Esther, Angela Li Rosi, and Tim Morris. 2011. *States of Denial: A Review of UNHCR's Response to the Protracted Situation of Stateless Rohingya Refugees in*

Bangladesh. Policy Development and Evaluation Service, UNHCR. www
.unhcr.org/4ee754c19.pdf.

Kristeva, Julia. 1982. *Powers of Horror: An Essay on Abjection.* New York: Columbia
University Press.

Landau, Joseph. 2004. "Soft Immutability and Imputed Gay Identity: Recent
Developments in Transgender and Sexual-Orientation-Based Asylum
Law." *Fordham Urban Law Journal* 32: 237.

Longmire, Sylvia. 2011. *Cartel: The Coming Invasion of Mexico's Drug Wars.* New
York: Palgrave Macmillan.

Lopez, Rene. 2009. "Asesinan a familia del marino que cayó en operative contra El Barbas." *La Jornada,* December 23. Accessed June 3, 2016. www
.jornada.unam.mx/2009/12/23/politica/003n1pol.

Lowen, Matthew, and Caroline Isaacs. 2012. "Lifetime Lockdown: How Isolation Conditions Impact Prisoner Reentry." Arizona: American Friends
Service Committee.

Lydgate, Joanna Jacobbi. 2010. "Assembly-Line Justice: A Review of Operation
Streamline." *California Law Review* 98(2): 481–544.

Magaloni, Beatriz. 2003. "Authoritarianism, Democracy and the Supreme
Court: Horizontal Exchange and the Rule of Law in Mexico." In *Democratic
Accountability in Latin America,* edited by Scott Manwairing and Christopher
Welna, 266–305. Oxford Scholarship Online.

Maldonado Aranda, Salvador. 2012. "Drogas, violencia y militarización en el
México rural: El caso de Michoacán." *Revista mexicana de sociología* 74(1):
5–39.

Marcus, Anthony, and Edward Snajdr. 2013. "Anti-anti-trafficking? Toward Critical Ethnographies of Human Trafficking." *Dialectical Anthropology* 37(2): 191–94.

Marcus, George E. 1995. "Ethnography in / of the World System: The Emer-
gence of Multi-Sited Ethnography." *Annual Review of Anthropology* 24(1):
95–117.

Marks, Dana Leigh. 2014. "Immigration Judge: Death Penalty Cases in Traffic
Court Setting." *CNN,* June 26. Accessed December 17, 2018. www.cnn
.com/2014/06/26/opinion/immigration-judge-broken-system/index.html.

Martínez, Daniel E. 2013. "The Crossing Experience: Unauthorized Migration
along the Arizona-Sonora Border." PhD dissertation, Department of Sociology, University of Arizona.

———. 2015. "*Coyote* Use in an Era of Heightened Border Enforcement: New
Evidence from the Arizona-Sonora Border." *Journal of Ethnic and Migration
Studies* 42(1): 103–19.

Martínez, Daniel E., Ricardo D. Martínez-Schuldt, and Guillermo Cantor. 2017. "Providing Sanctuary or Fostering Crime? A Review of the Research on 'Sanctuary Cities' and Crime." *Sociology Compass* 12(1).

Martínez, Daniel E., Robin C. Reineke, Raquel Rubio-Goldsmith, and Bruce O. Parks. 2014. "Structural Violence and Migrant Deaths in Southern Arizona: Data from the Pima County Office of the Medical Examiner, 1990–2013." *Journal on Migration and Human Security* 2(4): 257–86.

Martinez, Daniel, and Jeremy Slack. 2013. "What Part of 'Illegal' Don't You Understand? The Social Consequences of Criminalizing Unauthorized Mexican Migrants in the United States." *Social and Legal Studies* 22(4): 535–51.

Martínez, Daniel E., Jeremy Slack, and Ricardo D. Martínez-Schuldt. 2018. "Repeat Migration in the Age of the 'Unauthorized Permanent Resident': A Quantitative Assessment of Migration Intentions Postdeportation." *International Migration Review* 50(1): 197–230.

Martínez, Daniel E., Jeremy Slack, Kraig Beyerlein, Prescott Vandervoet, Kristin Klingman, Paola Molina, Shiras Manning, Melissa Burham, Kylie Walzak, Kristen Valencia, and Lorenzo Gamboa. 2017. "The Migrant Border Crossing Study: A Methodological Overview of Research along the Sonora-Arizona Border." *Population Studies* 71(2): 249–264.

Martínez, Daniel E., Jeremy Slack, and Josiah Heyman. 2013. *Bordering on Criminal: The Routine Abuse of Migrants in the Removal System.* Edited by American Immigration Council. Washington, DC: AIC.

Martinez, Jorge. 2017. "La Ley General de Víctimas duerme el sueno de los justos." *Milenio,* June 26. Accessed June 25, 2018. www.milenio.com/policia /la-ley-general-de-victimas-duerme-el-sueno-de-los-justos.

Martinez, Oscar. 2010. *Los migrantes que no importan: En el camino con los centroamericanos indocumentados en México.* Barcelona: Icaria.

Martinez, Paris. 2017. "Ellas y ellos son las madres y padres asesinados por buscar a sus hijos desaparecidos." *Animal Politico,* May 15. Accessed January 4, 2018. www.animalpolitico.com/2017/05/madres-padres-hijos-desaparecidos/.

Marx, Karl, and Friedrich Engels. 2001. "The 18th Brumaire of Louis Bonaparte." Electric Book Co. http://site.ebrary.com/id/2001665.

Massaro, Vanessa A., and Jill Williams. 2013. "Feminist Geopolitics." *Geography Compass* 7(8): 567–77.

Massey, Douglas S., Jorge Durand, and Nolan J. Malone. 2002. *Beyond Smoke and Mirrors: Mexican Immigration in an Era of Economic Integration.* New York: Russell Sage Foundation.

Mastrogiovanni, Federico. 2014. *Ni vivos ni muertos: La desaparición forzada en México como estrategia de terror.* Barcelona: Grijalbo.

Mbembe, J. A., and Libby Meintjes. 2003. "Necropolitics." *Public Culture* 15(1): 11–40.

McCombs. 2008. "Matan en Nogales a jefe policíaco estatal." *Arizona Daily Star,* November 7. Accessed December 6, 2018. https://tucson.com/news/foreign-language/spanish/matan-en-nogales-a-jefe-polic-aco-estatal/article_4744eaf7-c0b2-571a-b89b-b6230e627b66.html.

Meyers, Deborah Waller. 2003. "Does 'Smarter' Lead to Safer? An Assessment of the US Border Accords with Canada and Mexico." *International Migration* 41(4): 5–44.

Miranda, Roger, and William E. Ratliff. 1992. *The Civil War in Nicaragua: Inside the Sandinistas.* Piscataway, NJ: Transaction.

Morrissey, Kate. 2017. "Complaint: Border Officials Illegally Turn Away Asylum Seekers." *San Diego Tribune,* January 19. Accessed June 1, 2018. www.sandiegouniontribune.com/news/immigration/sd-me-asylum-seeker-20170119-story.html.

Mountz, Alison. 2010. *Seeking Asylum: Human Smuggling and Bureaucracy at the Border.* Minneapolis: University of Minnesota Press.

Movimiento Migrante Mesoamericano. 2017. "Seguiremos gritando y exigiendo hasta que sepamos qué pasó con nuestros hijos." Last modified December 10. Accessed December 12, 2018. https://movimientomigrante-mesoamericano.org/2017/12/10/seguiremos-gritando-y-exigiendo-hasta-que-sepamos-que-paso-con-nuestros-hijos/.

Muehlmann, Shaylih. 2013. *When I Wear My Alligator Boots: Narco-Culture in the US-Mexico Borderlands.* Berkeley: University of California Press.

Nail, Thomas. 2015. *The Figure of the Migrant.* Stanford, CA: Stanford University Press.

Nathan, Debbie. 2018. "Hidden Horros of 'Zero Tolerance': Mass Trials and Children Taken from Their Parents." *The Intercept,* May 29. Accessed June 1, 2018. https://theintercept.com/2018/05/29/zero-tolerance-border-policy-immigration-mass-trials-children/.

Nevins, Joseph. 2002. *Operation Gatekeeper: The Rise of the 'Illegal Alien' and the Making of the U.S.-Mexico Boundary.* New York: Routledge.

——— and Mizue Aizeki. 2008. *Dying to Live: A Story of U.S. Immigration in an Age of Global Apartheid.* San Francisco: Open Media / City Lights Books.

Nieto, Jorge. 2017. "Hallan en Tijuana una fosa con 300 restos óseos: Los trasladan a la CDMX para su análisis." *Animal Político,* August 16. Accessed December 11, 2018. www.animalpolitico.com/2017/08/

Notimex. 2008. "Guerra: Mueren 10 sicarios en Nogales, Sonora durante tres balaceras." *Cronica*, October 24. Accessed December 6, 2018. www.cronica .com.mx/notas/2008/393292.html.

Núñez, Guillermina Gina, and Josiah McC. Heyman. 2007. "Entrapment Processes and Immigrant Communities in a Time of Heightened Border Vigilance." *Human Organization* 66(4): 354–65.

O'Neill, Kevin Lewis. 2015. *Secure the Soul: Christian Piety and Gang Prevention in Guatemala*. Berkeley: University of California Press.

Oglesby, Elizabeth, and Amy Ross. 2009. "Guatemala's Genocide Determination and the Spatial Politics of Justice." *Space and Polity* 13(1): 21–39.

Orrenius, Pia M., and Roberto Coronado. 2005. *The Effect of Illegal Immigration and Border Enforcement on Crime Rates along the US-Mexico Border*. Center for Comparative Immigration Studies, University of California, San Diego.

Osorno, Diego Enrique. 2010. *El Cartel de Sinaloa: Una historia del uso politico del narco*. Mexico, D.F.: Grijalbo.

———. 2012. *La guerra de los Zetas*. Mexico, D.F.: Grijalbo.

Peck, Jamie. 2004. "Geography and Public Policy: Constructions of Neoliberalism." *Progress in Human Geography* 28(3): 392–405.

Powell, Robert Andrew. 2012. *This Love Is Not for Cowards: Salvation and Soccer in Ciudad Juárez*. New York: Bloomsbury.

Price, Patricia L. 2005. "Of Bandits and Saints: Jesus Malverde and the Struggle for Place in Sinaloa, Mexico." *Cultural Geographies* 12(2): 175–97.

Raeymaekers, Timothy. 2013. *Violence on the Margins: States, Conflict, and Borderlands*. New York: Springer.

Ramji-Nogales, Jaya, Andrew I. Schoenholtz, and Philip G. Schrag. 2007. "Refugee Roulette: Disparities in Asylum Adjudication." *Stanford Law Review* 60: 295–411.

———. 2011. *Refugee Roulette: Disparities in Asylum Adjudication and Proposals for Reform*. New York: NYU Press.

Reineke, Robin C. 2016. *Naming the Dead: Identification and Ambiguity along the US-Mexico Border*. Tucson: University of Arizona.

——— and Bruce E. Anderson. 2016. "Missing in the US-Mexico Borderlands." In *Missing Persons: Multidisciplinary Perspectives on the Disappeared*, edited by Derek Congram, 126. Toronto, Ontario: Canadian Scholars Press.

Ríos, Viridiana. 2014a. "The Role of Drug-Related Violence and Extortion in Promoting Mexican Migration: Unexpected Consequences of a Drug War." *Latin American Research Review* 49(3): 199–217.

———. 2014b. "Security Issues and Immigration Flows: Drug-Violence Refugees, the New Mexican Immigrants." *Latin American Research Review* 49(3): 3.

Robben, Antonius C. G. M. 2005. *Political Violence and Trauma in Argentina*. Philadelphia: University of Pennsylvania Press.

Robertson, Angela M., M. Gudelia Rangel, Remedios Lozada, Alicia Vera, and Victoria D. Ojeda. 2012. "Male Injection Drug Users Try New Drugs Following US Deportation to Tijuana, Mexico." *Drug and Alcohol Dependence* 120(1): 142–48.

Robles, Abdel. 2008. "Cuatro muertos en Sonora: Tres decapitados y un embolsado." *Zócalo*, August 29. Accessed December 6, 2018. www.zocalo.com .mx/new_site/articulo/cuatro-muertos-en-sonora-tres-decapitados-y-un-embolsado.

Rose, John. 2011. "Risk Atlas: The Global Kidnapping Epidemic." *Risk Management* 58(3): 20–21. Accessed October 30, 2018. www.rmmagazine.com/2011 /04/01/the-global-kidnapping-epidemic/.

Rubio-Goldsmith, Raquel, Melissa McCormick, Daniel Martínez, and Inez Magdalena Duarte. 2006. *The "Funnel Effect" and Recovered Bodies of Unauthorized Migrants Processed by the Pima County Office of the Medical Examiner, 1990–2005*. Tucson: Binational Migration Institute, University of Arizona.

Sandoval-Cervantes, Ivan. 2017. "Navigating the City: Internal Migration of Oaxacan Indigenous Women." *Journal of Ethnic and Migration Studies* 43(5): 849–65.

Sanford, Rachealle, Daniel E. Martínez, and Ronald Weitzer. 2016. "Framing Human Trafficking: A Content Analysis of Recent US Newspaper Articles." *Journal of Human Trafficking* 2(2): 139–55.

Schenk, Todd Stewart. 1994. "A Proposal to Improve the Treatment of Women in Asylum Law: Adding a 'Gender' Category to the International Definition of 'Refugee.'" *Indiana Journal of Global Legal Studies* 2(1): 301–44.

Schmidt, Samantha. 2018. "After Losing DACA and Facing Deportation, He Returned to Mexico. He Was Killed Weeks Later." *Washington Post*, June 11. Accessed August 9, 2018. www.washingtonpost.com/news/morning-mix /wp/2018/06/08/after-losing-daca-and-facing-deportation-he-returned-to-mexico-he-was-killed-weeks-later/?utm_term=.b558f6dc009f.

Schuster, Liza, and Nassim Majidi. 2015. "Deportation Stigma and Remigration." *Journal of Ethnic and Migration Studies* 41(4): 635–52.

Shay, Jonathan. 2003. *Odysseus in America: Combat Trauma and the Trials of Homecoming*. New York: Simon and Schuster.

———. 2010. *Achilles in Vietnam: Combat Trauma and the Undoing of Character.* New York: Simon and Schuster.

———. 2014. "Moral Injury." *Psychoanalytic Psychology* 31(2): 182.

Sicario, Molly Molloy, and Charles Bowden. 2011. *El Sicario: The Autobiography of a Mexican Assassin.* New York: Nation Books.

Sinha, Anita. 2001. "Domestic Violence and US Asylum Law: Eliminating the Cultural Hook for Claims Involving Gender-Related Persecution." *New York University Law Review* 76: 1562.

Slack, Jeremy, and Daniel E. Martínez. 2018. "What Makes a Good Human Smuggler? The Differences between Satisfaction with and Recommendation of Coyotes on the US-Mexico Border." *Annals of the American Academy of Political and Social Science* 676(1): 152–73.

Slack, Jeremy, and Daniel E. Martínez. n.d. "Post-Deportation Geographies: State Practices, Immigration Enforcement and Organized Crime on the U.S.-Mexico Border."

Slack, Jeremy, Daniel E. Martínez, Alison Elizabeth Lee, and Scott Whiteford. 2016. "The Geography of Border Militarization: Violence, Death and Health in Mexico and the United States." *Journal of Latin American Geography* 15(1): 7–32.

Slack, Jeremy, Daniel Martinez, Scott Whiteford, and Emily Peiffer. 2013. *In the Shadow of the Wall: Family Separation, Immigration Enforcement and Security.* Edited by the Ford Foundation. Tucson: University of Arizona.

Slack, Jeremy, Daniel E. Martínez, Scott Whiteford, and Emily Peiffer. 2015. "In Harm's Way: Family Separation, Immigration Enforcement Programs and Security on the US-Mexico Border." *Journal on Migration and Human Security* 3(2): 109–28.

Slack, Jeremy, and Scott Whiteford. 2011. "Violence and Migration on the Arizona-Sonora Border." *Human Organization* 70(1): 11–21.

Spener, David. 2009. *Clandestine Crossings: Migrants and Coyotes on the Texas-Mexico Border.* Ithaca, NY: Cornell University Press.

Staff. 2010. "Asesinada una mujer en Chihuahua por pedir justicia por la muerte de su hija." *El Mundo*, December 17. Accessed November 3, 2017. www.elmundo.es/america/2010/12/17/mexico/1292605079.html.

———. 2012a. "24 mil 91 desaparecidos en Mexico: CNDH." *Pagina3.* Accessed December 16, 2012. www.pagina3.mx/derechoshumanos/6473–24-mil-91-desaparecidos-en-mexico-cndh.html.

———. 2012b. "El día que los Zetas decapitaron a 'La Nena de Laredo'." Accessed September 27, 2015. www.valorportamaulipas.info/2015/06/el-dia-que-los-zetas-decapitaron-la.html.

————. 2015. "El día que murio Arturo Beltrán Leyva." *El Debate*, December 15. Accessed December 12, 2017. www.debate.com.mx/mexico/El-dia-que-murio-Arturo-Beltran-Leyva-20151215–0054.html.

————. 2016a. "Linchan a violador en Nuevo Laredo: Murio seis horas despues." *El Manana,* June 8. Accessed September 21, 2016. www.elmanana.com/linchan avioladorennuevolaredomurioseishorasdespues(video)-3309923.html.

————. 2016b. "Lo Linchan tras violar a nena de 4 anos: Reynosa." *Blog del Narco,* September 21. www.blog-del-narco.com/2016/09/tamaulipas-lo-linchan-tras-violar-nena.html.

————. 2017a. "Los grupos delincuenciales que pelean por Michoacán." *La Bandera Noticias,* February 7. Accessed September 25, 2017. http://labanderanoticias.com/inseguridad/2017/02/07/los-grupos-delincuenciales-pelean-michoacan/.

————. 2017b. "Mexico, el país donde hay más de 32,000 disaparecidos." *CNN Espanol,* September 13. Accessed November 2, 2017. http://cnnespanol.cnn.com/2017/09/13/mexico-el-pais-donde-hay-mas-de-32–000-desaparecidos/—0.

————. 2017c. "Muro antimigrante se encuentra en una comunidad de Oaxaca, México." *desinformémonos,* April 1. Accessed December 18, 2018. https://desinformemonos.org/muro-antimigrante-se-encuentra-una-comunidad-oaxaca-mexico/.

————. 2017d. "Diputado del PAN se echa para atrás y pide retirar su propia inciativa contra tatuajes." *Animal Politico,* May 11. Accessed June 6, 2017. www.animalpolitico.com/2017/05/tatuajes-pan-iniciativa/.

Starn, Orin. 1991. "Missing the Revolution: Anthropologists and the War in Peru." *Cultural Anthropology* 6(1): 63–91.

Stillman, Sarah. 2018. "When Deportation Is a Death Sentence." *New Yorker,* January 15. Accessed January 11, 2018. www.newyorker.com/magazine/2018/01/15/when-deportation-is-a-death-sentence.

Tate, Winifred. 2015. *Drugs, Thugs, and Diplomats: US Policymaking in Colombia.* Stanford, CA: Stanford University Press.

Thompson, Ginger. 2017. "How the U.S. Triggered a Massacre in Mexico." *Propublica,* June 12. Accessed February 6, 2018. www.propublica.org/article/allende-zetas-cartel-massacre-and-the-us-dea

Tilly, Charles. 1998. *Durable Inequality.* Berkeley: University of California Press.

Tully, Sheila R. 1995. "A Painful Purgatory: Grief and the Nicaraguan Mothers of the Disappeared." *Social Science and Medicine* 40(12): 1597–610.

Turati, Marcela. 2015. "El Pozolero, un albanil que acabo disolviendo en sosa caustica 300 cadaveres." *Proceso*, June 5. Accessed September 8, 2016. www.proceso.com.mx/406456/el-pozolero-un-albanil-que-acabo-disolviendo-en-sosa-caustica-300-cadaveres.

Tyner, James, and Joshua Inwood. 2014. "Violence as Fetish: Geography, Marxism, and Dialectics." *Progress in Human Geography* 38(6): 771–84.

Ureste, Manuel. 2015. "A 5 anos de massacre de 72 migrantes en San Fernando, caso sigue impune: Amnistía Internacional." *Animal Politico*, August 22. Accessed September 8, 2016. www.animalpolitico.com/2015/08/a-5-anos-de-masacre-de-72-migrantes-en-san-fernando-caso-sigue-impune-amnistia-internacional/.

USBP. 2017. *Border Patrol, Mexican Government Partner to Combat Human Smuggling.* Edited by United States Border Patrol, Tucson, AZ.

USCIS. 2017. *Number of Form I-914, Application for T Nonimmigrant Status, by Fiscal Year, Quarter, and Case Status 2008–2017.* Edited by United States Citizenship and Immigration Services. Washington, DC: Department of Homeland Security.

Vélez-Ibáñez, Carlos, and James Greenberg. 2005. "Formation and Transformation of Funds of Knowledge." In *Funds of Knowledge: Theorizing Practices in Households, Communities, and Classrooms,* 47–70. Tempe: Lawrence Erlbaum Associates, Arizona State University.

Vigil, James Diego. 2010. *Barrio Gangs: Street Life and Identity in Southern California.* Austin: University of Texas Press.

Vogt, Wendy. 2016. "Stuck in the Middle with You: The Intimate Labours of Mobility and Smuggling along Mexico's Migrant Route." *Geopolitics* 21(2): 366–86.

Weber, Max. 1965. *Politics as a Vocation.* Philadelphia: Fortress Press.

Weitzer, Ronald. 2011. "Sex Trafficking and the Sex Industry: The Need for Evidence-Based Theory and Legislation." *Journal of Criminal Law and Criminology* 101(4): 1337–69.

Wright, Melissa W. 2005. "Paradoxes, Protests and the Mujeres de Negro of Northern Mexico." *Gender, Place and Culture: A Journal of Feminist Geography* 12(3): 277–92.

———. 2006. *Disposable Women and Other Myths of Global Capitalism.* New York: Routledge.

———. 2011. "Necropolitics, Narcopolitics, and Femicide: Gendered Violence on the Mexico-U.S. Border." *Signs* 36(3): 707–31.

Young, Jock. 1999. "Cannibalism and Bulimia: Patterns of Social Control in Late Modernity." *Theoretical Criminology* 3(4): 387–407.

Zaitch, Damián. 2002. *Trafficking Cocaine: Colombian Drug Entrepreneurs in the Netherlands.* Vol. 1. Springer Science & Business Media.

———. 2005. "The Ambiguity of Violence, Secrecy, and Trust among Colombian Drug Entrepreneurs." *Journal of Drug Issues* 35(1): 201–28.

Zilberg, Elana. 2004. "Fools Banished from the Kingdom: Remapping Geographies of Gang Violence between the Americas (Los Angeles and San Salvador)." *American Quarterly* 56(3): 759–79.

INDEX

drug cartels *(continued)*
rules of, 141; in Tijuana, 44; violence against migrants by, 1–3, 28–29; violence and, 129–130. *See also* Beltran Leyva; Cartel Jalisco Nueva Generación; Gulf Cartel; La Familia Michoacana cartel; La Linea; Los Rojos; Sinaloa cartel; Zetas cartel
drug mules, 51–52, 124–25
drugs, 34–36
drug traffickers: crackdown on, 193; deportations and, 15; kidnappings and, 94–95, 97–98; migrants and, 1–3, 15; motivations for, 97–98; poverty and, 98; seasonal agricultural workers as, 116, 124; violence and, 99
drug trafficking: crime and, 149; desperation and, 109; friendships and, 153–54; gender and, 149; human smugglers and, 99; human smuggling and, 42–43; migration and, 109; poverty and, 109, 137–38; protests against, 137; risks of, 115; violence and, 59
Durango, 28–29

Ecuador, 4–5, 220n19
El Chayo, 47
El Hongo, 42
El Salvador, 5, 82, 113, 117, 120, 137, 147, 153, 176
enganchador (recruiter), 72
Entry Without Inspection (EWI), 182
Eschbach, Karl, 28
Escobedo Ortiz, Marisela, 138
Esmeralda, 61
Espenshade, Thomas J., 28
Eusebio, 156–57

facism, 204
families: asylum seekers and, 180; as a commodity, 123–24; deportations and, 26; of deportees, 135, 197; kidnappings and, 53–54, 65, 72–73,

94, 96, 103, 135, 157; of migrants, 23, 29, 53–54, 65, 72–73, 87, 94, 96, 103, 126–27, 153, 184; migrations and, 153; of missing migrants, 135–38, 147–48; separation of, 14, 26, 39, 153–54, 174, 183–85, 189–190, 195–96, 200–201, 205; as a support network, 35–36, 39, 66, 72–73, 80–81, 92, 94, 108–9, 123–24, 126; transnational, 26; violence against, 14, 26, 39, 153–54, 174, 183–85, 189–190, 195–96, 200–201, 205
fear: asylum and, 134, 225n1, 227n10; blaming the victim and, 144; of deportees, 16, 18–19, 119, 171; immigration policies and, 170; loss of possessions and, 154–58; in Mexico, 172; of migrants, 16, 18–19, 32, 70–71, 133; in migrant shelters, 18; organized crime and, 144; stigmas and, 144; of Zetas cartel, 222n24
Female Genital Mutilation, 178
feminicide, 138–39, 149, 224–25n59
Fernando, 72–73
fieldwork, 207–11
Fisher, Mike, 24–25, 215n44
flophouses, 126

gender, 149, 166–67
Gerardo, Don, 83–85
global capitalism, 149
Grupos Beta, 91, 131, 220n15, 222n1
Guatemala, 5, 121–22, 137, 147, 156–57, 163–64, 176
guest houses, 60, 125–26
guia, 52–53
guides, 52–53, 60, 70, 157–163, 170
Gulf Cartel, 76, 111, 117
Guzman, Joaquin "El Chapo," 46–47, 125, 222n24

halcones, 2, 68, 71, 110, 118
Helga, 164–65
Hernandez, Ezikiel, 191–92
Hernández, Oscar Misael, 132, 194
heroin, 35, 49, 191

CALIFORNIA SERIES IN PUBLIC ANTHROPOLOGY

The California Series in Public Anthropology emphasizes the anthropologist's role as an engaged intellectual. It continues anthropology's commitment to being an ethnographic witness, to describing, in human terms, how life is lived beyond the borders of many readers' experiences. But it also adds a commitment, through ethnography, to reframing the terms of public debate—transforming received, accepted understandings of social issues with new insights, new framings.

Series Editor: Robert Borofsky (Hawaii Pacific University)

Contributing Editors: Philippe Bourgois (University of Pennsylvania), Paul Farmer (Partners In Health), Alex Hinton (Rutgers University), Carolyn Nordstrom (University of Notre Dame), and Nancy Scheper-Hughes (UC Berkeley)

University of California Press Editor: Naomi Schneider